JOURNEYS TO THE PAST

A Traveler's Guide to Indiana State Historical Markers

by
Alan J. McPherson

Other Indiana Books by Alan McPherson

Temples of Knowledge: Andrew Carnegie's Gift to Indiana
Indiana Best Hikes
Nature Walks in Southern Indiana
Nature Walks in Northern Indiana
Paddle Indiana: An Access Guide to Canoeing & Kayaking Indiana's Lakes & Streams
Indian Names in Indiana
Wild Food Plants of Indiana and Adjacent States
Hoosier: Illustrated Origins of Indiana's Sobriquet

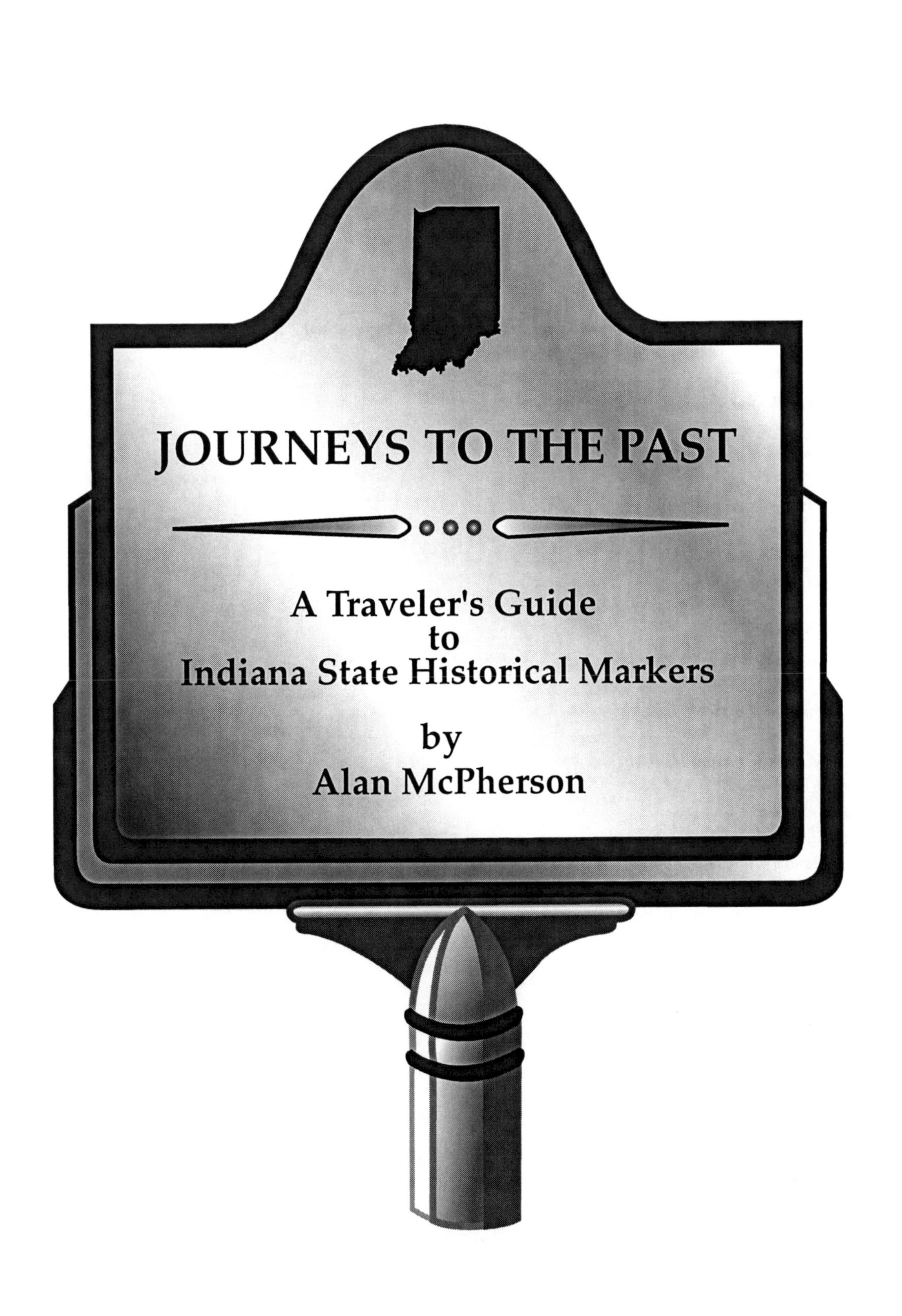
JOURNEYS TO THE PAST
A Traveler's Guide
to
Indiana State Historical Markers
by
Alan McPherson

AuthorHouse™
1663 Liberty Drive, Suite 200
Bloomington, IN 47403
www.authorhouse.com
Phone: 1-800-839-8640

First published by AuthorHouse 04/15/08

ISBN: 978-1-4343-1644-8 (sc)

Printed in the United States of America
Bloomington, Indiana

This book is printed on acid-free paper.

McPherson, Alan 1947-
Journey's To The Past: A Traveler's Guide To Indiana State Historical Markers

Includes recommended reading bibliography and indexes.
ISBN 0-9636978-5-4 (paperback)
1. Historical Markers--Indiana--Guidebooks
2. Indiana--History--Local
3. Indiana--Guidebooks
4. Indiana--Historical Geography
5. Travel--Indiana--Guidebooks

Cover and book design by Judy Wu, Patricia Linehan, SAMy Anderson

Portrait of Abraham Lincoln. Indiana Picture Collection, MS. Section, Indiana State Library.

"Fellow citizens, we cannot escape history."
Abraham Lincoln
From the December 1, 1862, Message To Congress

Lincoln's Indiana formative years (1816-1830)

TABLE OF CONTENTS

TABLE OF CONTENTS

Foreword

Alan McPherson's expertise, energy, and resources have brought about the publication of this book. He deserves congratulations for accomplishing the task, and we are extremely grateful that this project caught his attention. Beyond the book, his work will also reach people throughout the world via the Internet.

McPherson undertook a complete survey of the state historical markers in Indiana, including photographs and location descriptions, working with former Indiana Historical Bureau staff Carole M. Allen and Judy A. Rippel. His current information was provided to Alan to update the Indiana Historical Bureau Web database. His photographs will be added to the database as well. The book–and the Web database—will continue to be a rich resource to learn more about Indiana's history. As new markers are approved, they will be added to the Indiana Historical Bureau Web database.

Historical markers are a valuable part of state tourism. Research has shown that many people use marker guides to plan their trips. Markers are also an educational tool, used by teachers and students as they learn about their state, region, or community.

First and foremost, however, historical markers are a tangible reminder of the state's history. They make that history accessible to every member of the community and to visitors. They also demonstrate the value that the state and community place on that history for future generations.

Indiana's historical marker program, administered by the Indiana Historical Bureau, has grown in popularity. The combination of state and private funds has enabled many communities to obtain much-deserved markers. Researching and installing a historical marker has often brought together members of a community interested in this common goal. Historical markers continue to be a point of local and state pride in Indiana.

This book will enable travelers—in vehicles or armchairs—to sample the richness of Indiana's history as it is presented on the state historical markers along the roads of Indiana.

Pamela J. Bennett
Director, Indiana Historical Bureau

Preface

"History as record embraces the monuments, documents, and symbols which provide such knowledge as we have or can find respecting past actuality. But it is history as thought that is really meant when the term history is used in its widest and most general significance."

Charles A. Beard (1874-1948) U. S. historian, born in Knightstown, Indiana
Annual address of the President, American Historical Association,
December 28, 1933

During the course of my travels over the years throughout Indiana, I usually take the time to pull off the highway and read the historical markers I encounter. A healthy mix of curiousity and a long time interest in history drives me to stop and become informed of the rich heritage of the landscape through which I am passing. This guide was compiled for history-minded travelers like myself who are interested to learn the chronology of events which have shaped the cultural and historical development of Hoosierdom.

The main text of this guide contains all the information given on the markers installed under the State of Indiana Historical Marker Program which is administered by the Indiana Historical Bureau. The text is arranged alphabetically by county for ease of use. Each marker entry includes a number (county, year installed, and sequence in that year), title, text, sponsor credit, and directional location. I personally visited each individual historical marker the summer of 2003, inventorying and photographing their condition.

Unfortunately not every historical marker in Indiana is included in this guide. Several county historical societies and private organizations such as the Daughters of the American Revolution (D. A. R.) have their own historical marker programs. This guide only includes the nearly 500 Indiana Historical Bureau markers that are clearly recognizable by the uniform shape with the state geographical outline at the top of the marker. Be advised that not all markers are easily accessed with roadside pullouts. Occasionally markers are removed for repair, highway construction or theft. Time takes its toll on these signs of history.

The invaluable assistance of many individuals in compiling this guide is gratefully acknowledged. Special recognition is due the always helpful staff of the Indiana Historical Bureau especially Judy Rippel, Carole Allen, and Pamela Bennett. A special debt of gratitude goes out to the Indiana State University graduate students, Judy Wu and Patricia Linehan, and their instructor, Professor SAMy Anderson, for their professional design and formating of this book. I want to acknowledge the assistance of the librarians at the Indiana State Library for helping to locate many of the historic photographs that are reproduced herein. Many thanks to the staff of Photo Solutions, Bloomington, for their technical expertise. Finally, and most of all, a deep appreciation to my family and community who inspired me to learn all that is around us growing up. Thank you all very much.

Alan McPherson

Introduction

Marking Indiana's History

by Judy A. Rippel
Former Coordinator, Indiana Historical Marker Program

In order to give the history of historical markers in Indiana, one must first give a brief history of the Indiana Historical Bureau, the state agency mandated to provide the official Indiana Historical Marker Program.

The predecessor of the Indiana Historical Bureau was the Indiana Historical Commission, established by the Indiana General Assembly in 1915 to prepare and execute plans for the Centennial celebration in 1916 of Indiana's admission to statehood.

No appropriated state funds were available for the installation of markers or memorials when the Commission was created. It was noted by the Commission, however, that "It would thus be strange and a source of some inquietude, had the year 1916 seen no Centennial markers and memorials placed here and there throughout Indiana." With the encouragement of the Commission many historic sites, including historic highways and trails across the state were marked with monuments, plaques, tablets, and memorials. They were installed by cities, counties, individuals, groups, and historical organizations.

In 1921, the Indiana General Assembly specifically authorized the Indiana Historical Commission to cooperate with and advise local historical societies, clubs, and other organizations interested in locating and marking historical sites. There were no funds made available to the Commission for the purchase of historical markers.

In order to determine the status of marking historical sites in Indiana, the Commission in a 1921 *Indiana History Bulletin* issued a preliminary list of markers by county; an updated survey was published in February 1922. More than 150 signs, plaques, and memorials were installed in 1923 through the cooperative effort led by the Commission. A follow-up survey was published in the April 1924 *Indiana History Bulletin*.

When the members of the Indiana Historical Commission met in April 1925, the meeting marked the end of the Commission. Their activities became the mandate of the Indiana Historical Bureau, a part of the Indiana Library and Historical Department, created by the Indiana General Assembly in 1925.

The Historical Bureau continued with the listing of historical markers, plaques, and public memorials. In 1934, the Historical Bureau raised the question of state government becoming involved in the placing of historical markers. The reasons put forth were that markers could be made uniform throughout the state, it would increase the number of markers, and perhaps a better selection of historical sites and subjects would be marked.

Works Progress Administration Historical Markers Project

From 1936 to 1942, the Indiana Historical Bureau administered the Historical Markers Project of the Works Progress Administration. More than 2,200 signs, similar to this one, were made by WPA workers. It is not known how many of these signs are still in existence. Courtesy Indiana Historical Bureau, State of Indiana

Not until 1936, however, did a state government program for marking sites become a reality; the Works Progress Administration (WPA) project of marking historical sites was approved with funding. The program was authorized twice—January 9, 1936-June 30, 1937 and January 26, 1938-January 31, 1942—as a jobs program for Hoosiers. In the first phase, the WPA furnished the material for the signs and the labor for making and painting them. The signs were three feet wide and two feet high and were made of thin sheet metal framed in angle iron. They were painted white, and the inscriptions (text) were hand-painted in black capital letters. The posts and braces (mounting) for the markers were uniform and made under contract for the state, but the cost of ninety cents each was be paid with private funds.

The location of each sign and the text was to be approved by the Historical Bureau. The work and expense of installing the signs was provided by the Indiana State Highway Commission. The Historical Bureau requested that county historical societies send locations of sites that should be marked and text suggestions for each sign.

In 1939, there were improvements in the signs. They were made of rolled steel, the painting was improved with lower-case lettering—making the signs easier to read—and a small sketch of the subject commemorated appeared next to the text. The cost of these signs was $2.50 payable by the applicant. The labor of making the signs was still provided by the WPA.

These WPA signs were considered temporary because of the type of material used; it was expected that they would be illegible and rusty in a few years. They served, however, to call the attention of citizens and travelers to persons and places of historical interest in Indiana.

Under the project, more than 2,200 signs were installed from 1936 to 1942. Most of the signs became shabby with age. In 1942, the State Highway Commission made plans to remove all unsightly WPA signs and collect the metal, which could be utilized as scrap iron during the war.

A New Historical Markers Program

In 1947, a search was begun for a more permanent type of marker. It was decided that the markers should be made of cast aluminum, with raised gold letters against a blue enamel background, and mounted on a post. This is the same format that is used today. The Historical Bureau squeezed $1,000 from the agency's operating budget and purchased a dozen of these new permanent historical markers to replace some of the nearly illegible WPA signs on sites of statewide interest. The Historical Bureau requested a special appropriation from the Indiana General Assembly to purchase additional markers, but the request for funds was denied.

The Battle of Mississinewa marker (27.1947.1) is located on SR 15 in Marion, Grant County. Only three of these 1947 markers remain today. Courtesy Indiana Historical Bureau, State of Indiana

Since funds were not approved to purchase markers, the Historical Bureau tried to interest local historical societies, patriotic societies, luncheon clubs, chambers of commerce, and other organizations in purchasing markers. The Bureau offered the markers at a cost of about $85.00 each. By the year 1951, forty of these markers had been installed using private funds.

In 1957, a concerted effort was made by the Historical Bureau and the historic sites committees of the Society of Indiana Pioneers and the Indiana Historical Society to revive the marker program in the state. Between the years 1957 and 1965, approximately twenty markers were installed using private donations.

Civil War Centennial Commission Historical Markers

In September 1959, the Indiana Civil War Centennial Commission was authorized by the Indiana General Assembly to plan and conduct the commemoration of the centennial of the Civil War from 1961 to 1965. One purpose of the Commission was to identify, locate, and mark those places historically significant to Indiana's Civil War effort. Working with the Indiana Historical Bureau, the Commission installed thirty-nine permanent historical markers relating to Indiana's involvement in the Civil War.

Indiana Sesquicentennial Commission Historical Markers

The Indiana Sesquicentennial Commission was created by the 1957 Indiana General Assembly to celebrate Indiana's 150th birthday as a state in 1966. Installation of permanent state historical markers was one of the activities suggested to celebrate the sesquicentennial of statehood. Several hundred proposals resulted from a promotional mailing. The markers ranged in price from $150.00 to $195.00. Sixty-five markers were purchased by the Commission. In almost every instance the markers were dedicated with a proper ceremony attended by

The New Purchase Boundary (Treaty of St. Mary's) marker (4.1966.1) is located west of Fowler on SR 18 in Benton County. It was installed by the Indiana Sesquicentennial Commission in 1966 and restored in 2000 by volunteers. Courtesy Indiana Historical Bureau, State of Indiana

prominent national, state, and local citizens and interested groups. An attempt was made not to call any particular site the "first," "only," or "most important" unless sufficient proof existed to do so. It was the hope of the Commission that its marker program would stimulate others to pursue the installation of historical markers.

Something new in the state historical marker program was added when maps were incorporated with the texts. Since the text was limited to about thirty-five words, it was felt that the diagrams would provide considerably more information.

The Indiana Historical Bureau prepared a new listing of historical markers of the state in the Indiana Sesquicentennial year, the first since 1929. It was published in the April 1966 *Indiana History Bulletin* and updated in the July 1967 issue.

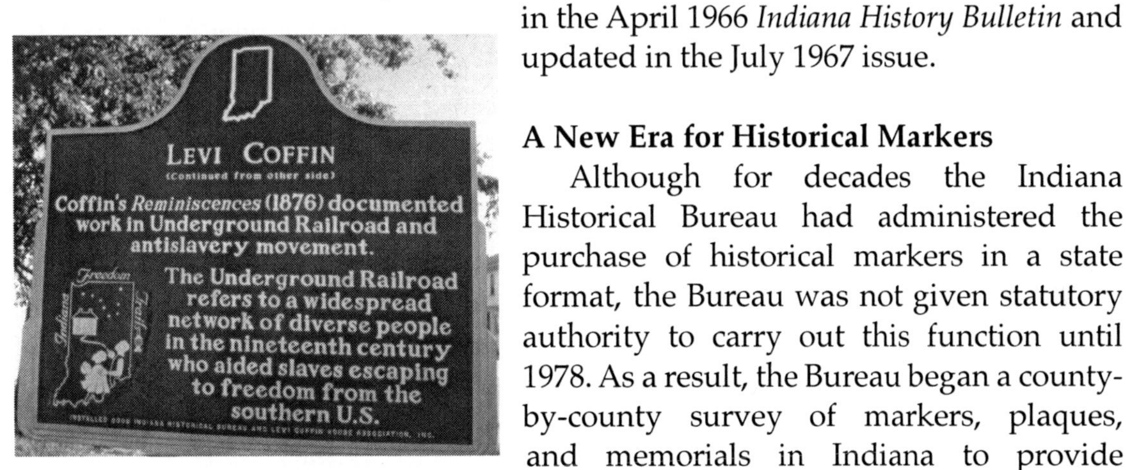

The Levi Coffin marker (89.2002.1) is located in Fountain City, Wayne County. This is an Underground Railroad Initiative marker with the Indiana Freedom Trails logo. Courtesy Indiana Historical Bureau, State of Indiana

A New Era for Historical Markers

Although for decades the Indiana Historical Bureau had administered the purchase of historical markers in a state format, the Bureau was not given statutory authority to carry out this function until 1978. As a result, the Bureau began a county-by-county survey of markers, plaques, and memorials in Indiana to provide a comprehensive and orderly central repository of marker information. Volunteers across the state completed survey forms, and the results—although incomplete—were published in 1978 and 1979 issues of the *Indiana History Bulletin*.

In 1989, there was a dramatic change to the Indiana Historical Marker Program. For the first time since the 1966 Sesquicentennial Commission Marker Program, the Indiana General Assembly appropriated funds to the Indiana Historical Bureau to purchase markers. Thirty-eight markers were installed, using these state funds and local donations.

In 1993, continuing appropriations from the Indiana General Assembly to purchase markers began. From 1947 to 1988, a period of forty-one years, a little over 200 markers were installed. As a result of the infusion of state funds, in the fifteen year period from 1989 to 2004, over 225 markers have been installed using state and private funds.

What about the future? Since historical markers are cast in aluminum, are fixed solidly in place, and are not amenable to revision, marker texts are being thoroughly documented with primary source material. With historically accurate texts, markers can serve the purpose of communicating history to the general public in capsule form. The markers may be used as educational tools for teachers,

By 1998, a searchable database containing all Indiana state historical markers was made available on the Historical Bureau Web site; it is regularly updated. The database contains the marker county, title, text, credit line, and location and is searchable in all of those fields. In 2003, the Historical Bureau began adding texts with footnotes for current and future markers to provide additional learning opportunities. Also available on the Historical Bureau Web site will be examples of Applications with copies of some materials used to document the information in the text.

A goal of the program is to increase the diversity of marker topics so that persons reading Indiana state markers can realize that Indiana is like a tapestry, an overall image made up of countless single strands, each with its own unique history worth celebrating. Markers should reflect the rich political, social, cultural, economic, intellectual, and scientific history of the state.

In 2001, the opportunity came to collaborate with the Division of Historic Preservation and Archaeology, Indiana Department of Natural Resources, on an Underground Railroad Initiative, which will help document this important facet of Indiana history. The numbers of markers about women, American Indians, and ethnic groups are also increasing.

The past, present, and continued success of the Indiana Historical Marker Program has been—and will be—dependent on the many volunteers across the state who have given—and will give—of their time, energy, and money to see that markers are installed which present, preserve, and celebrate the history of Indiana. To those people who have worked on the program, thank you! To those of you who have not yet become involved with the program, please join the effort to continue marking Indiana's history for future generations!

For more information about the Indiana Historical Marker Program, including how to apply for a historical marker, visit the Indiana Historical Bureau Web site at www.IN.gov/history or call 317-232-2535.

How to Use this Guidebook

Tailor-made for Indiana, this easy-to-use guidebook enhances the traveling pleasure for motorists by featuring the location and story text for each Indiana State historical marker, nearly 500 total. The historical markers are arranged and presented alphabetically by Indiana county. The Indiana county map (on page 16) identifies the State's 92 counties and their geographic locations. The historical markers are organized and listed in the Index by County and by Sign Title or Name. A sample text page illustrates the format:

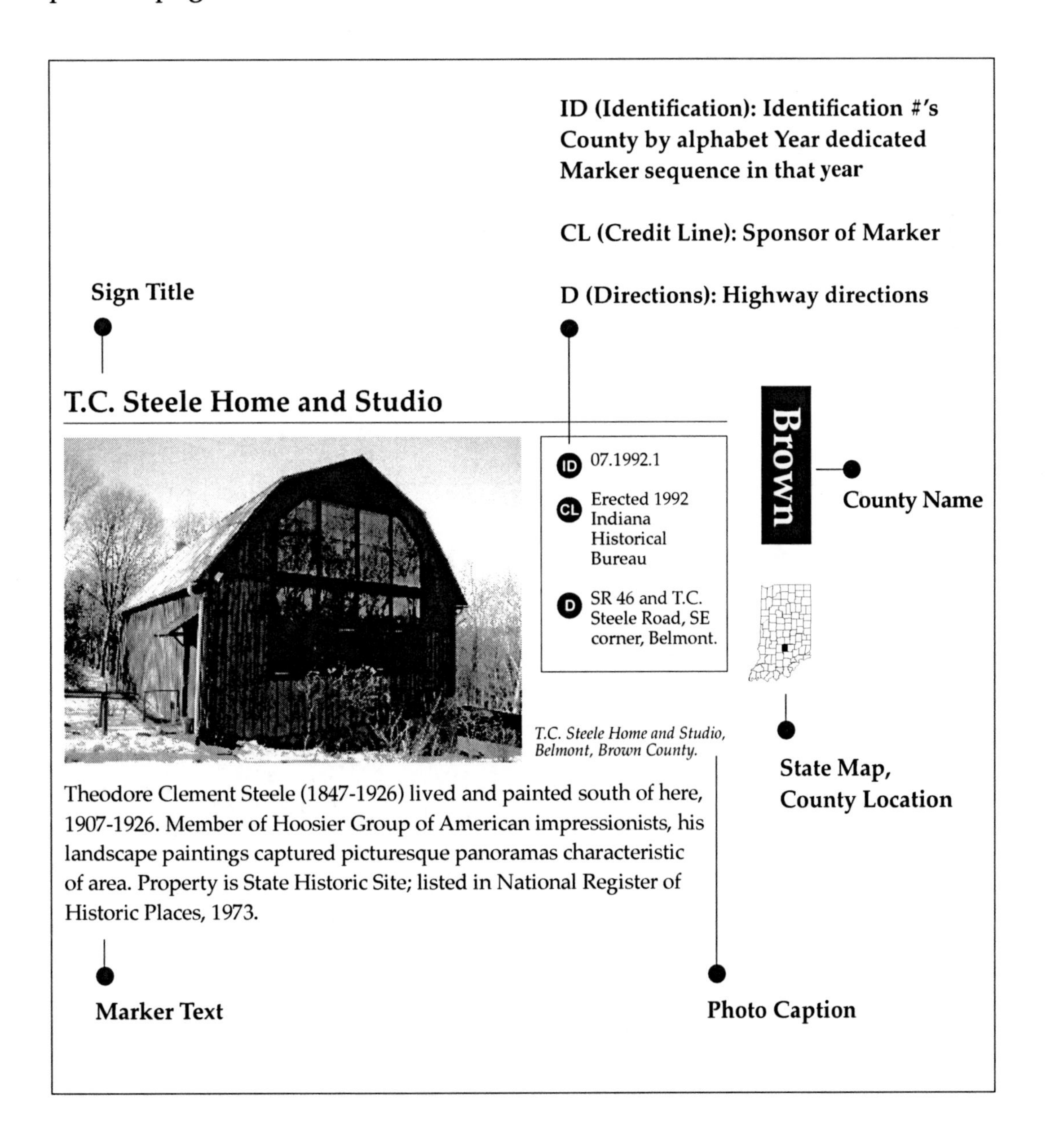

Indiana County Map

HISTORICAL
MARKER

The Wayne Trace

ID 01.1977.1
Formerly
01.1966.1

CL Erected by
the Society of
Indiana Pioneers
1977

D 0.1 mile north of
SR 101 and US
224, 6640 N SR
101, west side of
road, 3 miles east
of Decatur.

General Anthony Wayne and the Legion of the United States passed this way on October 30, 1794, in route from Fort Wayne to Fort Greenville, ending the western campaign against the Indian Confederacy. The Legion spent the previous night camped 2.6 miles N.N.W. of here.

Geneva Downtown Historic District

ID 01.2006.1

CL Installed
2006 Indiana
Historical
Bureau,
Adams County
Community
Foundation,
and Geneva
Proud/Geneva
Chamber of
Commerce

D Decatur and
Line Streets,
Geneva

Side one:
Adams County formed 1835. Geneva incorporation 1874 included early towns Alexander and Buffalo. During 1890s oil boom, population and businesses grew. Fire destroyed much of town 1895; Geneva Board of Trustees banned wooden buildings, mandated stone, iron, or brick buildings along part of Line Street.
Side two:
By end of 1895, twenty-four new brick business buildings completed here. District (144-455 East Line Street) retains look of late 1800s commercial center because most buildings were constructed concurrently, as evidenced by architectural details. Listed in National Register of Historic Places 2002.

Camp Allen 1861-64

Civil War Mustering-In Camp. Colonel Hugh B. Reed served as first Commandant. Here the 30th, 44th, 74th, 88th, and 100th Indiana Regiments and the 11th Indiana Battery were organized.

ID 02.1963.1

CL Erected by the Indiana Civil War Centennial Commission, 1963

D SE corner of Center & Huron Streets at playground entrance, Fort Wayne.

Site of Hardin's Defeat

Hardin's Defeat, Little Turtle, Allen County, Indiana Picture Collection, MS. Section, Indiana State Library.

Colonel John Hardin, of the Kentucky Militia, with 180 men and Captain John Armstrong, U.S. Army, with 30 men, were routed here on October 19, 1790, by Indians under Miami Chief Little Turtle during General Harmar's Campaign.

ID 02.1966.1

CL Erected by Indiana Sesquicentennial Commission, 1966

D 0.3 mile east of US 33 on Carroll Road near Madden Road across from church and cemetery, NW of Fort Wayne

Home of Philo T. Farnsworth

ID 02.1992.1

CL Erected 1992 Indiana Historical Bureau.

D St. Joseph & E. State Boulevards, Fort Wayne.

Home of Philo T. Farnsworth, Ft. Wayne, Allen County.

Home 1948-1967 of Farnsworth, inventor of television. Farnsworth (1906-1971) was instrumental in perfecting the image formation mechanism which enabled the first effective image transmission in 1927. Farnsworth Radio and Television Corporation in Fort Wayne 1938-1949.

Wabash and Erie Canal Groundbreaking

ID 02.1992.2

CL Erected 1992 Indiana Historical Bureau.

D 1716 West Main Street at Growth Avenue, NE corner, Fort Wayne.

Wabash & Erie Canal, St. Marys River Aqueduct, Ft. Wayne, Allen County, from J. P. Dunn's, Indiana and Indianans, Vol. I, page 386, 1919.

On February 22, 1832, ground was broken two blocks north for the canal, which would link Lake Erie at Toledo with the Ohio River at Evansville. Jordan Vigus, Canal Commissioner, Charles W. Ewing, Samuel Hanna, and Elias Murray participated in the ceremony.

Allen

Fort Miamis

Side one:
French built a palisaded fort on this strategic site in 1722; named Fort Saint Philippe des Miamis. One of three French forts built in what is now Indiana to protect French fur trade from encroaching English. First of five forts built over time within a square mile of the center of present-day Fort Wayne.
Side two:
Nearby confluence of St. Mary's and St. Joseph's rivers forms Maumee River, a strategic central part of the waterways system connecting Great Lakes regions with Mississippi River Valley. Using a portage between Maumee and Wabash rivers, travelers could journey nearly 2,500 miles by water from French Canada to Louisiana.

ID 02.2000.1

CL Installed 2000 Indiana Historical Bureau and Society of Colonial Wars in the State of Indiana

D Guldin Park, Van Buren Street Bridge, SW corner, and St. Marys River boat ramp at Michaels Avenue, Fort Wayne.

Gronauer Lock No. 2

Side one:
Wabash and Erie Canal lock was discovered here June 1991 during excavation for highway construction. It was built 1838-1840 by Henry Lotz and named for lock keeper Joseph Gronauer. The rare, well-preserved timber-frame design lock measured 115 by 40 feet; lock chamber was 90 by 15 feet; two-thirds of total structure was excavated and removed.
Side two:
Numerous artifacts and 750 pieces of timber were recovered. After extensive preservation treatment, approximately 5 percent of total lock structure is included in an Indiana State Museum exhibit. Wabash and Erie Canal, America's longest at approximately 460 miles, linked Lake Erie at Toledo, Ohio with Ohio River at Evansville 1853.

ID 02.2003.1

CL Installed 2003 Indiana Historical Bureau, Canal Society of Indiana, and New Haven Kiwanis

D US 24 just beyond east interchange of I-469 bypass, New Haven.

Lowell Mills

ID 03.1988.1

CL Erected 1988 Union Community Extension Homemakers

D CR 325 W & Driftwood Road at Driftwood River public access site, west of Columbus and I-65.

From 1830 to 1880 the community of Lowell Mills thrived here along Driftwood River. There were two grist mills, a cooperage, a shoemaker's shop, a distillery, a saw mill, a woolen mill, an inn and general store. When the mills closed, the town was abandoned.

Private Barton W. Mitchell

ID 03.1992.1

CL Erected 1992 by Indiana Historical Bureau

D SW corner of town square, SR 46/East Harrison Street & North Washington, Hartsville.

Mitchell, Co. F, 27th Indiana Volunteers, is buried in Hartsville Baptist Cemetery. He found Confederate General Lee's "Lost" Special Orders No. 191 Near Frederick, MD, September 13, 1862. Union General McClellan then engaged Lee at the Battle of Antietam.

Hartsville College

ID 03.1995.1

CL 1995 Indiana Historical Bureau and Cross Cliff Little Hoosiers.

D SE corner of town square, SR 46/East Harrison Street & North Jackson, Hartsville.

Original site of coeducational United Brethren school founded 1850 as Hartsville Academy by public act of Indiana General Assembly. Campus moved four blocks south, circa 1865; destroyed by fire, January 1898. Many graduates became distinguished citizens in their communities throughout the state and nation.

Booker T. Washington School

Site of only African-American school (grades 1-7) in Columbus. By circa 1899, town's African-American population had increased enough to qualify for separate school under 1869 Indiana law. Like other African-American schools around the state, it was a symbol of community pride and achievement; closed in 1922.

ID 03.1998.1

CL Erected 1998 Indiana Historical Bureau, Cummins Engine Foundation, and Historic Landmarks Foundation of Indiana.

D NE corner 14th & Union Streets, Columbus.

Second Baptist Church

Second Baptist Church, Columbus, Bartholomew County.

Congregation was formed in 1879; reorganized in 1882 by the Reverend John R. Miller and a core of determined members. The present building, formerly a theatre, was acquired in 1913. This African-American church, like many others, has served its members as an educational and social foundation as well as a religious institution.

ID 03.1998.2

CL Erected 1998 Indiana Historical Bureau, Cummins Engine Foundation, and Historic Landmarks Foundation of Indiana.

D 1328 9th Street, at Reed Street, Columbus.

Madison and Indianapolis Railroad

ID 03.1999.1

CL Erected 1999 Indiana Historical Bureau and Joseph Hart Chapter, Daughters of the American Revolution.

D 204 Railroad Road between 2nd & 3rd Streets on grassy median, Elizabethtown.

Mandated by Indiana's 1836 Internal Improvement Act, construction began in Madison 1836. Completed along this site 1843; Elizabethtown platted 1845 as a result of the railroad. Completed to Indianapolis 1847. Linked Ohio River and interior of state.

Bartholomew County Courthouse

ID 03.2000.1

CL Installed 2000 Indiana Historical Bureau and Joseph Hart Chapter, Daughters of the American Revolution

D SE corner of courthouse, 234 Washington Street, Columbus.

Bartholomew County Courthouse, Columbus.

Side one: County formed by Indiana General Assembly 1821. Thirty acres of land were purchased, and John Tipton donated thirty acres, for county seat. State commissioners named county seat Tiptona--after Tipton; local elected commissioners renamed it Columbus. Tipton served as state representative, Indian agent, and United States senator.

Side two: Second Empire Style courthouse, designed by Isaac Hodgson, completed 1874, is county's fourth courthouse. Constructed of red brick with white limestone trim. Foundation is rusticated blue limestone. Original slate roof replaced 1953 with standing-seam copper. Extensive remodeling 1968; interior restoration completed 1998. Listed in National Register of Historic Places 1979.

Orinoco Furniture Company

Side one: Incorporated and its factory built here 1890. Reorganized 1891; William H. Lincoln then led the company to great success, stressing quality and artistic merit in fine, high-grade furniture. By 1895, production included parlor, library, and tea tables and ladies' desks; furniture was sold throughout U.S. Lincoln Chair Company established 1913.
Side two: The companies were important in Columbus' economy; they were part of Indiana's extensive furniture industry. Employees included many skilled craftsmen. Lincoln died 1935; the companies were reorganized into Lincoln-Orinoco, Inc. The company closed 1940; buildings and all assets were sold at auction. Buildings have had various uses over time.

ID 03.2007.1

CL Installed 2007 Indiana Historical Bureau and Nugent Foundation

D 1720 17th St. Columbus.

Atterbury Army Air Field

Side one: Construction begun summer 1942 under Captain Stratton O. Hammon, who used broad authority over laborers, suppliers, and railroad; base in used February 1943. More than 1,000 workers employed during construction. Base was over 2,000 acres, cost over four million dollars, and included more than one hundred buildings, intended to be temporary.
Side two: WWII uses included training B-25, B-26, and glider pilots; by 1944, wounded from Europe received here for Wakeman Hospital. Wounded soldiers during Korean War received here. Renamed 1954 to honor Lt. John Bakalar. Base closed 1970. Original building made into chapel; restored and renamed for Women's Air Service Pilot Jean Lewellen Norbeck in 1990s.

ID 03.2007.2

CL Installed 2007 Indiana Historical Bureau and Atterbury-Bakalar Air Museum.

D Jean Lewellen Norbeck Chapel, Atterbury Army Air Field, intersection of Middle Road and Grissom Avenue, Columbus.

New Purchase Boundary (Treaty of St. Mary's)

ID 04.1966.1

CL Erected by Indiana Sesquicentennial Commission, 1966

D SR 18, 2.5 miles west of US 52 in Fowler, 0.5 mile east of US 41.

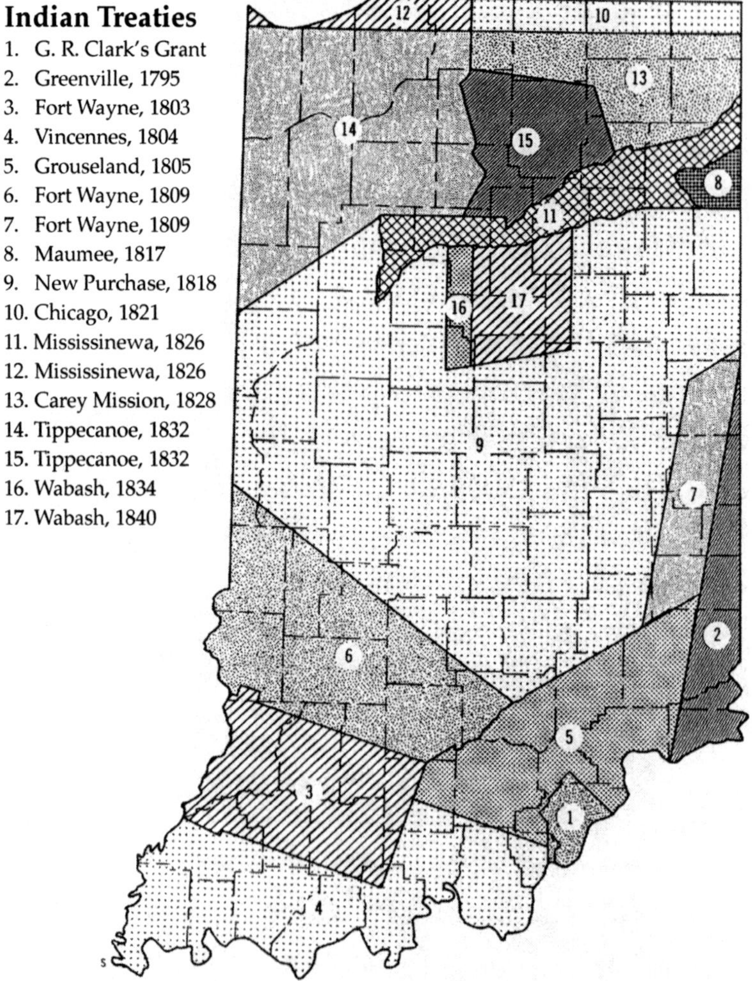

New Purchase Boundary, Fowler, Benton County, from Indian Treaty Map, Robert Kingsbury's, An Atlas of Indiana, Dept. of Geography, Indiana University, Bloomington, page 7, 1970.

In October 1818, Purchasing Commissioners Lewis Cass, Benjamin Parke and Governor Jonathan Jennings acquired Indian claims on the land shown on this marker. About one-third of modern Indiana was involved in this transaction. [map]

Benton County Courthouse

Benton County formed by General Assembly in 1840. Oxford first county seat; Fowler became second, 1874. Designed in Second Empire Style by Gorden P. Randall and built 1874 by Levi L. Leach. Located at geographical center of county on land donated by Moses Fowler family.

ID 04.1995.1

CL Erected 1995 Indiana Historical Bureau, Benton County Indiana Historical Society, Inc., and Benton County Commissioners

D 705 East Sixth Street at east entrance of courthouse, Fowler.

Dan Patch

Dan Patch, Race Horse, Oxford, Benton County, Indiana Picture Collection, MS. Section, Indiana State Library.

Side one: Standard-bred colt (sire Joe Patchen, dam Zelica) foaled 1896 Oxford, Benton County; raised by Daniel A. Messner, Jr. on this farm. A natural pacer, trained for harness racing, a very popular sport in late 1800s and early 1900s. Dan Patch began his racing career at county fairs in 1900; he became famous in Grand Circuit racing and never lost a race.

Side two: In 1902, sold to M. E. Sturgis, New York, then to Marion W. Savage, owner of International Stock Food Company, Minneapolis, Minnesota, who used horse's racing fame to market his stock food and many other products from toys to automobiles. Dan Patch's 1906 world record 1:55 mile held for thirty-two years. Was retired from racing 1909 for stud. Took part in exhibitions; died 1916.

ID 04.1999.1

CL Erected 1999 Indiana Historical Bureau, descendants of Daniel A. Messner, Jr., Oxford Lions Club, Oxford Citizens and Town Board, Benton County Indiana Historical Society, Inc.

D 203 South Michigan Road, near intersection of SR 352 & SR 55 at east edge of Oxford.

Blackford

Godfroy Reserve

ID 05.1989.1

CL Erected by Francois Godfroy Chapter NSDAR 1989

D SE corner of Main Street & Huntington Street/SR 18, Montpelier.

Reserved by U.S. to Chief Francois Godfroy of the Miami Nation of Indians by treaty at St. Mary's, Ohio, 6 October 1818, 3,840 acres on Salamonie River at La Petite Prairie, Harrison Township, Blackford County; reserve lands sold 1827, 1836.

Blackford County Courthouse

ID 05.1994.1

CL Erected 1994 Indiana Historical Bureau and Blackford Lodge #106 F. & A.M.

D 110 W. Washington Street at south entrance to courthouse, Hartford City.

Blackford County Courthouse, South Entrance, Hartford City.

Blackford County's second courthouse, featuring a 165 foot high clock tower, was built on foundation stones from nearby Montpelier quarries. At a cost of $129,337.83, this Richardsonian Romanesque structure was constructed 1893-1895. Listed in National Register of Historic Places, 1980.

Indian Cemetery/Eel River Tribe of Miamis

Ka-wi-a-ki-un-gi Village "Place of Thorns" (Thorntown) was center of 64,000 acre Thorntown Indian Reserve. Granted to Eel River Miamis in 1818, ceded to U.S. in 1828.

ID 06.1961.1

CL Indiana Historical Society, 1961

D North side of SR 47, 0.5 mile east of Thorntown.

Patrick H. Sullivan 1794-1879

was the first white settler in Boone County, 1823, and built the first log cabin. In 1857, he bought this site and lived here until 1872. He served in the War of 1812.

ID 06.1962.1

CL Erected by the Zionsville Historical Society 1962

D 225 W. Hawthorne at the P. H. Sullivan Museum, entrance Zionsville.

Michigan Road

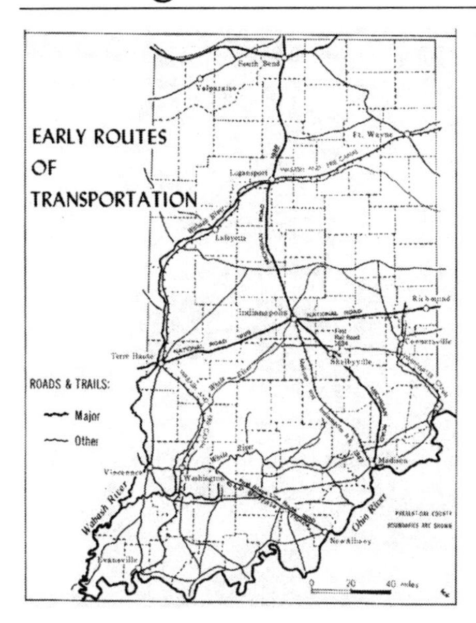

Michigan Road, near Zionsville, Boone County, from Early Routes of Transportation map, Robert Kingsbury, An Atlas of Indiana, Dept. of Geography, Indiana University, Bloomington, page 74, 1970.

With proceeds from the sale of 170,580 acres of Indian land granted by the Federal Government, Indiana built its first north-south road. Surveyed 1829, passable by 1834, "completed" in 1837, its cost was $242,000.00. [map]

ID 06.1966.2

CL Erected by Indiana Sesquicentennial Commission, 1966

D West side of US 421, north of 121st Street, north & east of Zionsville.

The Boone County REMC

ID 06.1985.1

CL Indiana Statewide Association of Rural Electric Cooperatives, Inc. 1985

D I-65 northbound rest stop, 1 mile north of exit 146 & SR 47, 7.5 miles north of Lebanon.

The Boone County REMC built Indiana's first electric cooperative line to the Clark Woody farm 5 miles west of this site with funds borrowed from the Rural Electrification Administration, July 22, 1935.

The Boone County REMC

ID 06.1985.2

CL Indiana Statewide Association of Rural Electric Cooperatives, Inc. 1985

D I-65 southbound rest stop, 1 mile north of exit 146 & SR 47, 7.5 miles north of Lebanon.

The Boone County REMC built Indiana's first electric cooperative line to the Clark Woody farm 5 miles west of this site with funds borrowed from the Rural Electrification Administration, July 22, 1935.

T.C. Steele Home and Studio

Brown

07.1992.1

Erected 1992 Indiana Historical Bureau

SR 46 and T.C. Steele Road, SE corner, Belmont.

T. C. Steele Home & Studio, Studio, Belmont, Brown County.

Theodore Clement Steele (1847-1926) lived and painted south of here, 1907-1926. Member of Hoosier Group of American impressionists, his landscape paintings captured picturesque panoramas characteristic of area. Property is State Historic Site; listed in National Register of Historic Places, 1973.

Sycamore Row

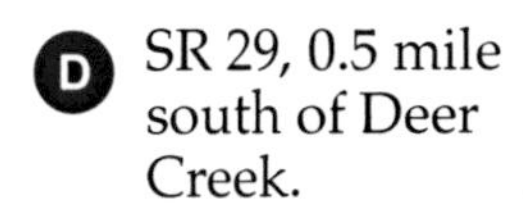

Sycamore Row and Historical Marker, Deer Creek, Carroll County.

This row of sycamores sprouted from freshly cut logs used in the 1830's to corduroy a swampy section of the historic Michigan Road, the first state road in Indiana, running from Madison to Michigan City.

New Purchase Boundary (Treaty of St. Mary's)

ID 08.1966.1

CL Erected by Indiana Sesquicentennial Commission, 1966

D US 421 south of the Wabash River bridge and north of South Road, Pittsburg.

In October 1818, Purchasing Commissioners Lewis Cass, Benjamin Parke and Governor Jonathan Jennings acquired Indian claims on the land shown on this marker. About one-third of modern Indiana was involved in this transaction. [map]

Wabash and Erie Canal

ID 08.1992.1

CL Erected 1992 Indiana Historical Bureau

D Bicycle Bridge Road, 0.1 mile north of US 421 & SR 25 intersection at the trailhead access & parking for Historic Delphi Trails, west edge of Delphi.

Wabash & Erie Canal, Conference & Interpretive Center, Delphi , Carroll County.

Constructed 1832-1853, canal was nation's longest, connection Lake Erie at Toledo with Ohio River at Evansville. Key portion in Carroll County included Deer Creek Lake Dam, constructed 1838-1840 (1 mile west). Various canal structures are still in evidence.

Wabash & Erie Canal

Trade and emigration route from Lake Erie to Evansville. Completed through Logansport 1840. Followed Erie Avenue and 5th Street, crossing Eel River by wooden aqueduct. Abandoned about 1876.

ID 09.1966.1

CL Erected by Indiana Sesquicentennial Commission, 1966

D SE corner of High & Fifth Streets, Logansport.

Cass

Clarksville

First American settlement in the Northwest Territory. 150,000 acres granted to George Rogers Clark and his troops by Virginia in 1781 for war services. Town named and tracts occupied by 1784.

ID 10.194?

CL Indiana Historical Bureau

D Clark Boulevard & Harrison Avenue, on landscaped median, Clarksville.

Clark

Civil War Hospital 1864-66

Site of Jefferson General Hospital, the third largest hospital in the United States during the Civil War. Under Dr. Middleton Goldsmith's command it served over 16,000 patients.

ID 10.1962.1

CL Erected by the Indiana Civil War Centennial Commission, 1962

D 301 Park Place at Crestview, northeast lawn, Holt Masonic Orphan's Home, Port Fulton neighborhood, Jeffersonville.

General Jefferson C. Davis 1828-1879

ID 10.1963.1

CL Erected by the Indiana Civil War Centennial Commission, 1963

D US 31 and Court Street, Memphis.

General Jefferson C. Davis (1828-1879), Memphis, Clark County, Indiana Picture Collection, MS. Section, Indiana State Library.

was born in Clark Co., Ind. Appointed colonel of the 22nd Indiana Infantry. After promotion to brigadier general for service at Pea Ridge, he saw action at Corinth, Murfreesboro, and Chickamauga and the Atlantic Campaign.

Grave of Jonathan Jennings (1784-1834) (Two blocks east)

ID 10.1966.1

CL Erected by Indiana Sesquicentennial Commission, 1966.

D Market/SR 3 at Pleasant Street, Charlestown.

Indiana Territorial delegate to Congress, 1809–1816. President of Indiana Constitutional Convention, June, 1816. First Governor of Indiana, 1816–1822. Member of Congress, 1822–1830.

Birthplace and Childhood Home of Col. Harland Sanders

ID 10.1987.1

CL See listing (right)

D South side of SR 160 & exit 16 of northbound I-65, Henryville.

Founder of Kentucky Fried Chicken [image}
Erected 1987 by these Local Franchisees

Mr. & Mrs. Robert Bagshaw, Mr. & Mrs. William Bridges, Mr. & Mrs. William Bright, Mr. & Mrs. Roy Burchel, Mr. & Mrs. Lee Cummings, Mr. & Mrs. Ralph Fordyce, Mr. & Mrs. Henry Gilley, Mr. & Mrs. Robert Heil, Mr. & Mrs. Everitt Houchen, Pauline Houchen & Joe Ann, Mr. & Mrs. Charles Howser, Mr. & Mrs. William Mullins, Mr. & Mrs. Marvin Payne, Mr. & Mrs. Raymond Popp, Mr. & Mrs. Henry Rothbaur, Mr. & Mrs. Bud Stotts, Mr. & Mrs. Hershel Wells, Mr. & Mrs. T. J. White.

Lewis & Clark Expedition 1803-1806

Portraits of William Clark & Captain Meriwether Lewis, by artist Charles Wilson Peale, Philadelphia, 1810.

William Clark *Captain Meriwether Lewis*

Near this site on October 26,1803, Meriwether Lewis and William Clark with the nucleus of the Corps of Discovery together set off down the Ohio River on their epic journey to explore the Louisiana Purchase and Pacific Northwest.

ID 10.1991.1

CL Erected by the Lewis & Clark Trail Heritage Foundation, Inc. 1991

D Falls of the Ohio State Park, George Rogers Clark Homesite, 1200 South Harrison Street, Clarksville.

Clark State Forest

Clark State Forest, Pine Lake, Henryville, Clark County.

Indiana's oldest state forest, established 1903. Portions of Clark's Grant (1781) included in original 2,000 acres. Experimental plantings and reforestation began 1904; became national models in scientific forestry. Multiple land uses include timber management, recreational activities, wildlife areas, and watershed protection.

ID 10.1992.1

CL Erected 1992 Indiana Historical Bureau and Henryville Elementary Little Hoosiers

D US 31, Clark State Forest, 100 yards past entrance on south side of forest road, north Henryville.

Borden Institute Site

ID 10.1995.1

CL Erected 1995 Indiana Historical Bureau and West Clark Community Schools—Gifted/ Talented Program

D 301 West Street at school drive, Borden or New Providence.

Coeducational school founded 1884 by William W. Borden primarily to serve children of southern Indiana farmers. Low-cost, progressive program included teacher preparation and laboratory-based scientific studies. School closed 1906. Borden also established library and museum with extensive geological collections.

Fern Grove and Rose Island Resorts

ID 10.1998.1

CL Erected 1998 Indiana Historical Bureau and Clark's Grant Historical Society.

D SR 62, at entrance to Charlestown State Park, Charlestown.

Fern Grove & Rose Island Resorts, Charlestown State Park, Clark County, Postcard, Dancing Pavilion, Indiana Picture Collection, MS. Section, Indiana State Library.

Side one:
Nearby is site of former popular Ohio River regional recreation area known from 1880s as Fern Grove. David Rose expanded facilities in 1923-including an amusement park and a swimming pool-and named it Rose Island. Major access was by car to swinging foot bridge over creek and by steamboats on river. Closed after extensive damage from 1937 flood.
Side two:
The peninsula at the confluence of Fourteen Mile Creek and the Ohio River near here was known as Fern Grove-Rose Island. Part of the Indiana Army Ammunition Plant circa 1940. Included in Charlestown State Park, established 1993. The rugged and scenic area is rich in geological features, archaeological remnants, and habitat for wildlife.

Tunnel Mill

Side one:
John Work (1760-1832), one of area's most prominent businessmen, settled on Fourteen Mile Creek 1804; had this house built circa 1811; built grist mill, tunnel, and dam on creek circa 1814-1816. Over time, Work operated three grist mills, four saw mills, powder mill, distillery, stone sawing mill, and general store.
Side two:
Tunnel dug near here was six feet tall, five feet wide, over 385 feet long, and considered major engineering feat. Blasting through limestone hill took nearly 2.5 years. Tunnel served as mill race providing consistent water supply. Mill was three stories tall with limestone foundation. Upper two floors made of wood. Mill burned 1927.

ID 10.2001.1
Installed

CL 2001 Indiana Historical Bureau and Descendants of John and Rebecca Work Drummond

D 3709 Tunnel Mill Road, Charlestown. Missing.

Indiana State Prison

Side one:
First state prison authorized January 9, 1821, opened October 1822 on lower Market Street in Jeffersonville; prisoners were confined to hard labor. Prisoners were moved to new state prison, opened here in Clarksville October 1847. Warden was elected by Indiana General Assembly. Inmates worked in shops set up by manufacturing companies on the grounds.
Side two:
In 1873, female inmates were transferred to Indiana Reformatory for Women and Girls in Indianapolis. In 1897, prison became Indiana Reformatory for men 16-30 years old; males over 30 sent to Michigan City prison. In 1918, fire swept through Reformatory. State sold land and buildings to Colgate Company 1921. Some original buildings still remain.

ID 10.2006.1

CL Installed 2005 Indiana Historical Bureau and Clarksville Historical Society

D 1400 block, South Clark Blvd., Clarksville.

Crosscut Canal Eel River Feeder Dam

ID 11.1999.1

CL Erected 1999 Indiana Historical Bureau, Canal Society of Indiana, and local citizens.

D 4 miles north of Clay City on SR 59 at Eel River bridge, northwest corner. Reinstallation pending as of 3/9/04.

Side one:
Eel River Feeder Dam, 180 feet long and 16.5 feet high, was completed 300 yards downriver from here 1839. It was constructed to carry enough water from the river to enable navigation of boats on the proposed Crosscut Canal, included in Indiana Internal Improvement Act 1836. State halted construction of canal 1839.
Side two:
Crosscut Canal construction resumed 1847; in service 1850-circa 1861 from Terre Haute on Wabash River to Worthington on West Fork White River. Feeder Dam, deteriorated with neglect, repaired and extended to 264 feet long by 1850. Part of Wabash and Erie Canal, America's longest at approximately 460 miles; linked Lake Erie at Toledo, Ohio with Ohio River at Evansville 1853.

Crosscut Canal

ID 11.1999.2

CL Erected 1999 Indiana Historical Bureau, Norman Klass, Local Organizations, and Citizens

D 6.5 miles south of Clay City on SR 59 at CR 1300 S, northwest corner of old K & E Canal Bridge.

Located here was part of Crosscut Canal, in service circa 1850-1861 from Terre Haute on Wabash River to Worthington on West Fork White River; sale of land in Clay County helped finance. Part of Wabash and Erie Canal, America's longest, linked Lake Erie at Toledo, Ohio with Ohio River at Evansville 1853; included in Indiana Internal Improvement Act 1836.

Clay County Courthouse

Clay County Courthouse, Brazil.

ID 11.2001.1

CL Installed 2001 Indiana Historical Bureau, Clay County Commissioners, and Clay County Historical Society, Inc.

D 609 E. National Road/US 40, Brazil.

Side one:
County formed by Indiana General Assembly 1825; named for national statesman Henry Clay. First county seat at Bowling Green; had three courthouses: first built 1827 was two-story log structure; second and third built 1839-1840 and 1852-1853 were two-story brick. County seat moved to Brazil 1877 after fourth courthouse completed there in 1876.
Side two:
This fifth courthouse designed by John W. Gaddis of Vincennes in Classical Revival Style. Built 1912-1914 of limestone; stained-glass skylight in central rotunda. Interior features marble wainscoting, granite columns, inlaid tile floors. Skylight restored, four tower clocks installed 1986. Listed in National Register of Historic Places 1999.

Leavenworth

ID 13.1992.1

CL Erected 1992 by Indiana Historical Bureau

D SR 62 & West Street, north side of highway on grassy median near general store & post office, Leavenworth.

Leavenworth, Overlook Above Horseshoe Bend, Crawford County.

Founded 1818 by Seth and Zebulon Leavenworth. Ohio River port for keelboats, flatboats, packets. Shipped pork, spirits, produce, corn, lumber, etc. Manufactured skiffs, flatboats, pearl buttons. Crawford County seat, 1843-c. 1895, when "stolen" by town of English. Town relocated to present site after 1937 flood.

Early Mining at Wyandotte Caves

ID 13.1992.2

CL Erected 1992 by Indiana Historical Bureau

D Wyandotte Cave entrance road, 0.5 mile north of SR 62, 5 miles east of Leavenworth.

Big Wyandotte Cave, Monument Mountain, Leavenworth, Crawford County, from G. S. Cottman's, Centennial History & Handbook of Indiana, page 232, 1915.

Chert and aragonite were mined prehistorically. Land containing Wyandotte and Saltpeter Caves was purchased by Levi Brashear on September 30, 1810 for saltpeter mining and by Dr. Benjamin Adams on December 27, 1815 for epsomite mining.

Hines' Raid

Capt. Thomas H. Hines, Leavenworth, Crawford County, from J. P. Dunn's, Indiana & Indianans, Vol. II, page 618, 1919.

ID 13.1992.3

CL Erected 1992 Indiana Historical Bureau

D SR 62 near Dry Run Road & Old Town Leavenworth Road, Leavenworth.

Confederate Captain Thomas Hines with fewer than 100 cavalrymen, crossed the Ohio River into Perry County June 17,1863, seeking horses. Warned here of impending ambush by Home Guards, they fled to upper Blue River Island where most were captured or killed June 19.

Marengo Academy

ID 13.2006.1

CL Installed 2005 Indiana Historical Bureau, Crawford County Historical and Genealogical Society, and Community Foundation of Crawford County

D Meridian Road, near Old Main Street, Marengo.

Side one:
John M. Johnson opened a private school in Marengo 1869 with 60 students. He designed a course of study to provide an opportunity for students to move beyond common school (elementary) education. In 1874, Johnson renamed it Marengo Academy in a new building located here. School open to all students, male and female, regardless of ability to pay.
Side two:
Courses included algebra, geometry, surveying, German, Latin, Greek. Johnson retired from teaching 1902. By 1910, Marengo Academy building had been torn down. Johnson died 1918. Academy was one of many private institutions that provided expanded educational opportunities for Indiana students before public secondary education was widely available.

Vincennes Donation Lands

ID 14.1966.1

CL Erected by Indiana Sesquicentennial Commission, 1966

D Intersection of US 50 bypass & SR 57, grassy median between restaurant & motel, 7 Cumberland Drive, Washington.

In 1788 Congress granted 400 acres of land to each French family of this area. The tract was laid off in a square containing 160 separate plots. Additional grants were made affecting the five counties shown.[map]

Mimi's House

ID 14.1989.1

CL Erected in 1989 by the Indiana Historical Bureau with funding from David and Stuart Graham

D 101 W. Maple & NW 1st Streets, Washington.

Residence of Robert C. Graham (1885-1967), pioneer glass, truck and auto manufacturer. Placed on the National Register of Historic Places in 1983 by the U.S. Department of the Interior because of its history and Prairie Style architecture.

Robert C. Graham

Robert Cabel Graham (1885-1967), a native of Washington, Daviess County, with his brothers Joseph and Ray, contributed much to the economy and quality of life in that city, Evansville, and other towns. Glass factories, truck manufacturing, and Graham automobiles were early endeavors. Graham was active later with his four sons in Graham Farms, Inc., and the Graham Cheese Corporation.

ID 14.1989.2

CL Erected 1989 by the Indiana Historical Bureau with funding from the Grandchildren of R. C. Graham

D Maysville Road exit, north of US 50 & US 150 bypass, east side of Maysville Road/CR 300 W, 2 miles west of Washington.

Odon, Formerly Clarksburg

Platted in 1846 by John Hasting; town named Clarksburg reportedly after George Rogers Clark; post office name was Clark's Prairie, 1858-1881. Both names changed to Odon, 1881; Odon incorporated, 1885. By tradition, name Odon coined by combining names of two prominent citizens.

ID 14.1991.1

CL Erected 1991 by the Daviess County Visitors Bureau

D North side of SR 58 near John Street, east edge of Odon.

Baltimore & Ohio Southwestern Railroad Depot

ID 14.1992.1

CL Erected 1992 Indiana Historical Bureau

D 1 Train Depot & Meridian Streets, Washington.

Baltimore & Ohio Southwestern Railroad Depot, Washington, Daviess County.

Mission Revival Style depot, built 1906, restored 1990; part of Washington Commercial Historic District. Link to city's trading and industrial history, with substantial railroad machine shops and car works. Indiana stop of former President Dwight D. Eisenhower's funeral train, April 1, 1969.

Burial Site of Captain Eli McCarty

ID 14.1993.1

CL Erected 1993 Indiana Historical Bureau and Daviess County Visitors Bureau

D United Methodist Ebenezer Cemetery, SR 257 & CR 725 S, east side of highway, 6 miles south of Washington.

Burial Site of Captain Eli McCarty, south of Washington, Daviess County.

During the Civil War, on October 3, 1864, Daviess County draft officer Eli McCarty was murdered by antiwar draft protesters. Five men were convicted of his murder. Reportedly, several other men involved fled west.

Indiana's Early Bird Pilot

Roderick M. Wright (1887-1960), one of Indiana's first pilots, received Federation Aeronautique Internationale pilot license No. 254 in 1913. Member of Early Birds, a national group of pilots who flew solo between 1903 and 1916. He was a flight instructor and a test, charter, and cargo pilot. Served in Indiana General Assembly, 1953-1957.

ID 14.1997.1

CL Erected 1997 Indiana Historical Bureau and Children and Grandchildren of Daviess County native Roderick M. Wright.

D Daviess County Airport, Sugarland Road, NE of Washington.

Fort Flora

Built on this site by civilians to protect approximately ten families during War of 1812. Named for landowner David Flora. Ten such forts were built circa 1811-1813 in area that became Daviess County. Area was Knox County, part of Indiana Territory 1800-1816. Daviess County was carved out of Knox County 1817, following Indiana's statehood 1816.

ID 14.1999.1

CL Erected 1999 Indiana Historical Bureau and Daviess County Visitors Bureau.

D SW corner of E. Main & NE 2nd Streets, Washington.

Homer E. Capehart / GOP Cornfield Conference

ID 14.1999.2

CL Erected 1999 Indiana Historical Bureau and Daviess County Visitors Bureau.

D Junction of CR 600 N & CR 150 W on SW side of the railroad tracks, 1.5 miles west of SR 57 on CR 600 N, about 6 miles NW of Washington.

Portrait of Homer E. Capehart, marker north of Washington, Daviess County, Indiana Picture Collection, MS. Section, Indiana State Library.

Side one:
Born into Indiana farming family 1897. Manufactured and pioneered sales of automatic phonographs, creating Capehart Corporation. Executive of Rudolph Wurlitzer Company 1933-1944. Organized 1938 Republican Party "Cornfield Conference" on Capehart farm land across the road. Became influential in party; served as U.S. senator 1945-1963. Died 1979.
Side two:
Republican Party rally organized by Homer E. Capehart took place August 26-27, 1938 on the Capehart farm. Thousands from Indiana and other states attended; received significant national news coverage. Event sparked revival of Republican Party in Indiana and nationally and launched Capehart's political career.

Daviess

Wabash and Erie Canal

Side one: A canal from Terre Haute to Evansville authorized 1846. Maysville Division along White River was over 23 miles long from Newberry through Owl Prairie (now Elnora) to Maysville; part of it paralleled what is now S.R. 57. Contracts were let June 1849. Construction was delayed by cholera outbreaks among workers, many of whom were Irish immigrants.
Side two:
Navigation between Newberry and Maysville opened June 1852. By 1853, Wabash and Erie Canal, America's longest at approximately 460 miles, linked Lake Erie at Toledo, Ohio with Ohio River at Evansville. By 1860, most of southern section no longer used because of repair costs and railroad competition. Entire canal in Indiana sold at auction 1876.

ID 14.2007.1

CL Installed 2007 Indiana Historical Bureau and Elmore Township Community Association, Inc.

D State Highway 58 & 57, Elnora.

Dearborn

Canal Junction

Side one:
The Whitewater Canal and the Cincinnati and Whitewater Canal joined in Harrison to provide better access to Cincinnati markets and Ohio River. Indiana Internal Improvement Act 1836 authorized Whitewater Canal; completed from Brookville to Lawrenceburg 1839. Nearby Dam No. 1 on Whitewater River created a pool for canal boats to cross the river.
Side two:
Cincinnati and Whitewater Canal incorporated by Ohio General Assembly 1837. Completed seven miles from Harrison (now West Harrison), Indiana to Dry Fork Creek, Ohio 1840. Twenty-five mile canal opened 1843 when 1,782 foot tunnel completed at Cleves, Ohio. Traffic diverted to Cincinnati on this interstate transportation link diminished Lawrenceburg's importance as a market.

ID 15.1999.1

CL Erected 1999 Indiana Historical Bureau, Canal Society of Indiana, and Dearborn County Historical Society.

D NW corner of Whitewater River bridge at Campbell & State Streets across railroad tracks, south side of West Harrison.

Decatur County Court House

ID 16.1980.1

CL Erected by the Decatur County Bicentennial Commission 1980

D Courthouse Square, Main Street/SR 46, SW lawn, Greensburg.

Decatur County Courthouse, Greensburg.

Site of the original court house built in 1827 and occupied until 1854. Present building completed in 1860. Large tooth aspen tree appeared in 1870 on the roof of the 115 foot clock tower. In July, 1863, it became a temporary armory while troops bivouacked on the lawn. The treasurer's office held provisions to feed 10 regiments. The 7th Regimental Band had played weekly on the square before being militarized. Many political figures have given speeches from the steps. It was placed on the National Register of Historic Places in 1973.

Civil War General John T. Wilder

Side one:
Wilder (1830-1917), resident of Greensburg circa 1858-1869, built this home 1865-1866. He was millwright and inventor; provided major employment in the area. Enlisted in Civil War; appointed lieutenant colonel of Seventeenth Indiana Volunteer Infantry 1861 by Indiana Governor Oliver P. Morton.

Civil War General John T. Wilder, 1863, Greensburg, Decatur County, Indiana Picture Collection, MS. Section, Indiana State Library.

ID 16.2001.1

CL Installed 2001 Indiana Historical Bureau and Wal-Mart

D North side of 446 E. Main Street/SR 46 at Poplar Street, Greensburg.

Side two: In 1863, Wilder commanded a brigade which included mounted infantry equipped with new Spencer repeating rifles. Use of rifles helped troops defeat Confederates at Hoover's Gap; earned them nickname Wilder's Lightning Brigade. Wilder was breveted Brigadier General 1864, after Chickamauga.

Donnell v. State

Side one: Luther Donnell was convicted in Decatur Circuit Court (1849) of aiding fugitive slaves, Caroline and her four children, to escape to Canada. In *Donnell v. State,* Indiana Supreme Court reversed the conviction, claiming that under U.S. Supreme Court decision in *Prigg v. Pennsylvania,* federal law superseded a state law regarding aid to fugitive slaves.
Side two: *Prigg,* a pro-slavery decision, was used in this case and elsewhere to benefit the anti-slavery cause. The Underground Railroad refers to a widespread network of diverse people in the nineteenth century who aided slaves escaping to freedom from the southern U.S.

ID 16.2007.1

CL Installed 2007 Indiana Historical Bureau, Division of Historic Preservation & Archaeology, IDNR; and Decatur Freedom Trails Association.

D Decatur County Courthouse, 150 Courthouse Square, Greensburg.

Auburn Automobile Company

ID 17.1992.1

CL Erected 1992 Indiana Historical Bureau

D 1600 S. Wayne Street at Gordon M. Buchrig Place, Auburn-Cord-Duesenberg Museum, Auburn.

Auburn Automobile Company, Auburn, DeKalb County.

Auburn Automobile Company (1900-1937) Art Deco Style Administration building, built 1929-1930. Housed departments of Cord Corporation, manufacturer of Auburn, Cord, and Duesenberg automobiles. Became Auburn-Cord-Duesenberg Museum, 1974; listed in National Register of Historic Places, 1978.

Spencerville Covered Bridge

ID 17.1996.1

CL Erected 1996 Indiana Historical Bureau and DeKalb County Board of Commissioners, Council, and Highway Department

D CR 68 & CR 57 at St. Joseph River, Spencerville.

Spencerville Covered Bridge, DeKalb County.

Built 1873, by John A. McKay, spanning Saint Joseph River; a Smith Truss, Variant Four, by Smith Bridge Company, Toledo, Ohio; has remained in use with regular maintenance, repairs, and extensive 1981 restoration. Listed in National Register of Historic Places, 1981.

First Indiana Gas Well

A. H. Cranell, Civil War Veteran, drilled Indiana's First Gas Well, 1876, Eaton, Delaware County, Indiana Picture Collection, MS. Section, Indiana State Library.

ID 18.1981.1

CL Placed by the Indiana Historical Bureau under grant from Panhandle Eastern Pipe Line Company

D Norsemen Park in front of town hall at 600 East Harris Street, Eaton.

The first significant commercial gas well came in Sept.15, 1886, near here south of the Mississinewa River and East of the railroad, ushering in the gas boom era. Almeron H. Crannell, a Civil War veteran and later resident of Hartford City, drilled the well.

Shaffer Chapel African Methodist Episcopal Church

Shaffer Chapel, Muncie, Delaware County.

ID 18.1996.1

CL Erected 1996 Indiana Historical Bureau and The Delaware County Historical Alliance

D 1501 E. Highland Avenue & Wolf Street, 3 blocks east of McCullough Park, Muncie.

Structure, circa 1893, is Muncie's oldest standing public school building. Purchased by church congregation, circa 1928. Rallying point in August 1930 when bodies of two African-American men, lynched in Marion, were brought to Muncie for embalmment by church's pastor J.E. Johnson, a mortician.

Delaware

Slickville Tile Works

ID 18.1996.2

CL Erected 1996 Indiana Historical Bureau

D Near Delaware-Madison County line, about 1.2 miles NW of I-69 exit145 via US 35/SR 28, west to CR 1000 W/CR 500 E/County Line Road, then north to CR 650 N, then east 100 yards near farm, west of Gaston.

Site of production mill and three beehive kilns, first fueled by wood and then by natural gas, circa 1883-1910, owned & operated by Manassa Myers, Sr. family. Produced drainage tiles (hollow cylinder-shaped sections) from adjacent clay pit for local use. Drainage tiles have been used throughout Indiana to develop and maintain farm land.

Elkhart

Indiana Territory Line

ID 20.1966.1

CL Erected by Indiana Sesquicentennial Commission, 1966

D South side of US 33 between Dunlap and Goshen, south of Elkhart.

The boundary between Indiana and Michigan territories was established in 1805. Just before Indiana became a state in 1816, the line was moved ten miles north to give Indiana frontage on Lake Michigan.

A. E. Kunderd Gladiolus Farm

ID 20.1997.1

CL Erected 1997 Indiana Historical Bureau, Goshen Historical Society and A. E. Kundred Family

D US 33 at corner of CR 28, Goshen.

Amos E. Kunderd (1866 - 1965) owned and resided on a 100-acre farm on this site. Respected internationally for hybridization of varieties of gladioli which were exhibited, and grown in gardens, throughout the world. Originated the ruffled and laciniated types. His floricultural business, operated 1911-1971, was important to the area economy.

Howard W. Hawks

Born 1896 in house on this site into locally prominent family. Moved with parents to Neenah, Wisconsin 1899 and to Pasadena, California 1906. Hawks-director, producer, screenwriter-is recognized as one of Hollywood's greatest filmmakers. His more than forty-six movies include fine examples of traditional film genres, both comedy and drama. Died 1977.

ID 20.1998.1

CL Erected 1998 Indiana Historical Bureau, Elkhart County Historical Society, and Goshen Historical Society.

D 301 S. Fifth Street at Jefferson, SW corner, Goshen.

Ambrose G. Bierce

Born in Ohio 1842; family moved to Kosciusko County, Indiana 1846. Bierce lived and worked in Elkhart 1860-1861. Union officer wounded in Civil War. Moved to California 1866; became nationally prominent as journalist, short story writer, and critic. Assumed dead, circa 1914, on a trip to Mexico. This property purchased 1870 by his parents.

ID 20.1998.2

CL Erected 1998 Indiana Historical Bureau, Elkhart County Historical Society, and Elkhart County Community Foundation.

D 518 West Franklin Street, Elkhart.

Krider Nurseries World's Fair Garden

ID 20.2001.1

CL Installed 2001 Indiana Historical Bureau, Middlebury Park Board, Town of Middlebury, Michiana Master Gardeners, and Elkhart County

D Bristol & Railroad Streets, Middlebury.

Side one:
Krider Nurseries constructed and exhibited Krider's Diversified Garden at Century of Progress International Exposition in Chicago 1933-1934. Some plants and structures were returned to Middlebury, and garden was reconstructed here 1935. After falling into decay, garden was restored by community 1995.

Side two:
Founded 1896 by Vernon Krider (1876-1955), Krider Nurseries produced its first catalog 1906. Primarily regional wholesale business; also served mail-order market. Bought patent to produce and sell first thornless rose. For many years, Krider's was one of Middlebury's largest industries. Ceased operation 1990.

Elkhart County Courthouse

Elkhart County Courthouse, Goshen.

ID 20.2001.2

CL Installed 2001 Indiana Historical Bureau, Elkhart County Commissioners, Elkhart County Historical Society, Jimtown Historical Museum, and Goshen Historical Society

D First & Lincoln Streets, SE corner of courthouse, Goshen.

Side one:
Elkhart County was formed by the Indiana General Assembly 1830; the first county seat was located in Concord Township. County commissioners relocated the county seat to Goshen 1831. Jacob Studebaker, Goshen, designed first brick courthouse, completed 1833. Barrows and Garnsey, Chicago, designed second brick courthouse, completed 1870.
Side two:
Patton and Miller, Chicago, redesigned and enlarged Renaissance Revival style structure, completed 1909. Contractor, P. H. McCormick, Columbus, dismantled south end tower and dome, added north and south wings, and built new central dome and tower incorporating original 1870 clock. Listed in National Register of Historic Places 1980.

Goshen's Carnegie Library

ID 20.2003.1

CL Installed 2003 Indiana Historical Bureau, City of Goshen, Elkhart County Historical Soc., Goshen Historical Soc., and Friends of the Goshen Public Library

D 202 S. Fifth Street, Goshen.

Goshen's Carnegie Library, Elkhart County.

Side one:
Indiana's first Carnegie library opened here 1903 with 3,000 volumes. Goshen Library Association received $25,000 in Carnegie grants 1901. Public donations, land purchase, and tax levy met Carnegie grant conditions. Architects Patton & Miller, Chicago, designed Beaux-Arts style structure. Library moved 1968; commercial and nonprofit uses followed.
Side two:
Listed in National Register of Historic Places 1983. Renovated building reopened 2001 housing city offices. Original features of decorative marble, fireplaces, and domed rotunda retained. One of 1,679 libraries built in U.S. with funds from philanthropist Andrew Carnegie. Indiana built more Carnegie libraries than any other state.

Nappanee Cartoonists

Side one:
Merrill Blosser was first Nappanee artist to gain national recognition as a professional cartoonist. *Freckles and His Friends*, his most popular cartoon, ran from 1915 to 1973, syndicated by Newspaper Enterprise Association. In 1965, National Cartoonists Society honored Blosser on fiftieth year of *Freckles* and its "wholesome entertainment."
Side two:
Five other Nappanee artists became nationally recognized cartoonists. Henry Maust and Francis "Mike" Parks drew newspaper editorial cartoons; Bill Holman's best was *Smokey Stover* (1935-1973); Fred Neher's *Life's Like That* ran 1934-1977; Max Gwin drew *Slim and Spud* for *Prairie Farmer* 1955-1991. Town, training, and careers connected these artists.

ID 20.2005.1

CL Installed 2005 Indiana Historical Bureau, City of Nappanee, Nappanee Historic Preservation Commission, Nappanee Public Library, Elkhart County Historical Society, Nappanee "Smokey Stover" Fire Department, Mayor Larry and Linda Thompson, E. Newcomer and Son Jewelers

D 57 North Main Street, Nappanee.

Nappanee Furniture

ID 20.2005.2

CL Installed 2005 Indiana Historical Bureau, City of Nappanee, Nappanee Historic Preservation Commission, Nappanee Public Library, Elkhart County Historical Society, Nappanee, E. Newcomer and Son Jewelers

D 452 East Market Street, Nappanee.

Side one:
Nappanee platted 1874 on Baltimore & Ohio Railroad line. Sawmill opened 1873 produced ties for railroad construction. Coppes and Mutschler brothers were partners in lumber, milling, and furniture business, 1902-1913, becoming significant part of local furniture industry. By 1919, Indiana's furniture industry ranked fourth in nation.
Side two:
As separate companies, Coppes focused on kitchen cabinets and sideboards, the sawmill and flour mill, and Mutschler on manufactured tables and porcelain top kitchen tables. Coppes and Mutschler families continued to manage the companies, adapting to changing times. In 1969, outside corporations acquired both companies, ending local ownership.

C.G. Conn Company

C.G. Conn, Poster by Hughes and Johnson Lithographers, Chicago, Illinois, ca. 1885.

Side one: Charles Gerard Conn began the musical instrument industry in Elkhart; city has been called the Band Industry Capital of the World. By 1874 producing rubber mouthpiece; was granted patent 1875; began producing musical instruments 1875. Factory here until 1910. C.G. Conn Company incorporated 1904. Conn sold business to Carl D. Greenleaf 1915.

Side two: Innovations by C.G. Conn, Ltd. under Greenleaf included promoting school band programs and one of first musical instrument research labs. Other instrument companies came to Elkhart, employing many skilled workers. By 1970s, about 40% of worldwide band instruments made in Elkhart. Conn Ltd. sold 1969; Conn-Selmer, Inc. continues name in Elkhart.

ID 20.2006.1

CL Installed 2006 Indiana Historical Bureau, The Truth, Elkhart Historic and Cultural Preservation Commission, Ray and Susan Enfield, and Elkhart County Historical Society

D Jackson Boulevard and Elkhart Avenue, Elkhart

E. Hill Turnock

ID 20.2006.2

CL Installed 2006 Indiana Historical Bureau, Elkhart Historic and Cultural Preservation Commission, Jack & Betty Foltz, George & Darlene Adkins, The Ruthmere Foundation, Inc., Goshen Historical Society, and Elkhart County Historical Society

D Municipal Building, 229 South Second Street, Elkhart

Side one: Added many buildings to the architectural significance of Elkhart, Goshen, and Nappanee. Born mid-1850s in England; his family moved to Elkhart early 1870s. In mid-1880s he moved to Chicago; worked until 1890 with architect William Le Baron Jenney. Began private practice 1890; Chicago designs include noted apartment building, Lincoln Park Palace.
Side two: He returned to Elkhart 1907; until his death 1926, designed public and private buildings here and in other Indiana cities. Designs here included Water Works, Masonic Temple, schools, hospital, factories, and houses. Harter residence (1913) in Elkhart embodies his design ideals. This Municipal Building, 1915, was designed by Turnock.

Graves et al. v. Indiana

ID 20.2007.1

CL Installed 2007 Indiana Historical Bureau, Division of Historic Preservation and Archaeology, IDNR;lkhart CountyHistorical Society, and Robert Weed Plywood Corporation.

D Memorial Park, corner of SR 15 and SR 120,Bristol.

Side one: In 1847, three Kentucky men tried to capture Thomas Harris, fugitive slave, in Bristol; a justice of the peace ruling freed Harris, who fled. In 1848, the Elkhart Circuit Court convicted the three men of causing a riot in 1847. In 1849, Indiana Supreme Court reversed Circuit Court decision based on 1842 *Prigg v. Pennsylvania* decision of U.S. Supreme Court.
Side two: this incident is an example of local judicial officers countering a proslavery federal decision. The Underground Railroad refers to a widespread network of diverse people in the nineteenth century who aided slaves escaping to freedom from the southern U.S.

Dr. Franklin L. Miles

Elkhart

Side one: Born circa 1845 in Ohio. Graduated from Rush Medical College 1874. Moved medical practice from Chicago to Elkhart 1875. Began the Dr. Miles Medical Company 1885 to sell Dr. Miles' Nervine, Restorative Nerve and Liver Pills, and other medicines; Miles was a Director and President of company. Purchased land here, on corner of Fourth and Franklin, 1900.
Side two: Began *Dr. Miles New U.S. Weather Almanac and Handbook of Valuable Information* 1902. Incorporated Grand dispensary Medical Company 1904; sold drugs and diagnosed patients by mail. Moved to Florida 1906; became a farmer. Medical Company's original corporation was dissolved 1912. Miles died 1929; is buried in Grace Lawn Cemetery, Elkhart.

ID 20.2007.2

CL Installed 2007 Indiana Historical Bureau, Elkhart County Historical Society, Radiology, Inc., & Ruthmere Foundation, Inc.

D 403 West Franklin Street, Elkhart.

The Whitewater Canal

Fayette

In 1836 construction began on this fifty-six lock, one hundred one mile canal. Opened from Lawrenceburg to Brookville (1839), it was extended to Laurel and Cincinnati (1843), Connersville (1845), Cambridge City (1846), and Hagerstown (1847). [map]

ID 21.1966.1

CL Erected by Indiana Sesquicentennial Commission, 1966

D S. Grand Avenue/SR 121 at Eastern Avenue, NE corner between railroad track and highway, south Connersville.

Site of Camp Whitcomb

ID 22.1966.1

CL Erected by Indiana Sesquicentennial Commission, 1966

D SE corner Beharrell Avenue & E. Spring Street, New Albany.

Five Indiana regiments were formed at this rendezvous point in 1846-1847 for service in the Mexican War. The first 3,000 men departed for active duty under Brigadier-General Joseph Lane during July, 1846.

New Albany

ID 22.1991.1

CL Erected 1991 by Indiana Historical Bureau and the City of New Albany

D W. Spring Street at I-64 southbound off-ramp, New Albany.

Founded 1813 along Ohio River by Joel, Nathaniel, and Abner Scribner. During 1840s and 1850s, New Albany was largest city and leading commerical and industrial center in Indiana. Industries included shipbuilding; glass and ironworks; hosiery, woolen, and cotton mills; woodworking plants.

Michael C. Kerr Home

ID 22.1992.1

CL Erected 1992 Indiana Historical Bureau, Floyd County Historical Society and Main Street Preservation Association

D 1109 E. Main Street, New Albany.

Built 1864 for Kerr (1827-1876), an attorney. Served five terms in the United States House of Representatives, 1865-1873 and 1875-1876. Elected Speaker of the House in 1875, the third Hoosier to serve in that capacity.

New Albany

Founded 1813 along Ohio River by Joel, Nathaniel, and Abner Scribner. During 1840s and 1850s, New Albany was largest city and leading commerical and industrial center in Indiana. Industries included shipbuilding; glass and ironworks; hosiery, woolen, and cotton mills; woodworking plants.

ID 22.1992.2

CL Erected 1992 by Indiana Historical Bureau

D E. Spring Street & Woodrow Avenue, New Albany.

Clark's Grant

Grant Line Road marks the western boundary of the 150,000 acres of land granted in 1781 by Virginia to General George Rogers Clark and his officers and soldiers who fought to reduce the British presence in Illinois Country during the Revolutionary War.

ID 22.1992.3

CL Erected 1992 by Indiana Historical Bureau and Henryville Elementary Little Hoosiers

D Indiana University Southeast, 4201 Grant Line Road/SR 111, New Albany just north of I-265.

State Bank of Indiana

State Bank of Indiana, New Albany, Floyd County.

Second state bank was established in 1834 by General Assembly with ten branch banks; one of the most successful banks at the time in U.S. This Greek Revival Style structure, built 1837, housed New Albany branch, serving Floyd, Harrison, Washington, Crawford, and Clark counties until expiration of the bank charter in 1857.

ID 22.1996.1

CL Erected 1996 Indiana Historical Bureau and Develop New Albany, Inc.

D 203 E. Main Street, New Albany.

Culbertson Mansion

ID 22.1996.2

CL Erected 1996 Indiana Historical Bureau and Friends of Culbertson Mansion.

D 914 E. Main Street, New Albany.

Culbertson Mansion, New Albany, Floyd County.

French Second Empire Style structure. Construction began 1867 for William Stewart Culbertson (1814-1892), leading industrialist, financier, and philanthropist in New Albany area. Listed in National Register of Historic Places, 1974; accepted as state-owned historic site, 1976; part of Mansion Row Historic District, 1983.

Scribner High School

ID 22.1998.1

CL Erected 1998 Indiana Historical Bureau and Southern Christian Leadership Conference.

D Directions: SW corner of 1st & Spring Streets at City-County Building, New Albany.

In 1880, an 1822 school building on this site became Scribner High School for African-American students, under an 1869 Indiana law mandating public education for African-American children and allowing segregated schools. Modern facility completed and state commissioned 1907. Closed 1952 after 1949 state desegregation law.

Buffalo Trace Route

Side one:
American Bison, migrating in great herds, created a cluster of paths along the natural topography between Illinois prairies and salt licks in Kentucky. These paths, called the Buffalo Trace, used by Native Americans and became premier travel route for early settlers and military. Northern and southern routes existed between New Albany and Vincennes.
Side two:
Northern route became federal post road 1800, scheduled stage coach route 1824, and New Albany-Paoli Turnpike 1836 as part of Internal Improvement Act. Became New Albany and Vincennes State Toll Road 1840, was macadamized, and charged tolls until circa 1915. Became part of state highway system. On November 11, 1926 designated Route 150 of Federal Aid Highway System.

ID 22.1999.1

CL Erected 1999 Indiana Historical Bureau and Floyd County Historical Society

D 2212 State Street, NE corner, New Albany.

Culbertson Widows' Home

ID 22.2003.1

CL Installed 2003 Indiana Historical Bureau, Steven W. Goodman, and Carlus Holliday

D 704 E.Main Street, New Albany.

Culbertson Widow's Mansion, New Albany, Floyd County.

Side one:
William S. Culbertson, wealthy merchant, opened home November 18, 1873 to provide food, clothing, and shelter for town's destitute widows. Home had gas lighting, upstairs water closet, and up-to-date kitchen. Residents' lives were structured according to strict rules. Culbertson's will provided support for the home after his death in 1892.
Side two:
Board of Trustees for home was formed 1922; it turned the home into a boardinghouse with a monthly fee in 1947. Because of changing city regulations, the Board closed the home 1971. James Banes was builder of the brick Italianate structure, which is included in Mansion Row Historic District, listed in National Register of Historic Places 1983.

A Gateway to Freedom

Side one:
As early as 1821, enslaved blacks seeking freedom crossed the Ohio River from Louisville to New Albany. Antebellum and Civil War periods brought more fugitives. Many freedom-seekers were aided by other slaves, free blacks, and anti-slavery whites-all risking violence and arrest. Not everyone who tried to escape succeeded.
Side two:
Many freedom-seekers coming through New Albany achieved their goal, traveling as far north as Canada. The Underground Railroad refers to a widespread network of diverse people in the nineteenth century who aided slaves escaping to freedom from the southern U.S.

ID 22.2004.1

CL Installed 2004 Indiana Historical Bureau, Floyd County Historical Society, and Division of Historic Preservation & Archaeology, IDNR

D SE corner of Marin & Third Streets, New Albany.

New Albany Downtown Historic District

Side one:
New Albany lots were advertised for sale 1813. It was designated county seat 1819, incorporated as town 1836, then as city 1839. Area within the district was part of early plat of New Albany. District boundaries are roughly West 1st to East 5th streets and East Spring to East and West Main streets.
Side two:
District reflects the historical development and commercial growth of New Albany. It contains a collection of outstanding examples of nineteenth and twentieth century commercial and institutional buildings and a few domestic structures. Listed in National Register of Historic Places 1999.

ID 22.2004.2

CL Installed 2004 Indiana Historical Bureau, Develop New Albany, Inc., and Floyd County Historical Society

D NE corner Pearl & Market Streets, New Albany.

Division Street School

- ID: 22.2005.1
- CL: Installed 2005 Indiana Historical Bureau and Friends of Division Street School, Inc.
- D: 1803 Conservative Street, New Albany.

Side one: Because of the growing number of African-American school-age children, the New Albany School Board authorized a new elementary school for them June 1884. It opened here 1885. An 1869 Indiana law had mandated education of colored children, with separate enumeration and separate schools supported with tax revenue within the common school system.
Side two: Improvements and repairs were made over the years. The still-segregated school closed 1946. Friends of Division Street School was organized 1999 for restoration of the building. Restoration has been a joint project of the Friends and New Albany/Floyd County School Corporation. Building listed in National Register of Historic Places 2002.

Fairview Cemetery

- ID: 22.2005.2
- CL: Installed 2005 Indiana Historical Bureau and Friends of Fairview, Inc.
- D: Culbertson Avenue and East Sixth Street, New Albany.

Side one: New Albany's second city cemetery, Northern Burial Ground, was officially created July 30, 1841 when D. W. and Margaret Wilson sold land to the city. The first burial took place the following day. In 1864 and 1875, the city made additions and improvements, perhaps influenced by a national movement to create a park-like atmosphere in cemeteries.
Side two: In 1890, lot owners paid for construction of the iron entrance gate. Name was changed to Fairview Cemetery and ornamental archway added 1896. Some of earliest vaults date to mid-1800s. Many prominent individuals, including Indiana Governor Ashbel P. Willard, local civic leaders, and victims of an 1844 steamboat disaster are among those buried here.

New Albany's Carnegie Library

New Albany Carnegie Library, facade, Floyd County.

ID 22.2005.3

CL Friends of the New Albany-Floyd County Public Library, Floyd County Historical Society, and Carnegie Center for Art & History, Inc.

D 201 East Spring St., New Albany.

Side one:
New Albany School Board organized a public library on May 8, 1884. This library building, supported with funds from Andrew Carnegie, opened on March 2, 1904 with 11,125 volumes. Building is Neoclassical style, constructed of brick and limestone. Public Library moved to new building 1969.
Side two:
Floyd County Museum opened here 1971. Carnegie building included in Downtown Historic District, listed in National Register of Historic Places 1999. One of 1,679 libraries built in U.S. with funds from philanthropist Andrew Carnegie. Indiana built more Carnegie libraries than any other state.

New Albany Tornado of 1917

ID 22.2007.1

CL Installed 2007 Indiana Historical Bureau, Floyd County Historical Society, and Caesars Foundation of Floyd County

D 1111 Pearl Street, New Albany.

Side one: Tornado struck city at approximately 3:30 p.m. March 23, 1917. Moved through north side of town, affecting roughly ninety blocks. Mayor and others formed Citizens Relief Committee. Next morning Red Cross joined forces with Committee; within hours, workers deployed throughout affected area. Red Cross nurses treated injured at St. Edward Hospital.
Side two: Tornado killed at least 45 people, injured hundreds more, destroyed approximately 300 homes and buildings, left 2,500 homeless, cost over $1,000,000 in total damage. At this site, "Olden Street Colored School" collapsed during the storm, trapping teachers and students; there were several deaths. Tornado ranks among deadliest to strike Indiana since 1900.

New Albany and Salem Railroad (The Monon)

ID 22.2007.2

CL Installed 2007 Indiana Historical Bureau, Floyd County Historical Society, and Caesars Foundation of Floyd County

D Corner of Bank Street and Culbertson Avenue, New Albany.

Side one: Railroad organized 1847, after years of legislation to provide transportation to move goods and people to and from the state's interior. Completed to Michigan City 1854 when last rail was laid in Putnam County. New Albany's economy expanded with the Railroad's presence starting in 1850s.
Side two: Fugitive slaves' use of this Railroad in escapes caused regional controversy in the 1850s. Several changes of ownership and name occurred in the 1800s and 1900s. The name officially was changed to the Monon Railroad 1956. Owners sold the facilities in this area in 1990 to private interests.

Cardinal Joseph E. Ritter

Side one: Born in New Albany 1892. Was ordained 1917 after graduation from St. Meinrad College and Seminary and assigned to his first parish in Indianapolis. He advanced in the Church, becoming Bishop of Indianapolis 1934 and first archbishop of new Archdiocese of Indianapolis 1944. In the 1930s, he championed the rights of African Americans in Indiana.
Side two: He was named Archbishop of St. Louis 1946. In 1947, he desegregated five Catholic St. Louis high schools amid protests. In 1961 he was elevated to Cardinal by Pope John XXIII; only Roman Catholic Cardinal from Indiana. Was an outspoken, progressive participant in all three sessions of Vatican Council II. Died 1967; buried in St. Louis.

ID 22.2007.3

CL Installed 2007 Indiana Historical Bureau and Knights of Columbus, Cardinal Ritter Council 1221

D 1218 East Oak Street, New Albany.

Boyhood Home of Daniel W. Voorhees

ID 23.1970.1

CL Erected by Fountain Central Junior Historical Society

D US 41 & CR 100 N, about 0.25 mile north of I-74 exit 15, 2 miles north of Veedersburg.

Portrait of Daniel W. Voorhees (1827-1897), Veedersburg, Fountain County, Indiana Picture Collection, MS. Section, Indiana State Library.

"Tall Sycamore of the Wabash"
1827-1897
Famous orator - Representative in Congress, 1861-66, 1869-73; U.S. Senator, 1877-1897; chief promoter of the building of the Library of Congress.

Esther Test Wallace 1807-1834

ID 23.1970.2

CL Erected by Fountain Central High School Junior Historical Society

D SR 136/Liberty Street between 8th & 9th Streets, Oak Grove Cemetery, Covington.

The 1st wife of Governor David Wallace and mother of General Lew Wallace, soldier, author of Ben Hur, statesman & diplomat, is here buried. She influenced the lives of two important Hoosiers.

Attica & Covington Canal Skirmish

In fall 1846, residents of Covington and Attica skirmished at Lock 35 over lack of water to Covington. Heavy rains eventually resolved the problem. Competition among canal towns over water control was often intense. First boat reached Attica 1846 via Wabash and Erie Canal (connected Lake Erie with Ohio River in 1853).

ID 23.1997.1

CL Erected 1997 Indiana Historical Bureau and Historic Landmarks of Fountain County.

D 200 W. Washington Street at entrance to Potawatomi Park, Attica.

Ravine Park

Ravine Park, Attica, Fountain County.

Side one:
American Indians frequented this area, rich in natural resources. The ravine provided water from natural springs, marl for lime, and clay for bricks for nineteenth-century residents of Attica, platted 1825. City became owner of ravine 1906 when local business and professional men organized to donate fifty-five acres for a public park.
Side two:
City purchased thirty-five additional acres 1911, adding to eastern end. Park has served as center for social and recreational activities. Attica Chautauqua entertained many here 1907-1928. Donations, grants, and volunteers over the years have added swimming pool, nature trail, bridges, and other structures improving park as community asset.

ID 23.2003.1

CL Installed 2003 Indiana Historical Bureau and Historic Landmarks of Fountain County.

D Park Boulevard at E. Jackson Street entrance to Ravine Park, Attica.

Fountain

Attica's Carnegie Library

ID 23.2005.1

CL Installed 2005 Indiana Historical Bureau and Friends of Fairview, Inc.

D 305 South Perry Street, Attica.

Side one: Ladies Library Association of Attica, created 1885, deeded its library building to city; city library opened 1902 with a collection of 1,500 books. Funds from Andrew Carnegie made it possible to build a new library here on land originally owned by Daniel Stump. It opened 1904. Building is Neoclassical design. Tall Crane fountains placed in front.

Attica Carnegie Library, Facade, Fountain County.

Side two: Library underwent major interior renovation 1988; complementary addition completed 1995. Library included in Brady Street Historic District, listed in National Register of Historic Places 1990. One of 1,679 libraries built in U.S. with funds from philanthropist Andrew Carnegie. Indiana built more Carnegie libraries than any other state.

Franklin

Whitewater Canal

ID 24.19??

CL Indiana Historical Bureau

D US 52, north side of highway at Gordon's Lock #24, east Metamora.

Whitewater Canal, Ben Franklin II Packet Boat, State Historic Site, Metamora, Franklin County.

Important waterway of pioneer commerce. Built 1836-1847 from Lawrenceburg to Hagerstown, with branch to Cincinnati. Used until 1860. Fifteen-mile section restored by state.

Little Cedar Grove Baptist Church

Little Cedar Grove Baptist Church, Mound Haven, Franklin County.

Built in 1812, this is the oldest church building still on its original location in the state. Interior shows rifle openings in walls, a balcony and raised pulpit. Burial plot adjoins church.

ID 24.1949.1

CL Indiana Historical Bureau 1949

D US 52 & Little Cedar Road, north side of highway, 3 miles south of Brookville at Mound Haven village.

Whetzel Trace (1818-1823)

Here Edward Toner founded SOMERSET, 1816, & operated Toner's Tavern, 1816-1823, from which rallying point pioneers started west on Jacob Whetzel's Trace to the "New Purchase" of Central Indiana.

ID 24.1965.1

CL Erected by the Society of Indiana Pioneers 1965

D Main/SR 121 & Toner Streets, south Laurel.

Brookville, Franklin County (Platted 1808)

Home of four Indiana Governors: James B. Ray, 1825-1831; Noah Noble, 1831-1837; David Wallace, 1837-1840 and Abram A. Hammond, 1860-1861. Location of United States Land Office from 1820 to 1825.

ID 24.1966.1

CL Erected by Indiana Sesquicentennial Commission, 1966

D US 52, north side of highway, east Brookville.

Academy of the Immaculate Conception

ID 24.1971.1

CL Erected by the Society of Indiana Pioneers, 1971

D Washington & Wein Strasse, Academy grounds, Oldenburg.

Academy of Immaculate Conception, Oldenburg, Franklin County.

Sisters of Saint Francis.
Opened in 1852; enlarged in 1876 and 1901. The Academy Classroom Building and the Auditorium were completed in 1968.

Brookville Historic District

ID 24.1992.1

CL Erected 1992 by Indiana Historical Bureau and Historic Brookville, Inc.

D SR 1/US 52/ Main Street, Franklin County Courthouse west lawn, Brookville.

Brookville Historic District, Courthouse, Franklin County.

Platted 1808 along Whitewater River, Brookville was an important entry point to interior lands opened to settlement. The district's concentration of well-preserved buildings reflects the city's continued prosperity. Brookville Historic District listed in National Register, 1975.

Old Franklin United Brethren Church

Old Franklin United Brethren Church, Brookville Lake, Franklin County.

United Brethren among earliest settlers in eastern Indiana during territorial period. Original structure, built 1831, one of first United Brethren churches in Indiana. Evangelical United Brethren Church joined Methodist Church to become United Methodist Church, 1968. Listed in National Register of Historic Places, 1995.

ID 24.1995.1

CL Erected 1995 Indiana Historical Bureau and Church Congregation

D 14023 Franklin Church Road, near dead end, north of Mounds SRA office, west of SR 101, south of Fairfield Causeway Road, Brookville.

Brookville's Carnegie Library

Brookville's Carnegie Library, Franklin County.

Dedicated in 1912, starting with approximately 600 books; collections and services have expanded to meet needs of local patrons. One of 1,679 libraries built in U.S. with funds from philanthropist Andrew Carnegie. Indiana built more Carnegie libraries than any other state.

ID 24.1995.2

CL Erected 1995 Indiana Historical Bureau and Friends of Brookville Town-Township Library

D 919 North Main Street, east side of street, Brookville.

Intersection of Treaty Lines

ID 24.1995.3

CL Erected 1995 Indiana Historical Bureau

D Castle Road and St. Marys Road, about 2 miles west of Brookville via 6th Street.

One mile south is intersection of western boundary line of Treaty of Greenville, Ohio (1795) and Treaty of Grouseland, near Vincennes (1805), northeastern boundary line. By these treaties, Native American tribes ceded land to the United States government for settlement.

Brookville's Grandstand

ID 24.2002.1

CL Installed 2002 Indiana Historical Bureau, Franklin County Historical Society, and 50 Years of Franklin County Football Committee 2001.

D East 8th & Mill Streets, Brookville Town Park, Brookville

Brookville's Grandstand, Community Park, Franklin County.

Side one: This grandstand built 1922 to seat 1,000 and serve fans of new Brookville semi-pro team. Twenty box seats included to help pay for construction. Central platform included for community activities. Facility later used for youth sports. Structure renovated 1992 for continuing use by community.

Side two: Baseball has been played in Brookville since at least 1867 when local amateur teams played out-of-town teams. A local team joined semi-pro Southern Indiana Baseball Association 1922 and other regional leagues in later years. Land given for the public park by Amos and Mary Butler 1907. Wooden grandstand built here 1914 seated 300.

Snow Hill Covered Bridge

Side one: Built 1894-1895 over Johnson's Fork Creek by John H. Horn and William H. Butts to a Howe truss design by John Burkhart. All men were local residents. Bridge was important passageway to Cincinnati markets. Rests on stone abutments with wingwalls; includes X-braced framing. Bridge braced with iron bolts and vertical iron rods.
Side two: Bridge honors landowner Lemuel Snow, a Revolutionary War veteran. Deemed unsafe 1986 and closed to traffic. Community-supported restoration project resulted. Roof, wood flooring, and other elements replaced 1987; bridge reopened 1987. Listed in National Register of Historic Places 1995. Restoration and construction project begun 2000.

ID 24.2005.1

CL Installed 2005 Indiana Historical Bureau, Franklin County Commissioners, and Franklin County Citizens for Historic Preservation

D Snow Hill Road over Johnson Fork, Rockdale. Installation pending.

Brigadier-General CSA Francis Asbury Shoup

Side one: Remembered for service in Confederate States of America army, 1861-1865, and "Shoupade" fortification design; fought in battles of Shiloh, Vicksburg, and Atlanta. Advocated recruitment of African Americans for CSA army. After the war, he was a university professor, published author, and Episcopal rector.
Side two: Born near present-day Laurel 1834. Attended Indiana Asbury University, Greencastle. Graduated 1855 from United States Military Academy at West Point. Served in Federal army 1855-1860; resigned to pursue law career. In Indianapolis circa 1860. Died 1896; buried at Sewanee University Cemetery, Tennessee.

ID 24.2006.1

CL Installed 2006 Indiana Historical Bureau, Franklin County Historical Society, and Indiana Division, Sons of Confederate Veterans.

D Conwell Cemetery, State Road 121, Laurel.

Brigadier-General CSA Francis Asbury Shoup. Illustration by Lowell Hildebrandt.

Fulton

Michigan Road

ID 25.1949.1

CL Indiana Historical Bureau 1949.

D Old US 31 at Tippecanoe River bridge, SE corner, 3 miles north of Rochester.

Extending from Michigan City to the Ohio River at Madison. Begun by the state in 1832 with funds obtained from sale of land granted by the Potawatomi Indians. Opened northern part of state to settlers.

Gibson

Lyles Station

ID 26.2002.1

CL Installed 2002 Indiana Historical Bureau and Lyles Station Historic Preservation Corporation

D CR 500 W near CR 100 N in front of restored Lyles Consolidated School, 1 mile north of SR 64 & 65, Lyles Station, 5 miles west of Princeton.

Lyles Station, Restored School, Gibson County.

Side one: Settled in late 1840s by Joshua and Sanford Lyles, former slaves from Tennessee. African Methodist Episcopal Church (since 1860) and schools (1865-1958) played important roles in sustaining the community. On land donated by Joshua Lyles, railroad companies maintained a station circa 1870-1950s for passenger, freight, and mail service. Side two:
Named Lyles Station 1886. Community declined after widespread flooding in 1913. It remains probably most intact African-American settlement in the state; several present residents are descendants of original settlers. Lyles Consolidated School, built 1919, listed in National Register of Historic Places 1999; restoration began 2001.

James Washington Cockrum

Gibson

James Washington Cockrum, Oakland City, Gibson County, Indiana Picture Collection, Ms. Section, Indiana State Library.

ID 26.2005.1

CL Installed 2005 Indiana Historical Bureau, City of Oakland City, Oakland City University, Division of Historic Preservation & Archaeology, IDNR

D 411 W. Oak St., Oakland City.

Side one: Born 1799 in North Carolina. Purchased land 1818 in Gibson County. Cockrum and Jacob Warrick Hargrove laid out the town of Oakland (now Oakland City) on January 15, 1856. Cockrum and his son William Monroe Cockrum, along with sympathizers in Warrick, Gibson, and Pike counties, aided enslaved blacks seeking freedom. Cockrum died November 19, 1875.

Side two: James W. Cockrum's barn, originally located on this property, was used to hide freedom seekers. The Underground Railroad refers to a widespread network of diverse people in the nineteenth century who aided slaves escaping to freedom from the southern U.S.

Battle of Mississinewa

ID 27.1947.1

CL Indiana Historical Bureau

D SR 15 at CR 600 N, SE corner, Marion.

Two Miles West
Site of battle fought Dec. 18, 1812, in which British-allied Miami Indians were defeated by U.S. troops and Militia under Col. John Campbell.

New Purchase Boundary (Treaty of St. Mary's)

ID 27.1966.1

CL Erected by Indiana Sesquicentennial Commission, 1966

D NW corner Grant County Courthouse lawn, Marion.

In October 1818, Purchasing Commissioners Lewis Cass, Benjamin Parke and Governor Jonathan Jennings acquired Indian claims on the land shown on this marker. About one-third of modern Indiana was involved in this transaction. [map]

Miami Indian Cemetery

Miami Indian Cemetery & School, north of Marion, Grant County.

ID 27.1972.1

CL Society of Indiana Pioneers

D North of Marion on SR 15, 1.1 miles west on CR 600 N.

The largest Indian cemetery in Indiana. Few graves are marked. The Indians buried here are largely descendants of Chief Metocinya and include Meshingomesia and his family. The first burial was probably in 1873. Burial was contrary to Indian tradition and reflects Christian influence. An Indian Baptist Church and an Indian school were located here. Otho Winger taught at the school 1895-1898. This land is part of the last Indian reservation in Indiana. The site of the battle of Mississinewa (1812) may be seen along the Mississinewa River to the southwest.

[West Ward School]

ID 27.1988.1

CL Erected by Gas City Historical Society, 1988

D 210 W. North A Street, Gas City.

West Ward School, Historical Museum, Gas City, Grant County.

This Richardsonian Romanesque style structure, built 1900-1902, reflects the area's prosperity during the natural gas boom. The town of Harrisburg had been renamed Gas City in 1892.

Former Narrow Gauge Railroad/Railroad Construction

ID 27.1992.1

CL Erected 1992 by Indiana Historical Bureau and National Railway Historical Society

D E. 4th & McClure Streets, Marion.

Side one:
Tracklayers building narrow gauge railroad connecting Great Lakes at Toledo, Ohio, with Mississippi River reached this point October 1, 1880. In 1887, 2,000 men converted 206 miles of this to standard gauge railroad in 11 hours.
Side two:
A significant part of America's rail system in the 19th century was 18,000 miles of 3-foot-wide narrow gauge railroad in 44 states. Most subsequently converted to 4-foot, 8 1/2 inch standard gauge.

J.W. Patterson House

J. W. Patterson House, Historical Museum, Fairmount, Grant County.

ID 27.1995.1

CL Erected 1995 Indiana Historical Bureau.

D 203 E. Washington Street, Fairmount.

Built circa 1888. Occupied by civic leaders (Nixon Winslow, Levi Scott, and Joseph Patterson) who made significant contributions to Fairmount's economic, educational, and cultural development. Patterson was community's medical doctor, 1889-1913. Listed in National Register of Historic Places, 1979.

The Village of Trask

The Village of Trask, School turned Home, Grant County.

ID 27.1995.2

CL Erected 1995 Indiana Historical Bureau, Matthews Lions Club, Matthews Order of Eastern Star, Descendents of Trask and Issac G. Carter

D 1.4 miles east of I-69, exit 55 at SR 26 & S. Wheeling Pike, Trask.

Trask, like other pioneer villages, served an important commercial, social, and educational role for early settlers. The post office (1846-1901) marked the start and end of Trask's official existence. As travel improved, such villages disappeared or remained as residential communities like Trask.

Greene

Richland-Plummer Creek Covered Bridge

ID 28.1998.1

CL Erected 1998 Indiana Historical Bureau and Greene County Landmarks Foundation.

D NE end of Richland-Plummer Creek Covered Bridge, Baseline Road over Plummer Creek, about 2 miles south of Bloomfield.

Built 1883 by A. M. Kennedy and Sons to Burr arch truss design on stone abutments. Closed 1957; opened 1967 after foundation and roof rehabilitation; closed 1990. Bridge reopened 1998 following extensive structural renovation and replacement of timbers. Listed in National Register of Historic Places 1993.

Fred A. Jewell

ID 28.1998.2

CL Erected 1998 Indiana Historical Bureau , Matthew Huber, Director of Bands, Jackson Township Community Band, and Brazil Concert Band.

D US 231 & SR 157, Fountain Triangle Park, Worthington.

Born in Worthington 1875. Left home at sixteen and became performer, composer, and bandmaster for several circuses, including Ringling Brothers (1902-1904, 1907) and Barnum and Bailey (1908-1910). Brought his publishing company to Worthington 1923; died 1936. Nationally recognized as "Indiana's March King." Many of his marches are still performed.

The Central Canal

These canal-bed earthworks are remnants of construction on the Central Canal from 1836-39. It was planned to link the Hoosier interior with interstate markets, via the Wabash & Erie Canal, as part of the 1836 Internal Improvement Act. Indiana's bankruptcy in 1839 forced abandonment of the Central Canal project.

ID 29.1994.1

CL Erected 1994 Indiana Historical Bureau and Precedent Partners I

D SR 37 & 191st Street, Noblesville.

Hamilton

Conner Street Historic District

Side one: Hamilton County formed 1823. Noblesville platted 1823, selected county seat 1824, incorporated 1851. Located east of downtown commercial area; boundaries are Conner and Logan streets (east and west) and 10th and 17th streets (north and south). Listed in National Register of Historic Places 1999.

Side two: Available railroad transportation after 1851 and discovery of natural gas (1887) helped town to grow. District was a significant neighborhood, including a mix of structures and styles of the middle-class and affluent citizens who were active in business, politics, and civic affairs of the town.

ID 29.2005.1

CL Installed 2005 Indiana Historical Bureau and Noblesville Preservation Alliance

D Conner Street and 17th Street, Noblesville.

Conner Street Historic District

Text same as above.

ID 29.2005.2

CL Installed 2005 Indiana Historical Bureau and Noblesville Preservation Alliance

D 1039 Logan Street, Noblesville.

Potter's Covered Bridge

ID 29.2007.1

CL Installed 2007 Indiana Historical Bureau, Hamilton County Parks and Recreation Department, and Noblesville Preservation Alliance.

D Potter's Bridge Park, 19401 North Allisonville Road, Noblesville.

Side one:
First bridge spanning white river at Potter's Ford was commissioned 1860 and named after the landowner, William Potter. In 1870, Hamilton County Commissioners voted for construction of this "Howe Truss" bridge. It was finished 1871 and repaired 1937, 1959, 1961. Plans to replace this structure with a concrete bridge were introduced in 1969.
Side two:
After 100 years of use, county commissioners voted to close the bridge to traffic 1971 and lease it to Hamilton County Parks and Recreation Department. Listed in National Register of Historic Places 1991. During 1990s, plans to restore bridge and create a park were developed. Bridge was restored and rededicated when Potter's Bridge Park opened 1999.

Birthplace of Democratic Party Rooster

The use of the rooster as a Democratic party symbol originated in Greenfield in the 1840 campaign. The rooster was later adopted by the state and national Democratic parties.

ID 30.1966.1

CL Erected by Indiana Sesquicentennial Commission, 1966

D E. Main Street/ US 40, Riley Park, Greenfield.

Birthplace of Democratic Party Rooster, Greenfield, Hancock County, Indiana Picture Collection, MS. Section, Indiana State Library.

Birthplace James Whitcomb Riley "The Hoosier Poet" October 7, 1849-July 22, 1916

Birthplace of James Whitcomb Riley, "The Hoosier Poet", Historic Site, Greenfield, Hancock County.

ID 30.1967.1

CL Erected by Indiana Sesquicentennial Commission, 1967

D 250 W. Main Street/US 40, Greenfield.

Editor, author, poet, lecturer and entertainer. One of the best known Hoosiers of all time, Riley first wrote under the name of "Benj. F. Johnson of Boone" and was famous for his use of Hoosier dialect.

Indiana Capitol

ID 31.1948.1

CL Indiana Historical Bureau

D N. Capitol Avenue adjacent to Harrison County Courthouse, Corydon.

Indiana Capitol, State Historic Site, Corydon, Harrison County.

The capital of Indiana Territory was moved to Corydon from Vincennes, 1813. This building became first State Capitol, 1816. Offices were moved to Indianapolis in 1825.

Battle of Corydon July 9, 1863

ID 31.1961.1

CL Erected by the Society of Indiana Pioneers, 1961

D 300 N. Capitol, SW corner of Harrison County Courthouse lawn, Corydon.

A force of about 400, Indiana militia and citizen volunteers commanded by Col. Lewis Jordan, engaged John Hunt Morgan's raiders, 2,400 cavalry, along a wooded ridge a mile south of Corydon. The determined Hoosier defense caused General Duke, Morgan's second in command, to comment, "They resolutely defended their rail piles." Three Hoosiers and eight Confederates were killed. Morgan then brought up his cannon and flanked the militia forcing Jordan to retreat. After Morgan surrounded and began shelling Corydon, Jordan surrendered with 345 men.

First State Office Building

Built 1817. Housed offices of State Treasurer and Auditor until fall of 1824. The cellar was the treasury vault. Building used by Harrison County Seminary, 1829~51. Since 1871, home of Amzi Brewster heirs.

ID 31.1962.1

CL Erected by the Corydon Chamber of Commerce

D Walnut & Mulberry Streets, Corydon.

First State Capital

Corydon became the first state capital of Indiana in 1816. The first constitution was drawn up and the first sessions of the state legislature and supreme court convened here.

ID 31.1962.2

CL Erected by the Corydon Chamber of Commerce

D Directions: SR 62, 0.3 mile east of SR 135 intersection, between Dale & Williar Avenues, west Corydon.

Site of the Battle of Corydon July 9, 1863

Site of the Battle of Corydon, Memorial Park, Cannon, Harrison County.

ID 31.1963.1

CL Erected by the Indiana Civil War Centennial Commission, 1963

D Old SR 135, Battle of Corydon Memorial Park entrance, one mile south of Corydon.

Morgan's Raid July 8-13, 1863

ID 31.1963.2

CL Erected by the Indiana Civil War Centennial Commission, 1963

D SR 135 and SR 11 junction, before the Mauckport-Brandenburg Ohio River Bridge.

Despite naval and militia opposition, General John Hunt Morgan, commanding about 2,200 Confederate cavalrymen, began his Indiana Raid by crossing the Ohio at this point, July 8, 1863.

Posey House

ID 31.1965.1

CL Erected in memory of Misses Margaret, Mary Jane, and Olive Griffin and Helen Griffin O'Leary, 1965

D 225 Oak Street, Corydon.

Posey House, Corydon, Harrison County.

Built 1817-Home of Col. Thomas Posey, son of Gov. Posey. Col. Posey (1792-1863) served as Treasurer of Harrison County; Cashier of Corydon Branch of the Bank of Vincennes; U.S. Military Pension Agent in Indiana; Adjutant General of Indiana; Legislator representing Harrison County; early Corydon merchant; an active Mason; and an ardent Methodist. Although he never married, he reared fourteen orphans in his home. Since 1925, Museum and Chapter House of The Hoosier Elm Chapter, Daughters of the American Revolution.

Harrison County Jail

First Log Jail erected 1809. Spier Spencer, First Sheriff, was killed 1811 commanding the Harrison County Yellow Jackets in the Battle of Tippecanoe. During first twelve years, Harrison County had a whipping post where justice was meted out by floggings. Second Jail burned 1871 in one of Corydon's disastrous fires. Devin and Tennyson, two criminals, were taken from Jail 1889 by a band of White Caps and hanged on the West Bridge at Corydon. Third Jail, a brick structure, was razed 1964 to make way for present jail.

ID 31.1965.2

CL Erected by Corydon Chamber of Commerce, 1965

D SW corner of N. Capitol Avenue and Cherry Street, Corydon.

Governor's Headquarters

Governor's Headquarters, State Historic Site, Corydon, Harrison County.

Home of governor William Hendricks 1822-1825 while he was Governor of Indiana. Front room was Governor's Headquarters. Hendricks was also Secretary of Constitutional Convention. House was built 1817 by Davis Floyd, Territorical Auditor and Treasurer and member of Constitutional Convention. Floyd had been convicted 1806 of aiding Aaron Burr. House purchased 1841 by Judge William A. Porter, noted lawyer, judge, and staunch Whig leader who served many terms in State Legislature and was Speaker of House 1849. The home since 1841 of Judge Porter and descendants.

ID 31.1965.3

CL Erected by Dan P. Griffin, 1965

D E. Walnut Street & N. Elm, NE of the courthouse, Corydon.

Presbyterian Church

ID 31.1965.4

CL Erected in memory of Judge and Mrs. Clyde R. Lottick, 1965

D E. Walnut Street & N. Elm, NE of the courthouse, Corydon.

Presbyterian Church, Steeple, Corydon, Harrison County.

Organized under Louisville Presbytery, Synod of Kentucky, January 1819 by Rev. John Finley Crowe who later founded Hanover College. Early Church services were held in homes and in State Capitol prior to building first church 1826. Original church stood on South Capitol Ave. where present E.U.B. Church stands. This original church used as a Confederate Hospital following the Battle of Corydon, July 9, 1863. Congregation moved to new location and present church erected 1906. Oldest continuous church organization in Corydon.

Last Home of Squire Boone

ID 31.1966.1

CL Credit Line: Erected by Indiana Sesquicentennial Commission, 1966

D SR 135 and SR 11 junction, before the Mauckport-Brandenburg Ohio River Bridge.

Four miles northwest Squire Boone, wilderness scout, brother of Daniel, settled on Buck Creek in 1804. He built Harrison County's first mill. Squire Boone died in 1815.

Walter Q. Gresham

Union General In The Civil War; U.S. District Judge; Postmaster General Under President Arthur; Interim U.S. Secretary of Treasury in 1884; U.S. Secretary of State Under President Cleveland. Was Born in Lanesville in 1832, And Lived In Corydon For Many Years. 1832-1895

ID 31.1966.2

CL Indiana State Highway Commission, 1966

D 2415 Barron Avenue NE & SR 62 at post office, Lanesville.

Mt. Solomon Lutheran Church

Rev. George Forster preached to Lutherans in Harrison County as early as 1805. Mt. Solomon Church was organized in 1810 four miles southwest of this spot and is credited as being the first Lutheran Church established in Indiana.

ID 31.1966.3

CL Erected by Descendants and Friends of Former Members of Mt. Solomon 1966

D SR 62, 5 miles west of Corydon.

Cedar Hill Cemetery

Cedar Hill Cemetery, Corydon, Harrison County.

First burials date back to founding of Corydon 1808. Col. Thomas L. Posey, a public minded citizen, donated the original ground to the Town of Corydon for burial purposes. The Farquar family added a small addition and the remainder of the cemetery was part of the Kintner-McGrain farm of Cedar Glade. Cemetery contains graves of veterans of all wars starting with the American Revolution; also graves of Confederate soldiers killed or died following Battle of Corydon, July 9, 1863. Maintained by Town of Corydon.

ID 31.1966.4

CL Erected 1966 by Cedar Hill Cemetery Committee

D E. Summit & N. Maple Streets, Corydon.

Harrison County

ID 31.1966.5

CL Erected by County Commissioners, 1966

D 300 N. Capitol, SE corner Harrison County Courthouse lawn, Corydon.

Harrison County Courthouse, Corydon.

Organized 1808 from parts of Knox and Clark Counties. Named in honor of William Henry Harrison who owned land within the County and was Territorial Governor and later ninth President of U.S. Fourth county formed in Indiana Territory. Original Harrison County comprised a large area and parts went to form Washington, Perry, Orange, Crawford, and Floyd Counties. Two buildings have served as county courthouses-the original State Capitol and the present courthouse erected 1929. County records date from 1808.

First State Capital

ID 31.1978.1

CL Erected by the Corydon Chamber of Commerce

D NE corner of Old Capitol grounds, Corydon.

Corydon became the first state capital of Indiana in 1816. The first constitution was drawn up and the first sessions of the state legislature and supreme court convened here.

Corydon United Methodist Church

Site of the first Methodist church, Corydon. Lot purchased from Isaiah Boone, son of Squire Boone, in 1826. Earlier, Corydon was a station on Silver Creek Methodist Circuit. Services were held in Corydon as early as 1816.

ID 31.1980.1

CL This marker erected by Church Memorial Committee 1980

D 214 N. Elm Street, east of the courthouse, Corydon.

Cedar Glade

House built by Jacob Kintner, Sr. 1808. Named for giant native red cedars in area. Self-sustaining plantation traded 1849 to Thomas McGrain, Sr. for Louisville property. Sheltered Corydon residents July 1863 during Morgan's Raid. First marked 1966 by Mr./Mrs. M. Dowling McGrain. Listed in National Register, 1983.

ID 31.2006.1

CL Erected 1992 by Indiana Historical Bureau and Mr./Mrs. Thomas D. McGrain

D 772 N. Capitol Avenue, SE corner Indian Creek bridge, Corydon.

Leora Brown School

Facility built 1891 as elementary and secondary school for African Americans. Originally known as Corydon Colored School; first graduation was on May 14, 1897. Renamed 1987 for Leora Brown Farrow, a teacher at the school, 1924-1950. Rehabilitated as cultural and educational center, 1993.

ID 31.1995.1

CL Erected 1995 Indiana Historical Bureau.

D 400 E. Summit Street near Hill Street, Corydon.

St. Paul African Methodist Episcopal Church

ID 31.2003.1

CL Installed 2003 Indiana Historical Bureau and St. Paul's A.M.E. Building Fund Organization

D SE corner of Maple & High streets, Corydon.

Side one:
Free blacks and former slaves organized an African Methodist Episcopal congregation in Corydon by 1843. In 1851, church trustees purchased land in Corydon in order to build a church and for school purposes. In 1878, church trustees purchased land at this site and later built a frame church.
Side two:
In August 1975, the congregation dedicated the brick church adjacent to this site. William Paul Quinn, appointed A.M.E. missionary 1840, established many congregations in frontier Indiana; elected Bishop 1844. Many early churches served as schools and enriched black social, cultural, and political life.

John Shields Lewis and Clark Expedition Member

ID 31.2004.1

CL Installed 2004 Indiana Historical Bureau and Harrison County Convention & Visitors Bureau

D 310 N. Elm Street, Harrison County Convention & Visitors Bureau, Corydon.

Side one:
Shields, born 1769 in Virginia, served as a private for the entire Lewis and Clark Expedition from October 19, 1803 until October 10, 1806; one of its "Nine Young Men from Kentucky," he was a skilled gunsmith and blacksmith.
Side two:
The Corps of Discovery explored lands of Louisiana Purchase and Pacific Northwest, 1803-1806. Shields settled in southern Indiana by June 1807; appointed captain in Clark County militia July 1807. Died in Harrison County in December 1809.

Oswell Wright

Side one:
Born in Maryland early 1810s. Bought land in Corydon, May 1849. In November 1857, Kentuckians arrested Wright and two white men, Charles and David Bell; they were indicted and jailed in Kentucky for aiding escape of fugitive slave. Bells rescued in jailbreak 1858. Wright convicted May 1859; completed sentence in Kentucky Penitentiary; released June 1864.
Side two:
Wright, a free black, lost his own freedom for helping a slave escape. Died in Corydon March 31, 1875. The Underground Railroad refers to a widespread network of diverse people in the nineteenth century who aided slaves escaping to freedom from the southern U.S.

ID 2008

CL Installed 2008 Indiana Historical Bureau, Division of Historic Preservation and Archaeology, IDNR; Leora Brown School, and Community Unity

D 417 Chestnut Street, Corydon.

Western Yearly Meetinghouse

ID 32.1972.1

CL Erected by the Guilford Township Historical Society, 1972

D SR 267 & National Road/US 40, Plainfield.

Western Yearly Friends Meeting House, Plainfield, Hendricks County.

Has been the site of annual meeting of Religious Society of Friends since 1858. The Depository was erected to house Quaker records, 1873. Friends Central Academy served as a secondary school, 1881-1919.

Danville's Main Street Historic District

ID 32.2000.1

CL Installed 2000 Indiana Historical Bureau, Main Street Historical Association of Danville, and Town of Danville

D 256/260 W. Main Street/US 36, Danville.

Side one:
Residential district bounded by Main, East, Cross, and Marion streets. Nineteenth and early twentieth century homes reflect social and economic diversity of residents, including town's prominent citizens. Listed in National Register of Historic Places 1994.
Side two:
Part of original 1824 Danville plat; county seat of Hendricks County, formed by Indiana General Assembly 1824. Lies west of downtown commercial area and reflects town's growth and prosperity. Town was market center for area farmers 1820s into early 1900s. Industries developed along tracks of Indianapolis and St. Louis Railroad built 1870.

Danville's Carnegie Library

Danville's Carnegie Library, Hendricks County.

ID 32.2001.1

CL Installed 2001 Indiana Historical Bureau and Danville Junior History Club sponsored by Danville Public Library

D 101 S. Indiana Street, Danville.

Side one:
At May 1902 meeting newly-formed Library Board authorized lot purchase and tax levy to support a public library as required by philanthropist Andrew Carnegie for funding. Designed by S. C. Dark of Indianapolis in Classical Revival Style; built 1902-1903; dedicated 1903 as Danville Public Library with approximately 1,000 volumes.
Side two:
Library has played major role in community's educational and cultural development. Additions built 1979 and 1999, doubling original space. Currently houses Danville Center Township Public Library. One of 1,679 libraries built in U.S. with funds from philanthropist Andrew Carnegie. Indiana built

Central Normal College

ID 32.2001.2

CL Installed 2001 Indiana Historical Bureau and Danville Senior History Club sponsored by Danville Public Library

D Main Street/US 36 & Wayne Street, Danville.

Central Normal College, Danville, Hendricks County, Indiana Picture Collection, MS. Section, Indiana State Library.

Side one: Organized 1876 at Ladoga as second private Indiana normal school specializing in teacher training. Based on Alfred Holbrook's techniques at his normal college in Lebanon, Ohio which pioneered teacher training in America. Central Normal College was moved to old Danville Academy building. The campus eventually consisted of five buildings.
Side two: Central Normal College, last self-supporting private normal school in Midwest, closed 1946. School reopened as Canterbury College by Episcopal Church; declining financial situation forced closure 1951. Alumni include many prominent Hoosiers. Hargrave Hall, gymnasium, and well house remain as part of Danville Middle School.

Samuel Luther Thompson

ID 32.2006.1

CL Installed 2006 Indiana Historical Bureau and Thompson and McPheeters Families

D Ellis Park, 600 E. Main Street, Danville.

Side one: He was born in Danville March 5, 1860 and educated in Danville Grade School. He played for Danville Browns baseball team in 1883 and for Evansville and Indianapolis minor league ball clubs 1884 and 1885. He played for National League Detroit Wolverines (1885-1888) and Philadelphia Phillies (1889-1898) and with American League Detroit Tigers 1906.
Side two: Thompson and his wife retired to Detroit, where he died November 7, 1922; buried there in Elmwood Cemetery. Inducted into National Baseball Hall of Fame 1974 and Indiana Baseball Hall of Fame 1979. Thompson remains first in runs batted in per game, edging out Lou Gehrig. Local ball diamond and Danville High School award honor this native son.

Arthur L. Trester

Side one:
Born 1878 in Pecksburg (which was 2.1 miles east). Elected to Board of control of Indiana High School Athletic Association (IHSAA) 1911, appointed Permanent Secretary 1913, continued after 1929 as Commissioner of High School Athletics. Under Trester, showcase of IHSAA became high school basketball, reflected in term, "Hoosier Hysteria," still used today.
Side two:
Under Trester, widely referred to as czar of IHSAA and high school athletics, IHSAA excluded black and parochial schools until 1942, stating they were not public high schools because of exclusive enrollment. He died 1944. Trester Medal for Mental Attitude first awarded 1945. Inducted into national (1961) and Indiana (1965 Basketball Halls of Fame.

ID 32.2007.1

CL Installed Indiana Historical Bureau and Donald D. Stuart.

D Intersection of Pearl and Railroad Avenue Amo.

Henry

Birthplace of Wilbur Wright

ID 33.1966.1

CL Erected Indiana Sesquicentennial Commission, 1966

D 1525 N 750 E, 4 miles south of Mooreland & 3 miles north of Millville.

Birthplace of Wilbur Wright, Millville, Henry County.

April 16, 1867-May 30, 1912
Co-inventor of the airplane.
With his brother, Orville, he began studing flight, 1896; built first model airplane, 1899; began gliding, 1900; and achieved first successful powered flight at Kitty Hawk, North Carolina, December 17, 1903.

Underground Station

ID 33.1976.1

CL Erected by Greensboro Women's Auxiliary and Greensboro Corporation

D SE corner Main Street & Greensboro Pike, Greensboro.

Seth Hinshaw, (1787-1865), well-known abolitionist, operated a station of the Underground Railroad on this site, prior to the Civil War. He also operated a store in which he refused to sell goods produced by slave labor. In 1843, Hinshaw helped erect Liberty Hall, which was located one block west of this site, where many fiery anti-slavery meetings were held under his direction.

Haynes' Horseless Carriage

Howard

Haynes Horseless Carriage, Kokomo, Howard County, Indiana Picture Collection, MS. Section, Indiana State Library.

ID 34.1966.1

CL Erected by Indiana Sesquicentennial Commission, 1966

D SE corner, US 31 & Boulevard Street, Kokomo.

Here on July 4, 1894, Elwood Haynes made the first test run of an automobile which he designed and built. His car reached a speed of about seven miles per hour over a six mile course on the Pumpkinvine Pike.

Pioneer Medical Doctors/Chase S. Osborn

Huntington

Side one:
George A. Osborn, 1823-1902; Margaret Osborn, 1827-1914; Parents of Chase S. Osborn. The mother launched upon active practice here 1860. The father practiced in Ohio before 1850.
Side two:
Naturalist, "Iron Hunter," Author, World Citizen, Friend of the Indian, Governor of Michigan 1911 and 1912, born here in a log cabin January 22, 1866.

ID 35.1949.1

CL Huntington County Medical Society / The Turtle Society

D Directions: SE corner SR 124 & SR 105, west of Mt. Etna.

Home of Chief Richardville

ID 35.1966.1

CL Erected by Indiana Sesquicentennial Commission, 1966

D Forks of the Wabash Historic Park, SW corner US 24 & SR 9, Huntington.

Home of Chief Richardville, Huntington, Huntington County.

Jean Baptiste Richardville (Pe-she-wah), 1761-1841, last great chief of the Miamis, made the forks of the Wabash his principal residence. His mother was the influential Tau-cum-wah, sister of Chief Little Turtle.

Forks of Wabash

ID 35.1972.1

CL Society of Indiana Pioneers

D Business US 24/ W. Park Drive, east of SR 9 junction, Huntington.

Forks of the Wabash River, Huntington, Huntington County.

The junction of the Wabash and Little rivers, 100 yards south, was the western terminus of the Maumee-Wabash long portage and, in 1835, of the first section of the Wabash and Erie Canal. During the 18th century French and English traders passed this way and, in 1778, Henry Hamilton brought 171 British troops and 350 Indians with 40 boats through the portage enroute to retake Fort Sackville at Vincennes. Three Miami villages were located here and Chiefs Richardville and LaFontaine once lived here. The Forks was the scene of many Indian councils and the Miami Treaties of 1834, 1838 and 1840.

Canal Landing on Washington Street/ Jefferson Park Mall

Side one: The Huntington Landing started 120 feet west on Washington St. and continued to the lock at Cherry St. The Wabash & Erie Canal was 4 feet deep and 100 feet wide at this point. Other locks were at First St. and Byron St. The Canal was completed from Fort Wayne to Huntington on July 4, 1835, and from Toledo to Evansville, 459 miles, in 1854. The Canal preceded the railroad to Huntington by 20 years, spurring early settlement. The Canal was abandoned in 1873. [map]
Side two: Indiana's First Tax-Free Mall
Jefferson Street was closed to motor traffic and transformed into a landscaped and lighted walkway by private financial contributors in 1969. Jefferson Street was the Huntington segment of a pioneer route–the Fort Recovery to Goshen Road –travelled by settlers from Ohio to Lake Michigan and northwest areas in the 1830's. Here the Road bridged the Wabash & Erie Canal.

ID 35.1973.1

CL Huntington Mall Merchants Association

D Washington & N. Jefferson Streets, Huntington.

Drover Town

Drover Town, the first addition south of Little River was platted Aug. 22, 1857 by Henry Drover. It included about 20 of his 160 acres of woodland. Family first names were given to the streets. Additional subdivisions followed. Huntington's efforts to annex the prosperous settlement were an emotional issue for several years. The resolution to annex came in January 1874. Henry Drover (1815-1880) founder, an emigrant from Prussia, was an outstanding citizen and leader in the community. [diagram]

ID 35.1979.1

CL Huntington County Historical Society

D One block north of Etna Avenue & Henry Street, St. Peter's First United Church of Christ property, Huntington.

The "Lime City"

ID 35.1979.2

CL South Side Business Association

D W.Park Drive & Diamond Street, Sunken Gardens Park, Huntington.

Huntington, The "Lime City," so named for its many limestone quarries and kilns, the first kiln being built in this vicinity by Michael Houseman in 1843 or 1844. By 1885 there were 31 kilns in operation; eight were perpetual kilns, the others were occasional kilns. The lime was of such high quality it was shipped out of the state as well as being used locally. [image]

Huntington's Buildings over the River/ Huntington's Ford and First Bridge

ID 35.1979.3

CL South Side Business Association and Huntington County Historical Society

D Jefferson Street, Little River bridge, Huntington.

Side one:
Controversy to Controversy
After fighting off a city injunction, A. J. Johnson erected two-story buildings (c 1900) over Little River beside the south span of the steel twin bridge built in 1891. Shops, offices and dwellings were housed here until the structures were condemned unsafe. The Southside Businessmen's Association spruced up the fronts, and the Art Guild donated colorful murals to cover 18 upper windows. Following years of controversy, the buildings were razed in 1977 by order of the state. [image]
Side two:
Pioneers forded Little River from Charles Street diagonally across just below the Island to the Court House. A dugout canoe, when hailed, carried pedestrians across for .50 cents. Reportedly Indians had used this ford when traveling to The Forks. The first truss bridge over Little River was built here at the ford. It was accepted in December 1843. [image]

Wabash & Erie Canal Lock 4

First lock west of summit level of Wabash and Erie Canal (connected Lake Erie with Ohio River in 1853). Known as Dickey Lock. Built as Lock 1, 1834-1835, of wood construction; renumbered Lock 4 as result of canal completion to Ohio line (1840). Remnant of arch culvert nearby. Canal important to founding of Roanoke.

ID 35.1997.1

CL Erected 1997 Indiana Historical Bureau and Roanoke Area Heritage Center.

D 339 E. First Street & US 24, Roanoke

Kiilhsoohkwa (Kilsoquah)

Kiilhsoohkwa, Miami woman, age over 100 years. Ill. by Lowell Hildebrandt.

Side one:
Born 1810 in what is now Huntington County. She was a granddaughter of Miami Chief Little Turtle. Her second husband was Antoine Revarre; her son Anthony Revarre, lived with her near Roanoke and acted as interpreter since she spoke only Miami. Most Miami were removed from Indiana 1846; 1850 act of Congress exempted her only son and other Miami people.
Side two:
Honored with a grand celebration on her 100th birthday. Died September 4, 1915. For many years, Kiilhsoohkwa cared for the flag reportedly presented to her other grandfather, shimaakanehsia, at the Treaty of Greenville between the U.S. and several Indian tribes 1795. Flag is rare artifact significant in American history and Miami Indian tradition.

ID 35.2005.1

CL Installed 2005 Indiana Historical Bureau, Roanoke Area Heritage Center, Inc., and Miami Nation - Miami, Oklahoma

D Glenwood Cemetery, 1000 block North Main Street, Roanoke.

Huntington

Warren's Carnegie Library

ID 35.2007.1

CL Installed 2007 Indiana Historical Bureau, Library Gift Fund, and Friends of the Library.

D 123 East Third Street, Warren.

Side one:
A Warren Public Library Board was organized in June 1916 after a public fundraising campaign to buy books and periodicals. In 1917, a grant of $10,000 from the Carnegie Corporation was confirmed to support construction of a free public library. Library Board selected Samuel Craig as supervising architect 1917. Building is Neoclassical in design.
Side two: Supply and transportation problems as a result of World War I halted construction temporarily. Warren Free Public Library was dedicated June 5, 1920 with over 1,500 books. Improvements completed in 1990s. One of 1,679 libraries built in U.S. with funds from philanthropist Andrew Carnegie. Indiana built more Carnegie libraries than any other state.

Jackson

Fort Vallonia

ID 36.1951.1

CL Indiana Historical Bureau

D SW corner Main Street & SR 135, Vallonia

[arrow pointing right]
Site in town of stockade built in 1812 on old Indian trail for protection of the settlers in this area. Garrisoned by Maj. John Tipton and his militia Rangers in 1813. Marker on the site.

Indian Treaty Corner

ID 36.1966.1

CL Erected by Indiana Sesquicentennial Commission, 1966

D US 50 at Crane Cemetery, 1 mile west of Seymour, north side of road

800 feet northwest is the point which marks the junction of the Grouseland Treaty line of 1805 with the Fort Wayne Treaty line of 1809. These and other treaties permitted early white settlement of Indiana. [map]

In Memory of Col. John Ketcham 1782-1865/Time Capsule

Portrait of Col. John Ketcham (1782-1865), Brownstown, Jackson County, Indiana Picture Collection, MS. Section, Indiana State Library.

Side one: Fearless pioneer, Ranger, surveyor, public servant who dedicated this public square for seat of government of Jackson County, Ind. when Brownstown was founded April 8, 1816. Side two: Brownstown Area Sesquicentennial October 1-8, 1996. To be opened in preparation for Brownstown, Ind., Bicentennial 2016 A. D. Steering Committee Mrs. G. R. Gillespie, Chr.; R. A. Brodhecker, V. Chr.; R. R. Robertson, Sec.; John H. Robertson, Sec.; Kathryn Horstman, Tr.; Kenneth Ball; Alan D. Beickman; Mrs. James P. Heller; Thomas P. Kieffer; Harry McOsker; Joseph Nierman; Robert Nuss; William Sharp; Mrs. M. K. Summers.

ID 36.1966.2

CL Erected by Ralph L. Anderson great-great-grandson of Col. Ketcham

D SW corner of Jackson County Courthouse grounds, Main/ US 50 & E. Cross Streets, Brownstown.

Freeman Field

Freeman Field, Museum, Seymour, Jackson County.

Activated December 1942 as U.S. Army Air Forces advanced training school for World War II twin engine pilots; graduated over 4,000 by February 1945. Construction of 413 structures and four 5,500-foot runways supervised by U.S. Army Corps of Engineers; named for Indiana pilot Captain Richard S. Freeman (1907-1941). Deactivated in 1948.

ID 36.1997.1

CL Erected 1997 Indiana Historical Bureau, City of Seymour, and Seymour Municipal Airport Authority

D NW corner SR 11/Walnut Street & B Avenue East at east entrance to Freeman Field, Seymour

Freeman Field

ID 36.1997.2

CL Erected 1997 Indiana Historical Bureau, City of Seymour, and Seymour Municipal Airport Authority

D SW corner US 50 & Airport Road at north entrance to Freeman Field, Seymour

Activated December 1942 as U.S. Army Air Forces advanced training school for World War II twin engine pilots; graduated over 4,000 by February 1945. Construction of 413 structures and four 5,500-foot runways supervised by U.S. Army Corps of Engineers; named for Indiana pilot Captain Richard S. Freeman (1907-1941). Deactivated in 1948.

Medora Shale Brick Plant

ID 2008

CL Installed 2008 Indiana Historical Bureau, Stephen Graves, and State Bankof Medora.

D State Bank of Medora, 24 East Main Street, Medora.

Side one: West Lee Wright laid out Medora 1853. Sample of local shale was made into brick "excellent for building and paving" 1904. Medora Shale brick company organized 1904. Construction began by 1910, one mile south of here along Baltimore & Ohio Southwestern Railroad, with six beehive kilns–round structures wrapped with steel bands and squared chimneys.

Side two: By 1927, ten kilns were at the site. Plant closed 1990s. In 2007, ten kilns remained. Medora was part of a large industry making a variety of clay products for agriculture, street paving, and building construction, which contributed to Indiana's growth as a leading industrial state. In 1920, Indiana was seventh in U.S. for production of clay products.

Jasper

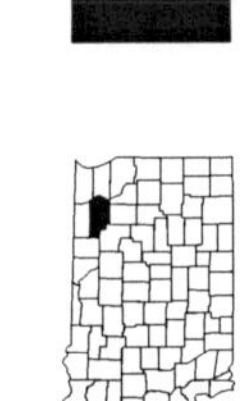

General Robert H. Milroy 1816-1890

General Robert H. Milroy (1816-1890), Rensselaer, Jasper County.

was appointed colonel of the 9th Indiana Infantry, later promoted to brigadier and major general. He saw extensive action in western Virginia. After the war he served as Indian agent in state of Washington.

ID 37.1964.1

CL Erected by the Indiana Civil War Centennial Commission, 1964

D Milroy Park, 3 blocks west of downtown between Washington & Milroy Streets & College Avenue, Rensselaer.

La Salle Expedition

In December, 1679, Robert Cavalier, Sieur de La Salle, with thirty men crossed northwestern Indiana by way of the Kankakee River in an attempt to find a water route to the Pacific Ocean.

ID 37.1966.1

CL Erected by Indiana Sesquicentennial Commission, 1966

D US 231 at Kankakee River, northern Jasper County. Missing.

St. Joseph's Indian Normal School 1888-1896

ID 37.1971.1

CL Erected by the Indiana Historical Society 1971

D East side of US 231, across from St. Joseph College main entrance, south Rensselaer.

St. Joseph's Indian Normal School (1888-1896), Rensselaer, Jasper County.

Erected by the Bureau of Catholic Indian Missions with funds from Katharine Drexel and operated by the Society of the Precious Blood with federal funds, 60 Indian boys from distant reservations were annually trained here.

Fountain Park Chautauqua

ID 37.1992.1

CL Erected 1992 by Indiana Historical Bureau and Fountain Park Chautauqua

D Fountain Park Chautauqua central grounds, CR 1600 S, 0.3 mile west of US 231, Remington

Fountain Park Chautauqua, Historic Hotel, Remington, Jasper County.

Fountain Park has been the site of annual Chautauqua sessions since 1895. The Chautauqua continues to promote traditional values and the religious, social, and educational activities upon which it was founded.

Remington Water Tower

Side one: Built 1897 by Challenge Wind and Feed Mill Company of Batavia, Illinois. Rare tower and wood tank structure is an original example of nineteenth century public water utility facility, construction methods, and technology. Tower has limestone foundation, is 104 feet tall and approximately 20 feet in diameter, with two-foot thick brick walls.
Side two: Original 1897 tank replaced 1924 by Challenge; 66,000 gallon tank is made of horizontally curved cypress battens held in place by metal binder rings. Additions made to structure, which has housed various governmental services. Awarded American Water Works Association's Water Landmark Award 1986. Listed in National Register of Historic Places 2003.

Remington Water Tower, Jasper County.

ID 37.2005.1

CL Installed 2005 Indiana Historical Bureau, Town of Remington, and Remington Historical Society

D 3 East Michigan St., Remington.

James Frederick Hanley

Side one: Born February 17, 1892 in Rensselaer; became part of New York Tin Pan Alley music scene. Wrote for Broadway musicals such hits as "Second Hand Rose" (Grant Clarke, lyrics) for Fanny Brice (1921 *Ziegfeld Follies*) and "Zing! Went the Strings of My Heart" (1934), popularized by Judy Garland 1938. Wrote scores for many Hollywood musicals in early 1930s.
Side two: "[Back home Again in} Indiana," by Hanley and Ballard MacDonald (lyrics) was hit in 1917, 1920s jazz classic recorded by Louis Armstrong, and a 1930s swing tune by Benny Goodman. .Song has remained popular and has been performed at every Indianapolis 500 since 1946. Hanley died February 8, 1942 in New York; buried there in Gate of Heaven Cemetery.

ID 37.2008

CL Installed 2008 Indiana Historical Bureau and Jasper County-Historical Society

D James F. Hanley Park, Intersection of Washington and Front, Rensselaer

Jay

West Grove

ID 38.1972.1

CL Erected 1972 by the Jay County Historical Society

D East of Balbec & SR 1 on CR 650 N 1.7 miles to cemetery entrance, 4.5 miles NE of Pennville.

Early Quaker settlement established 1836; center of Underground Railroad activity. Meeting house erected here, 1840, on land donated by Enos and Margaret Lewis; used by Congregational Friends, by Spiritualist society, as school, community hall; razed 1927.

Jefferson

Morgan's Raid July 8-13, 1863

ID 39.1963.1

CL Erected by the Indiana Civil War Centennial Commission, 1963

D Dupont Elmentary School, SR 7, Dupont.

Confederate forces under Gen. John Hunt Morgan camped near Dupont the night of July 11. They destroyed railroad track, burned bridges, freight cars and a warehouse, and stole 2,000 hams from Mayfield's pork house.

James F. D. Lanier 1800-1881

ID 39.1963.2

CL Erected by the Indiana Civil War Centennial Commission, 1963

D 511 First & Elm Streets near Ohio River at Lanier Mansion State Historic Site, Madison.

Portrait of James F. D. Lanier (1800-1881), Madison, Jefferson County, Indiana Picture Collection, MS. Section, Indiana State Library.

Rendered his most important public service during the Civil War when he loaned Governor Oliver P. Morton over $400,000 to equip Indiana's troops. He later arranged additional loans to save the credit of the state.

First Chartered Bank in Indiana

Legislature authorized the organization of the Farmers' and Mechanics' Bank of Madison. The bank operated on this site for about ten years when its charter was revoked.

ID 39.1966.1

CL Erected by Indiana Sesquicentennial Commission, 1966

D 308 Jefferson Street, Madison.

Harvey Washington Wiley, M.D. 1844-1930

Born near Kent, Jefferson County, Dr. Wiley graduated from Hanover College (1867), received his medical degree from Indiana Medical College (1871), and taught at Butler and Purdue universities. As Chief Chemist for the U.S. Department of Agriculture he led the nationwide movement which culminated in the Pure Food and Drug Act of 1906 and the establishment of the U.S. Food and Drug Administration.

ID 39.1981.1

CL Erected by the Association of Food and Drug Officials, 1981

D SW corner of SR 256 & CR 850 West, Kent.

Madison Historic District

Madison Historic District, Jefferson County.

Madison Historic District, listed in National Register, 1973, in over 130 blocks contains hundreds of structures of every type, size, and period, 1812-1920, including many outstanding examples of major 19th century architectural styles. Madison is significant in growth of Indiana historic preservation movement.

ID 39.1992.1

CL Erected 1992 by Indiana Historical Bureau and Cornerstone Society, Inc.

D Vaughn Drive & Jefferson Street at Ohio Riverside walk, Madison.

Madison Hill Incline and Cut

ID 39.1996.1

CL Erected 1996 Indiana Historical Bureau and Jefferson County Historical Society, Inc.

D 1001 W. Main & McIntire Streets, SW corner of railroad bridge, Madison.

Madison Hill Incline & Cut, Jefferson County, from G. S. Cottman's, Centennial History & Handbook of Indiana, page 281, 1915.

Built 1836-1841 as part of Indiana's 1836 Internal Improvement Act. Measures 7,012 feet long and elevates 413 feet to achieve a 5.89 percent grade; 500,000 tons of rock and earth were moved in construction. Still considered to be the steepest standard gauge main track ascended by wheel-adhesion locomotives in the U.S.

Alois O. Bachman

ID 39.1999.1

CL Erected 1999 Indiana Historical Bureau and Jefferson County Civil War Round Table

D SE corner of Alois O. Bachman Bridge at SR 7, Hanging Rock Hill, Presbyterian & Cragmont Streets, Madi-

Side one: Born in Madison 1839. Family home on West Main Street. Attended Hanover College 1856-1858 to pursue practice of law. Attended Kentucky Military Institute in Frankfort. Organized Madison City Greys 1858, which became part of Sixth Regiment Indiana Volunteers of Union Army in the Civil War. Side two: Lieutenant Colonel Bachman, commanding the Nineteenth Indiana Infantry Regiment of the Iron Brigade of the Army of the Potomac, was mortally wounded leading a charge during the Battle of Antietam on September 17, 1862. He was the highest ranking Hoosier in the Union Army killed in this battle. His grave is in adjacent Springdale Cemetery. Bridge named for him 1998.

Michael C. Garber

Side one: Born Staunton, Virginia 1813. Purchased Madison *Courier* 1849; transformed it from pro-Democratic to voice for newly forming Republican Party. Promoted the Union and objected to Fugitive Slave Law. Was active in Republican Party politics. Nominated to represent state's Third Congressional District at first Republican National Convention 1856.
Side two: Garber served in U.S. Volunteers in the Civil War, 1861-1866, and was mustered out with rank of colonel and chief quartermaster. Turned over editorship of the Madison *Courier* to his son Michael, Jr. 1875. Served as Madison postmaster 1875-1881. He died April 8, 1881 and is buried in Madison.

ID 39.2004.1

CL Installed 2004 Indiana Historical Bureau and The Madison Courier

D The Madison Courier office, 310 West Street, Madison.

Lyman Hoyt

Lyman Hoyt Home. Indiana Historical Bureau Photo. Lancaster, Jefferson County.

Side one: Born in Vermont 1804. Moved to Jefferson County 1834, where he owned land and had several manufacturing businesses. Active in Neil's Creek Anti-Slavery Society and in forming Liberty Party for abolition of slavery. He and his family supported Eleutherian College. He died 1857. Home listed in National Register of Historic Places 2003. Side two: Hoyt condemned the Fugitive Slave Law and participated in helping fugitives escaping through Jefferson County. The Underground Railroad refers to a widespread network of diverse people in the nineteenth century who aided slaves escaping to freedom from the southern U.S. [logo]

ID 39.2004.2

CL Installed 2004 Indiana Historical Bureau, Division of Historic Preservation & Archaeology, IDNR, African American Landmarks Committee of Historic Landmarks Foundation of Indiana, Inc., Historic Eleutherian College, Historic Madison, Jefferson County Preservation Council, Cornerstone Society, Jefferson County Civil War Roundtable, and City of Madison

D 7147 West SR 250, Lancaster

Eleutherian College

ID 39.2004.3

CL Installed 2004 Indiana Historical Bureau, Division of Historic Preservation & Archaeology, IDNR, African American Landmarks Committee of Historic Landmarks Foundation of Indiana, Inc., Historic Eleutherian College, Historic Madison, Jefferson County Preservation Council, Cornerstone Society, Jefferson County Civil War Roundtable, and City of Madison

D 6927 West SR 250, Lancaster.

1931, Eleutherian College, Hohenberger Picture Collection, MS. Section, Indiana State Library.

Side one:
College developed 1854 from Eleutherian Institute, founded 1848. Thomas Craven and antislavery advocates in the area created and supported the institution for education of students of all races and genders. This structure, built in the 1850s for classes and a chapel, was purchased for restoration 1990. Designated National Historic Landmark 1997.
Side two:
Eleutherian provided one of earliest educational opportunities for women and African-Americans before Civil War.
The Underground Railroad refers to a widespread network of diverse people in the nineteenth century who aided slaves escaping to freedom from the southern U.S. [logo]

Georgetown

Side one:
Free blacks settled in Madison as early as 1820. The growing black community began businesses and organized churches and schools in this area, later called Georgetown. Risking their own freedom, some free black residents here actively aided slaves seeking freedom. A few of these residents had to flee from Madison themselves in the late 1840s.
Side two:
Despite the danger, after the late 1840s some free blacks in Madison continued to aid freedom seekers.
The Underground Railroad refers to a widespread network of diverse people in the nineteenth century who aided slaves escaping to freedom from the southern U.S. [logo]

ID 39.2004.4

CL Installed 2004 Indiana Historical Bureau, Division of Historic Preservation & Archaeology, IDNR, African American Landmarks Committee of Historic Landmarks Foundation of Indiana, Inc., Eleutherian College, Historic Madison, Jefferson Co. Preservation Council, Cornerstone Society, Jefferson Co. Civil War Roundtable, and City of Madison; Georgetown part of Madison Historic District, 1973

D Jefferson & Fifth Streets, Madison.

Irene Dunne

ID 39.2006.1

CL Installed 2006 Indiana Historical Bureau and Friends of Irene Dunne

D Ohio Theatre, 105 E. Main Street, Madison

1940, Irene Dunne portrait, Indiana Picture Collection, Manuscript Section Indiana State Library.

Side one: Born in Louisville, Kentucky 1898; after father's death, moved with family to Madison. Graduated from Madison High School 1916. After voice training in Indianapolis and Chicago, began singing professionally. Won lead in road show of Florenz Ziegfeld's *Show Boat* 1929. Began Hollywood career 1930; in 42 films; nominated for five Academy Awards.

Side two:
Dunne maintained ties with Madison, which has honored her; she helped with restoration of Broadway Fountain 1976. She received Laetare Medal from University of Notre Dame 1949. President Dwight Eisenhower named her an alternate delegate to United Nations General Assembly 1957; was Kennedy Center Honors Awardee 1985. Died 1990 in Los Angeles.

John H. and Sarah Tibbets

ID 39.2006.2

CL Installed 2006 Indiana Historical Bureau, Historic Eleutherian College, Lena McDole and Tibbets' descendants.

D 6810 N. Boyd Road, Madison

Side one: The Tibbets provided assistance to fugitive slaves here in their home (now part of National Park Service, Network to Freedom); John piloted them to the next safe haven. Both were members of Neil's Creek Anti-Slavery Society and Anti-Slavery Regular Baptist Church at College Hill. John served as a trustee for the church and Eleutherian College.
Side two: Free blacks from Madison and surrounding area and white abolitionists helped fugitive slaves. The Underground Railroad refers to a widespread network of diverse people in the nineteenth century who aided slaves escaping to freedom from the southern U.S.

Grouseland Treaty Line (August 21, 1805)

Territorial Governor, William Henry Harrison, in a treaty with Indians held at Vincennes, secured lands which for the first time opened the entire north bank of the Ohio River for settlement.

ID 40.1966.1

CL Erected by Indiana Sesquicentennial Commission, 1966

D SR 7, SE of Scipio.

Hannah Milhous Nixon

Mother of President Richard M. Nixon was born on a farm four and a half miles southeast to which her grandparents came in 1854. Hannah's parents moved to California in 1897 when she was twelve years old.

ID 40.1969.1

CL Jennings County Junior Historical Society, an affiliate of the Indiana Junior Historical Society, 1969

D US 50 & CR 325 N, Butlerville.

Jonathan Jennings, 1784-1834

Jonathan Jennings (1784-1834), Indiana's First Governor (1816-1822), Vernon, Jennings County, Indiana Governors' Portraits Collection, Indiana Historical Bureau.

Jennings County, formed 1816, named in honor of Jonathan Jennings: territorial delegate to Congress, 1809-1816; president of Indiana Constitutional Convention, 1816; first governor of state, 1816-1822; member of United States House of Representatives, 1822-1831. The only Jennings County in the United States.

ID 40.1995.1

CL Erected 1995 Indiana Historical Bureau and Jennings County Community donations; B.S.A. Troop 532 Eagle Project by Charles Edward Dale Bentz.

D South corner of Courthouse Square, SR 7 & SR 3, Vernon.

Morgan's Raid

ID 40.1997.1

CL Erected 1997 Indiana Historical Bureau

D SW corner of Courthouse Square, Vernon. (Replaced 40.1963.1)

Portrait of Confederate General John Hunt Morgan, Vernon, Jennings County, L & N Railroad, Louisville, Kentucky.

During the Civil War, Confederate General John Hunt Morgan led a raid into southern Indiana, July 8-13, 1863. On July 11, he demanded the surrender of Vernon. Colonel Hugh T. Williams, Indiana Legion, replied that Morgan "must take it by hard fighting." No major battle occurred, and Morgan's cavalry withdrew toward Dupont, Jefferson County.

Kellar Grist Mill

ID 40.1997.2

CL Erected 1997 Indiana Historical Bureau and Jennings County Historical Society

D N. Base Road, 0.5 mile south of Brewersville, 0.5 mile north of the Sand Creek bridge, north of North Vernon.

Adam Kellar began constructing a stone mill race on Sand Creek, 1813, and opened grist mill, 1823. Mill was important to local economy and was an impetus for development: state road to mill established, 1834, and Brewersville founded, 1837. Flatboats carried mill products as far as New Orleans. Mill was closed after damage in 1937 flood.

Muscatatuck Park

Muscatatuck County Park, Vernon Fork, North Vernon, Jennings County.

Side one: Opened 1921 as Indiana's fourth state park for its natural beauty and recreation potential. Named Vinegar Mills State Park after stone-cutting mill in park. Renamed Muscatatuck State Park 1922. Stone shelters and stairways, fire tower, trails, and retaining walls were built by Works Progress Administration and Civilian Conservation Corps in 1930s.
Side two: Nearby home (built 1850) of William Read, owner of stone-cutting mill, was used as an inn by the state park. Quail were raised in park 1953-1962; park was renamed Muscatatuck State Park and Game Farm. State youth camp was started in park 1962. In 1968, park was returned to Jennings County for recreational uses. Walnut Grove Schoolhouse (1913) was moved here 1990.

ID 40.1999.1

CL Erected 1999 Indiana Historical Bureau and Jennings County Parks and Recreation Department

D CR 325 N & SR 7 at park entrance, North Vernon.

Vernon Historic District

Side one: Vernon platted 1815. Jennings County formed by Indiana General Assembly 1817; Vernon named county seat 1817. Madison-Indianapolis Railroad reached Vernon 1839; masonry arch, elevating track over Pike Street, remains. Vernon still operates under its amended 1851 incorporation by General Assembly authorizing a mayor and local elections in March.
Side two: Vernon listed as Historic District in National Register of Historic Places 1976. Many structures built before 1900, some from 1820s through 1840s. Fire October 13, 1859 destroyed homes and businesses on Pike Street opposite Court House Square. Federal, Greek Revival, Italianate, and composite architectural styles blend into a historic mosaic.

ID 40.2003.1

CL Installed 2003 Indiana Historical Bureau, Town of Vernon, Jennings County Parks & Recreation, and Jennings County Tourism Bureau

D SW corner of courthouse lawn, Vernon

Johnson

Birthplace of Paul Vories McNutt

ID 41.1992.1

CL Erected 1992 by Indiana Historical Bureau

D 200 N. Walnut Street, north of W. King Street, Franklin.

Governor Paul Vories McNutt (1933-1937), Franklin, Johnson County, Indiana Governors' Portraits Collection, Indiana Historical Bureau.

McNutt, born July 19, 1891 at 200 N. Walnut, was Indiana's 33rd Governor (1933-1937), state and national American Legion Commander, I. U. Law School Dean, High Commissioner and first U.S. Ambassador to Philippine Republic. Died March 24, 1955; buried at Arlington National Cemetery.

Johnson

Birthplace of Roger D. Branigin

Governor Roger D. Branigin (1965-1969), Franklin, Johnson County, Indiana Governors' Portraits Collection, Indiana Historical Bureau.

As Indiana's 42nd governor 1965-1969, championed equal opportunity in education and housing. Earned degrees from Franklin College and Harvard University. Deputy prosecutor of Johnson and Brown counties 1926-1929. Practiced law in Franklin, Louisville, and Lafayette. Served in World War II. Lived 1902-1975.

ID 41.2000.1

CL Installed 2000 Indiana Historical Bureau, Greater Johnson County Community Foundation, Inc., Glen Floyd, Fred W. Garver, Ivan D. Lancaster, Lee K. and Sian Napier, Daniel E. and Eva M. Poe, David P. Vandivier

D 250 N. Yandes Street, north of E. King Street on west side of street, Franklin.

Shakertown

First settlement, 1808-1812, of a religious society of celibates known as Shakers. The four hundred members of this communal group occupied 1,300 acres seven miles west of Carlisle.

ID 42.1966.1

CL Erected by Indiana Sesquicentennial Commission, 1966

D US 41 southbound & CR 1100 N/Gauger Road, 1 mile north of Oaktown. Formerly listed as being in Sullivan County (77.1966.1)

Fort Knox, First Site

ID 42.1966.2

CL Erected by Indiana Sesquicentennial Commission, 1966

D Buntin & 1st Streets, 2 blocks south of Old French House, Vincennes

Built in 1787 by Major John F. Hamtramck under command of General Josiah Harmar. United States Army's most western outpost for several years. Named for General Henry Knox, first Secretary of War.

Old French House

ID 42.1995.1

CL Erected 1995 Indiana Historical Bureau and Old Northwest Corporation

D 509 N. 1st Street, north of Seminary Street intersection, Vincennes

Home of French fur trader Michel Brouillet (1774-1838). French Creole cottage (built circa 1806) is typical of "posts-on-sill" construction technique used by French settlers in Mississippi Valley during eighteenth and early nineteenth centuries. Restoration 1974-1976. Located within Vincennes Historic District.

Samuel Thornton Scott (1777-1827)

ID 42.1995.2

CL Erected 1995 Indiana Historical Bureau

D Harrison Street, south of 2nd Street, Indiana Territory State Historic Site, east of Vincennes University, Vincennes.

First resident Presbyterian minister in Indiana Territory, 1808. Headed the first school under the authority of the board of trustees of Vincennes University (a grammar school), 1811-1815. Served as member of board of trustees of Vincennes University, 1813-1824.

Vincennes' Carnegie Library

Vincennes Carnegie Library, Knox County.

ID 42.2001.1

CL Installed 2001 Indiana Historical Bureau and Knox County Public Library

D NW corner of 7th & Seminary Streets, Vincennes.

Side one:
Designed by local architect John B. Bayard in Collegiate Gothic Style; built 1917-1918. Dedicated 1919, with 13,518 books and 4,207 registered borrowers, as Vincennes Public Library; Public Library located in City Hall since 1889. Modern addition 1976-1977; became Knox County Public Library 1978.
Side two:
Library has played major role in the community's educational and cultural development. Included in Vincennes Historic District, listed in National Register of Historic Places 1974. One of 1,679 libraries built in U.S. with funds from philanthropist Andrew Carnegie. Indiana built more Carnegie libraries than any other state.

Knox

William Henry Harrison & Lewis & Clark Expedition

ID 42.2006.1

CL Installed 2006 Indiana Historical Bureau, Ohio River Chapter – Lewis & Clark Trail Heritage Foundation, National Park Service, Indiana Lewis & Clark Bicentennial Commission & IDNR.

D Indiana Territory State Historic Site, 1 W. Harrison St., Vincennes

Side one:
Harrison became Governor of Indiana Territory 1800; he administered government of District of Louisiana 1804-1805. In Vincennes, he served as a contact during the expedition; surviving records document his support and his involvement in decisions about western Indian chiefs visiting Washington.
Side two:
In 1806, on their way to the Falls of the Ohio and then Washington after the expedition, Lewis and Clark stopped in Vincennes; Lewis wrote from Vincennes on October 30 to Secretary of War Henry Dearborn. The expedition explored lands of the Louisiana Purchase and the Pacific Northwest, 1803-1806.

Kosciusko

Papakeechie's Reserve

ID 43.1962.1

CL Indiana Historical Society 1962

D 7277 E. Eli Lilly Road, north shore Lake Wawasee, Syracuse.

You are now leaving Papakeechie's Reservation, 36 square miles. This Miami Chief, also known as Flat Belly, held this land from 1828 to 1834 when it was returned to the National Government. It was later owned by the Wabash & Erie Canal.

Indian Hill

Indians formerly wrapped their dead and secured them in the trees here. At the time of white settlement the wrappings were disintegrating and the bones were falling to the ground.

ID 43.1962.2

CL Indiana Historical Society 1962

D 877 N. Shore Drive, Syracuse Lake, Syracuse.

Indiana's Glacier Lakes

Indiana's Glacier Lakes, Wyland Lake, North Webster, Kosciusko County.

About 14,000 years ago melting blocks of ice from the last, or Wisconsin Glacier, formed the kettle hole lakes of northern Indiana. The largest lake, Wawasee, and the deepest lake, Tippecanoe, are in Kosciusko County.

ID 43.1966.1

CL Erected by Indiana Sesquicentennial Commission, 1966

D Kosciusko County Courthouse, NE lawn, Warsaw.

Continental Divide

This divide separates the Great Lakes drainage system from the Mississippi River drainage system. [map]

ID 43.1968.1

CL Erected by the Indiana Historical Society, 1968

D East side of SR 13 along frontage of the Northern Indiana Weather Forecast Office facility, 2 miles north of North Webster, south of Syracuse.

Site of Cowen Grove Seminary, 1851-1876

ID 43.1976.1

CL Kosciusko County Historical Society, 1976

D 311 S. Detroit Street, Warsaw.

One of the first secondary schools in the area. Built at the call of the Presbyterian Church by Robert Cowen and his wife Jane Cowen headmistress. A fire of unknown origin burned the Seminary to the ground in December, 1879.

Lawrence D. Bell

ID 43.1995.1

CL Erected 1995 Indiana Historical Bureau and Bell Aircraft Museum

D SR 25 W, Mentone.

Born in Mentone, Lawrence D. Bell (1894-1956) became one of America's foremost aviation pioneers. He founded Bell Aircraft Corporation in Buffalo, New York, 1935. Advanced aircraft manufactured included Bell helicopters, America's first jet, and Bell X-1, first plane to fly faster than speed of sound.

Chinworth Bridge

ID 43.2007.1

CL Erected 1999 Indiana Historical Bureau, Kosciusko County Historical Society, and Kosciusko County Convention and Visitors Bureau

D Tippecanoe River Rest Park, Old US 30/Lincoln Highway at CR 350 W, Warsaw.

Chinworth Bridge, Tippecanoe River, Warsaw, Kosciusko County.

Built 1897 across Tippecanoe River by Bellefontaine Bridge and Iron Company of Ohio. Single-span 140-foot iron bridge is last remaining Pratt through truss bridge in county. U.S. Highway 30 bypassed it in 1924. Closed to vehicle traffic 1975. Leased by Kosciusko County Historical Society 1975. Listed in National Register of Historic Places 1997.

Kosciusko County Jail

Kosciusko County Jail, Historic Society & Museum, Warsaw, Kosciusko County.

Side one: This third county jail, including a sheriff's residence, was built 1870 by Richard Epperson. Chicago architect, George O. Garnsey designed it in Neo-Gothic style. Rusticated stonework and turrets create the appearance of a small castle to provide a sense of security and strength. Two-story jail was located behind sheriff's three-story residence.
Side two: Listed in National Register of Historic Places 1978. Jail closed and building leased to Kosciusko County Historical Society for first county museum 1982. County jails were first established in 1792 under laws of the Northwest Territory; they continued under laws of the Indiana Territory and state constitutions of 1816 and 1851.

ID 43.2003.1

CL Installed 2003 Indiana Historical Bureau, Kosciusko County Historical Society, Kosciusko County Convention & Visitors Bureau, and The Hall Family

D 121 N. Indiana, Warsaw.

The LaGrange Phalanx

The Fourier System of communal living was attempted here between 1843 and 1848. Approximately thirty families lived by rules established in councils of industry, commerce, justice and education. Their "new social order" was a failure.

ID 44.1966.1

CL Erected by Indiana Sesquicentennial Commission, 1966

D US 20, 0.7 mile east of junction of US 20 & SR 3, west of Brushy Prairie.

First Physician

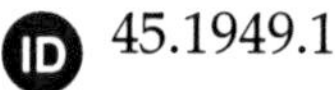

ID 45.1949.1

CL Woman's Auxillary, Lake County Medical Society

D 2985 W. 73rd Place, Merrillville

Henry D. Palmer, M.D. (1809-1877) located at this site in 1836. First physician in Lake County, he was also counselor to the pioneers for 40 years and member of the underground railroad aiding escaped slaves.

Great Sauk (Sac) Trail (east-west through this point)

ID 45.1966.1

CL Erected by Indiana Sesquicentennial Commission, 1966

D Van Buren Street at W. 73rd Avenue/Old US 30/Lincoln Highway on traffic median east of Calumet Cemetery & west of Broadway/SR 53, Merrillville

Part of a transcontinental trail used by prehistoric peoples of North America, it passed through modern Detroit, Rock Island and Davenport in the Midwest. The trail was important into the 19th century.

St. John's Lutheran Church Tolleston

ID 45.1976.1

CL none

D 2235 W. 10th Avenue at Taft Avenue, SE corner, Gary

St. John's Lutheran Church, Tolleston Neighborhood, Gary, Lake County.

St. John's Church, the oldest surviving institution in Gary and north of the Little Calumet River, began with the work of the Rev. Henry Wunder in the early 1860's. He regularly came from Chicago by horse and buggy. Baptism records date from 1863; the first church was built on this site in 1868 or 1869; 1870 is celebrated as date of organization. The church served German immigrants to Tolleston (named for George Tolle who came in 1856). Tolleston was annexed to Gary in 1910.

Dutch in the Calumet Region

Dutch immigrants after 1850 began moving to this area because of its similarties to their homeland. They helped to locate ditches to drain water from the extensive marshes, leaving rich land to expand sucessful horticultural activities.

ID 45.1992.1

CL Erected 1992 Indiana Historical Bureau and Lamprecht Florist & Greenhouse, established 1923

D 8941 Kleinman Road, Highland

St. John Township School, District #2

Built, 1853, approximately one half mile south; closed, 1907; moved to this site and restored for educational and community uses, 1993-1994. One of twelve St. John Township schools; structure typical of early one-room school buildings in Indiana.

ID 45.1995.1

CL Erected 1995 Indiana Historical Bureau and Committee to Save Township School #2

D 1515 Joliet Street/Lincoln Highway/US 30, east of St. John Road at the St. John Township Community Center, Schererville

The Lincoln Highway/ The "Ideal Section"

ID 45.1996.1

CL Erected 1996 Indiana Historical Bureau, Northwest Indiana Lincoln Highway Association, Dyer and Schererville Historical Societies, Sand Ridge Bank, Welsh, Inc

D US 30/Joliet Street and Calumet Avenue, about 30 yards west of the intersection on the southwest corner on the south side of Joliet Street/US 30, Dyer

Side one: United States' first transcontinental highway, constructed 1913-1928, from New York City to San Francisco. Dedicated to the memory of Abraham Lincoln. Conceived by Carl G. Fisher to encourage building "good roads." Sponsored by Lincoln Highway Association and supported by automotive industries.

Side two: "Ideal Section" - 1.5 miles - of Lincoln Highway, completed 1923, designed and built as a model for road construction. Funded by county, state, and U.S. Rubber Co. Features included 100 foot right-of-way, 40 foot paved width, 10 inch steel-reinforced concrete, underground drainage, lighted, landscaped, bridge, and pedestrian pathways.

The Lincoln Highway/ The "Ideal Section"

ID 45.1996.2

CL Erected 1996 Indiana Historical Bureau, Northwest Indiana Lincoln Highway Association, Dyer and Schererville Historical Societies, Sand Ridge Bank, Welsh, Inc.

D NE corner of Joliet Street/US 30 and Janice Drive, Schererville

Side one: United States' first transcontinental highway, constructed 1913-1928, from New York City to San Francisco. Dedicated to the memory of Abraham Lincoln. Conceived by Carl G. Fisher to encourage building "good roads." Sponsored by Lincoln Highway Association and supported by automotive industries.
Side two: "Ideal Section" - 1.5 miles - of Lincoln Highway, completed 1923, designed and built as a model for road construction. Funded by county, state, and U.S. Rubber Co. Features included 100 foot right-of-way, 40 foot paved width, 10 inch steel-reinforced concrete, underground drainage, lighted, landscaped, bridge, and pedestrian pathways.

Civil War Camps

Two Civil War training camps: Colfax and Jackson, were located near La Porte. The 9th and 29th Indiana Volunteer Infantry regiments were organized and trained here.

ID 46.1962.1

CL Erected by the Indiana Civil War Centennial Commission, 1963

D SR 2 W & Colfax Avenue, La Porte

La Porte

Chicago-New York Electric Air Line Railroad

Proposed in 1905 as a 742 mile, straight-line, high speed route, without crossings; estimated ten hours travel time at a cost of ten dollars. Just under twenty miles, between La Porte and Chesterton, were constructed, 1906-1911.

ID 46.1995.1

CL Erected 1995 Indiana Historical Bureau

D CR 250 & SR 39, south La Porte.

Camp Anderson

One of three Civil War training camps in La Porte County. Site is one fourth mile west. Named for Colonel Edward Anderson. Used 1863-1864 to train Indiana Union volunteers of the 127th, 128th, and 129th regiments.

ID 46.1996.1

CL Erected 1996 Indiana Historical Bureau and McDonald's Restaurant

D 2404 E. Michigan Boulevard at Carroll Street, Michigan City

Indiana Territory Boundary Line

ID 46.1999.1

CL Erected 1999 Indiana Historical Bureau, the Hinton Family, and La Porte County Historical Society, Inc.

D 213 Pine Lake Avenue, La Porte

Side one: Northwest Territory formed 1787; Indiana Territory formed 1800. Admission of Ohio 1803 and formation of Michigan Territory 1805 established Indiana Territory's northern boundary at southern tip of Lake Michigan. When Indiana became state in 1816, Congress moved boundary ten miles north giving Indiana part of Lake Michigan.

Side two: [Map of territorial boundary line at top of marker with following text under it]: Northern boundary of Indiana Territory established at southern tip of Lake Michigan when Michigan Territory formed in 1805.

La Porte County Courthouse

ID 46.2001.1

CL Installed 2001 Indiana Historical Bureau, La Porte County Board of Commissioners, and La Porte County Historical Society, Inc.

D 813 Lincolnway & Michigan Avenue, SE corner of La Porte County Courthouse lawn, La Porte

La Porte County Courthouse, La Porte County.

Side one: County formed by Indiana General Assembly and La Porte selected county seat 1832. Three courthouses built on this site: first 1833, second 1847-1848. Present courthouse constructed 1892-1894 of Lake Superior Red Sandstone; designed by Brentwood S. Tolan of Fort Wayne in Richardsonian Romanesque Style. Incorporates cornerstone from 1848 courthouse.

Side two: Features include open-arched central tower, stained glass window transoms, wood paneling, and gilded friezes. Goddess of Justice stained glass graces courtroom. Tower has 272-piece glass skylight; gargoyles decorate exterior. Included in Downtown La Porte Historic District, listed in National Register of Historic Places 1983.

La Porte's Carnegie Library

La Porte Carnegie Library, La Porte County.

ID 46.2002.1

CL Installed 2002 Indiana Historical Bureau and Friends of the La Porte County Public Library

D La Porte County Public Library, SW corner of 904 Indiana Avenue/ US 35 & Maple Avenue, La Porte

Side one:
La Porte's first public library was established 1896. La Porte City School Board was awarded $27,500 Carnegie grant 1916; by 1919 local support had been secured to meet grant requirements. Architect Wilson B. Parker designed the Neo-Classical style structure. Library opened in 1920 with 30,000 volumes.
Side two:
Renovation and expansion designed by architect William Koster; building dedicated 1991. Original 1920 section retained. Library has played a major role in community's development. One of 1,679 libraries built in U.S. with funds from philanthropist Andrew Carnegie. Indiana built more Carnegie libraries than any other state.

La Porte

The Rumely Companies

ID 46.2003.1

CL Installed 2003 Indiana Historical Bureau and Rumely Historic Recognition Committee

D NW corner of Madison Street & Lincolnway, La Porte

Side one:
Meinrad Rumely (1823-1904), a German immigrant, founded a blacksmith shop here 1853, which grew into a dominant company through reorganizations and acquisitions. Rumely companies in La Porte benefited from available rail transportation plus German and later Polish immigrant laborers. Products included a wide variety of agricultural machines.
Side two:
Rumely's prizewinning thresher later became one of the earliest powered by steam. Thousands of OilPull tractors sold worldwide 1910-1930. Rumely companies were at the forefront of mechanization of American and world agriculture and had significant impact on La Porte. Allis-Chalmers acquired the firm 1931 and closed La Porte plant 1983.

Lawrence

Indiana (Oolitic) Limestone Quarries

ID 47.1966.1

CL Erected by Indiana Sesquicentennial Commission, 1966

D Oolitic Town Hall, Main Street between Lafayette & Hoosier Avenues, Oolitic

Indiana's Limestone Quarries, Joe Palooka, Limestone Statue, Oolitic, Lawrence County.

Largest building stone quarries in the world, in continuous operation since the 1830s. These quarries have produced stone for many of the world's largest and finest memorials, buildings and bridges.

Astronaut Virgil I. Grissom April 3, 1926 - January 27, 1967

Portrait of Virgil I. Grissom (1926-1967), Astronaut, Mitchell, Lawrence County, Indiana Picture Collection, MS. Section, Indiana State Library.

ID 47.1967.1

CL Erected by Indiana Sesquicentennial Commission, 1966

D 8th & Main Streets, Mitchell. Reinstallation pending as of 12/2003

Born in Mitchell, Indiana. Lieutenant Colonel Grissom flew the project Mercury sub-orbital mission, July 21, 1961. He was command pilot, first Gemini flight, March 23, 1965, and died in an Apollo spacecraft at Cape Kennedy, January 27, 1967.

Bedford Courthouse Square Historic District

ID 47.1998.1

CL Erected 1998 Indiana Historical Bureau and Historic Preservation Committee of Bedford Revitalization, Inc.

D 1st between 15th & 16th Streets, east side of Lawrence County Courthouse square at sidewalk, Bedford.

Courthouse square, part of original 1825 plat, surrounded by nineteenth and early twentieth century commercial buildings in various architectural styles. Limestone facing quarried and milled by local industry. Listed in National Register of Historic Places 1995.

Lawrence

Dunn Memorial Hospital

ID 47.2005.1

CL Installed 2005 Indiana Historical Bureau and Dunn Memorial Hospital

D 1600 23rd St., Bedford

Side one:
Lawrence County Hospital Association was organized July 15, 1903 to build, maintain, and manage a hospital in Bedford. Opened first building 1904. State, district, and local Works Progress Administration officials and city and county officials approved and turned over this building—the hospital's third—to Lawrence County, October 22, 1941.
Side two:
Open House and public tours held October 23, 1941. State WPA felt it was one of the "most beautiful building construction jobs ever completed in the state by WPA workers." Removal of patients and equipment from second building completed November 1, 1941. Addition started 1949. Major modernization and expansion of hospital was dedicated May 9, 1982.

Madison

Massacre of Indians

ID 48.1966.1

CL Erected by Indiana Sesquicentennial Commission, 1966

D SR 38, 0.5 mile east of Markleville

In 1824, nine Indians were murdered by white men near this spot. The men were tried, found guilty, and hanged. It was the first execution of white men for killing Indians.

Indiana's First Interurban

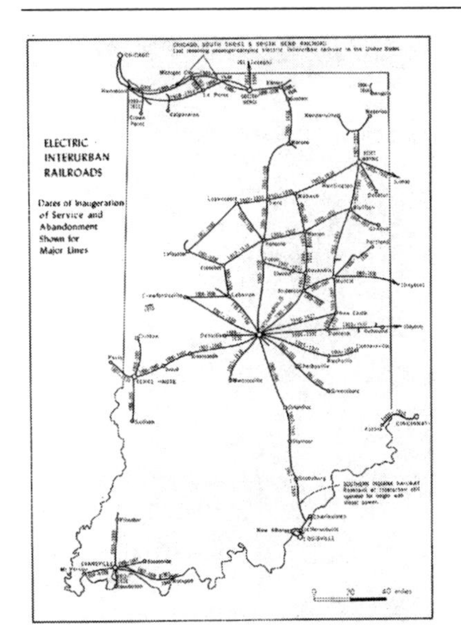

Electric Interurban Railroads. Map from Robert Kingsbury's, An Atlas of Indiana, Dept. of Geography, Indiana University, Bloomington, page 78, 1970.

Charles L. Henry's Union Traction Company, the first electric rail line specifically designed for interurban service, began operating through here on January 1, 1898. It ran from Alexandria to Anderson. Indiana became the traction center of the United States.

ID 48.1967.1

CL Erected by Indiana Sesquicentennial Commission, 1966

D SE corner, Harrison & Church Streets, Alexandria

Wendell Willkie

Side one:
Here in Callaway Park August 17, 1940, Willkie accepted Republican party presidential nomination after a nationwide grassroots campaign. An estimated crowd of 250,000 was in the park and along adjacent streets. Established campaign headquarters in Rushville. Lost election to Franklin Delano Roosevelt, but received 22,304,755 votes.
Side two:
Willkie was born in Elwood 1892. Earned bachelor and law degrees from Indiana University. Practiced law in Indiana, Ohio, and New York. President of Commonwealth and Southern Corporation, a New York utility holding company serving eleven states, 1933-1939. His book *One World* (1943) called for world peace. Died 1944; buried in Rushville.

ID 48.2001.1

CL Installed 2001 Indiana Historical Bureau and Team Starfleet Elwood Community Middle School

D 19th & N. J Streets, Callaway Park, picnic pavilion near Big Duck Creek, Elwood

State Capitol

ID 49.19??.1

CL Indiana Histori-cal Bureau

D Capitol Avenue & W. Market Street at the east entrance to the State House, Indianapolis

Indiana State Capitol, Indianapolis, Marion County.

State capital was moved to Indianapolis, 1825, from Corydon. The capitol built on this site in 1835 was razed in 1878 to make way for this State House, completed in 1888.

Anthony Wayne 1745-1796

ID 49.1960.1

CL Erected by Indiana Historical Society in conjunction with Junto Club, George Washington High School

D George Washington High School front yard, 2215 West Washington Street, Indianapolis.

Wayne Township was named for Gen. Anthony Wayne. This hero of the Revolution defeated the Indians at Fallen Timbers, 1794, and opened large areas for settlement by the Treaty of Greene Ville, 1795.

Sarah T. Bolton 1814-1893

Portrait of Sarah T. Bolton (1814-1893), Beech Grove, Marion County, Indiana Picture Collection, MS. Section, Indiana State Library.

A pioneer poet of Indiana, author of "Paddle Your Own Canoe" and "Indiana," crusader for women's rights, lived here at "Beech Bank" from 1871 to 1893.

ID 49.1960.2

CL Erected by the Society of Indiana Pioneers, 1960

D 107 E. Sherman Drive, west of Sarah T. Bolton Park, Beech Grove

Lincoln to the Citizens of Indiana

"...it is your business...if the Union of these States, and the liberties of this people, shall be lost....It is your business to rise up and preserve the Union...." From speech by President-elect Abraham Lincoln at intersection of Washington and Missouri Streets, Indianapolis, February 11, 1861.

ID 49.1961.2

CL Erected by the Indiana Historical Society, February 11, 1961

D 402 W. Washington Street at Missouri Street, Indianapolis

Toll House/Michigan Road

Operated by Augusta Gravel Road Co., circa 1866-1892.

First major state road, built in the 1830's, from the Ohio River to Lake Michigan.

ID 49.1961.3

CL Erected by the National Society of Colonial Dames of America in the State of Indiana, 1961

D 4702 N. Michigan Road/US 421, Indianapolis

Camp Morton 1861- 65

ID 49.1962.1

CL Erected by Indiana Civil War Centennial Commission, 1962

D 1900 block N. Alabama Street, Herron-Morton Place Historic Park, Indianapolis

Civil War Camp Morton (1861-1865), Indianapolis, Marion County, Indiana Picture Collection, MS. Section, Indiana State Library.

Site selected by Lew Wallace as training camp for volunteers on old State Fairgrounds in 1861 and named for Governor Oliver P. Morton. Used as a camp for Confederate prisoners, 1862-65. Col. Richard Owen, Commandant.

Brig. General Benjamin Harrison 1833-1901

ID 49.1963.1

CL Erected by the Indiana Civil War Centennial Commission 1963

D President Benjamin Harrison Home, 1230 N. Delaware Street, Indianapolis

Portrait of President Benjamin Harrison (1833-1901), Indiana Picture Collection, MS. Section, Indiana State Library.

Entered the Union Army as 2nd Lt. of the 70th Indiana Regiment. He insisted on turning raw recruits into disciplined soldiers. He later was United States Senator from Indiana and the twenty-third President of the United States.

Civil War Arsenal 1861-1864

Governor Oliver P. Morton established a state arsenal to supply Indiana's troops with ammunition. First located adjacent to the State Capitol, the arsenal was later moved to the present site of Arsenal Technical High School.

ID 49.1964.1

CL Erected by the Indiana Civil War Centennial Commission, 1964

D In storage

Home of Charles Warren Fairbanks May 11,1852 - June 4, 1918

Prominent lawyer of Indianapolis; Keynote convention speaker, 1896; United States Senator, 1897-1905; Vice-President of the United States, 1905-1909; and Vice-Presidential candidate in 1916.

Portrait of Charles Warren Fairbanks (1852-1918), U.S. Vice President (1905-1909), Indiana Picture Collection, MS. Section, Indiana State Library.

ID 49.1966.1

CL Erected by Indiana Sesquicentennial Commission, 1966

D 30th & Meridian Streets, front lawn of gated establishment, Indianapolis

The Central Canal

Central Canal, Indianapolis, Marion County.

Part of a statewide canal system begun in the late 1830's. The Central was projected from Peru to Worthington via Marion and Martinsville. Twenty-four miles were completed in this region. Railroads soon replaced the canals.

ID 49.1966.2

CL Erected by Indiana Sesquicentennial Commission, 1966

D Illinois Street & Westfield Boulevard, Indianapolis.

Milestones in Nursing

ID 49.1968.1

CL Erected by the Indiana League for Nursing in 1968

D 1001 W. 10th Street, Nursing Museum entrance, Wishard Hospital, Indianapolis

Wishard Hospital, Museum, Indianapolis, Marion County.

1859 Completion of the first building of the Indianapolis City Hospital, forerunner of Marion County General Hospital. Founder of this oldest general hospital in Indiana was Livingston Dunlap, M.D.

1861-1865 The first patients were admitted when the facility was opened as a Military Hospital by Governor Oliver P. Morton. Sister Athanasius Fogarty and other Sisters of Providence supplied the nursing care. John M. Kitchen, M.D., was chief medical officer. Henry M. Wishard, M.D., was resident surgeon.

1883 Professional nursing in Indiana was born with founding at City Hospital of the Flower Mission Training School for Nurses, Indiana's oldest school of nursing. Superintendent of the hospital was William N. Wishard, M.D. Margaret Iddings was the first graduate. Other early graduates organized training schools in the midwest and west and in Honolulu.

1891 Upon graduation from the training school Mae D. Currie '91 joined the staff of the Flower Mission Society to initiate professional home care for the sick poor in Indianapolis.

1913 Founding of the Public Health Nursing Association of Indianapolis by Abbie Hunt Bryce. Two fruitful years as superintendent of the Flower Mission Training School, 1885-1887, were followed by a lifetime of concern for every phase of nursing.

Mary Bryan, Pioneer Woman

Mary Bryan, one of the first American women to cross the Cumberland Mountains (c. 1776), is buried here with Samuel, her husband, a Revolutionary War veteran, who settled in Perry Township in 1830.

ID 49.1975.1

CL Erected by the Little Hoosiers of Homecroft Elementary School, 1975

D Pine Street & Southport Road at the cemetery, Southport

Indianapolis Motor Speedway

Indianapolis Motor Speedway, Museum, Marion County

Constructed in 1909, the Speedway has contributed significantly to the advancement of automotive technology and development of safety devices. It is unchallenged as the world's oldest continuously operated race course and the site of the largest one-day sports event anywhere. Listed on the National Register of Historic Places and dedicated on the 59th running of the "500," May 25, 1975.

ID 49.1975.2

CL Presented by Historic Landmarks Foundation of Indiana

D 4790 W. 16th Street at Indianapolis Motor Speedway Hall of Fame Museum, Indianapolis

Former U.S. Arsenal

ID 49.1976.1

CL Presented by the Military Order of World Wars, May 11, 1976

D West edge of Arsenal Technical High School Campus, Indianapolis

Established by an Act of Congress in 1862, this arsenal furnished munitions for U.S. Forces until 1903. It became the home of Arsenal Technical High School in 1912.

Crown Hill

ID 49.1976.2

CL Erected October 1976 by the Board of Corporators of Crown Hill Cemetery

D 738 W. 38th Street, Crown Hill Cemetery (road between chapel-crypt & 38th Street overpass), Indianapolis

Crown Hill, James Whitcomb Riley Gravesite, Indianapolis, Marion County.

Crown Hill Cemetery, founded in 1863, is the fourth largest cemetery in America. The history of Indiana and the United States is reflected in its monuments. President Benjamin Harrison, Vice-Presidents Charles Fairbanks, Thomas Hendricks, and Thomas Marshall, innovators Richard Gatling and Col. Eli Lilly, author Booth Tarkington and poet James Whitcomb Riley are among the many political, commercial, and literary leaders buried within its bounds. Crown Hill is the only cemetery in the state listed on the National Register of Historic Places.

Woodruff Place

Woodruff Place, Fountain, Indianapolis, Marion County.

Conceived by James Orton Woodruff, prominent citizen and industrialist, platted in 1872, as a residence park, this 77 acre landscaped enclave long existed as an incorporated town completely surrounded by the larger City. The district was finally annexed by the City of Indianapolis in 1962. Two hundred and forty dwellings of predominantly neo-Jacobean and Eastlake styles are aligned on three prominent esplanade drives adorned with handsome urns, fountains and statuary. The area was officially listed on The National Register of Historic Places July 31, 1972.

ID 49.1976.3

CL Presented in the Bicentennial Year of 1976 by Betsy Toy Hall in memory of her mother, Rose M. Toy and father, John H. Toy devoted residents of Woodruff Place for over 50 years

D Woodruff Cross Drive & Woodruff Middle Drive on median, south of fountain, Indianapolis

[The Indianapolis Times]

The Indianapolis Times, begun as The Indianapolis Sun in 1878, was published here from 1924 until it ceased publication October 11, 1965. The Times won journalism's highest award, the Pulitzer Prize, in 1928 for exposing the Ku Klux Klan.

ID Installation Pending

CL Erected by former staff members and the Marion County Historical Society 1979

D 300 block W. Maryland Street at Capitol Avenue, Indianapolis

First Presbyterian Church of Southport

ID 49.1983.1

CL Erected April 10, 1983 by Sesquicentennial Committee

D 6200 McFarland & Banta Roads, Southport

"Go therefore and make disciples of all nations . . . ." (*Matthew* 28:19) In recognition of its 150th year as a worshipping congregation, this sign marks the original location of the First Presbyterian Church of Southport, established March 30, 1833. Originally known as New Providence, the founding congregation met at this site in a log cabin called the "Old Mud Schoolhouse." This marker is dedicated to the glory of God in 1983, the congregation's sesquicentennial year. The past is prologue to the future.

William Forsyth 1854-1935

ID 49.1984.1

CL Erected by the family of William Forsyth, 1984

D N. Emerson & E. Washington Streets at Brown's Corner Park, Indianapolis

William Forsyth (1854-1935), Artist, Indianapolis, Marion County. Indiana Picture Collection, Ms. Section, Indiana State Library.

Indiana artist and teacher; member of the Hoosier Group; influential in Indiana and the World of Art. Studio and residence located at 15 South Emerson (on diagonal corner) from 1906-1935.

Macedonian Tribune

Original location of the Macedonian Tribune, 20 South West Street, from 1927-1949. Founded by immigrants from Macedonia as the voice of the Macedonian Patriotic Organization, the paper continues to be published in Fort Wayne, Indiana.

ID 49.1990.1

CL Erected September 2, 1990. Macedonia Patriotic Organization of the United States and Canada

D SE corner, West & Washington Streets, Indianapolis

North Meridian Street Historic District

Listed on the National Register of Historic Places, 1986 "One of America's Great Streets."

ID 49.1991.1

CL Erected by the Meridian Street Foundation 1991

D Westfield Boulevard & N. Meridian Street, Indianapolis

North Meridian Street Historic District

Listed on the National Register of Historic Places, 1986 "One of America's Great Streets."

ID 49.1991.2

CL Erected by the Meridian Street Foundation 1991

D 40th & N. Meridian Streets, Indianapolis

Crispus Attucks High School

ID 49.1992.1

CL Erected 1992 Indiana Historical Bureau

D 1140 Dr. Martin Luther King, Jr. Street, Indianapolis

Crispus Attucks High School, Indianapolis, Marion County

Built 1927 to serve as the only public high school for Indianapolis' black population. Integrated 1970 under court-ordered desegregation. Converted to junior high, 1986. Listed in National Register of Historic Places, 1989. Named for patriot of American Revolution.

North Western Christian University

ID 49.1992.3

CL Erected 1992 Indiana Historical Bureau, Old Northside Foundation, and Butler University

D 1325 N. College Avenue, east side of street north of I-65 overpass, Indianapolis

Ovid Butler.
Illustration by Lowell Hildebrandt.

Chartered by Indiana General Assembly, 1850. Opened at this site, 1855, on land provided by Ovid Butler. Became Butler University, 1877, after relocation in Irvington. Present location in Fairview Park was made possible through donations by prominent citizens; opened for classes, 1928.

Site of Golden Hill Totem Pole

A 30 foot 19th century Alaskan Haida totem stood on this site c. 1905-c. 1948. The totem, part of Brady Collection in Alaska Pavilion at 1904 St. Louis World's Fair, was given to David M. Parry, industrialist, whose estate once encompassed Golden Hill.

ID 49.1992.4

CL Erected 1992 by Indiana Historical Bureau and Golden Hill, Inc.

D Totem Lane, Golden Hill neighborhood, Indianapolis

Site of the Central Canal

Authorized by Indiana's 1836 Internal Improvement Act, Central Canal conceived as link in transportation system connecting Wabash and Erie Canal with Ohio River. State's bankruptcy in 1839 prevented completion of Central Canal. Canal has since provided hydraulic power, fresh water and recreation.

ID 49.1992.5

CL Erected 1992 by Indiana Historical Bureau and Marion County-Indianapolis Historical Society

D At Central Canal, behind Indiana Government Center North, at 100 N. Senate Avenue, Indianapolis

Ransom Place Historic District

Area includes subdivisions platted 1865 and 1871; most intact neighborhood associated with city's African-American population. Numerous prominent citizens lived in area, including attorney and civic leader Freeman B. Ransom (1882-1947). Listed in National Register of Historic Places, 1992.

ID 49.1993.1

CL Erected 1993 Indiana Historical Bureau and the Ransom-Cox and Brabham-Douglas families

D 830 Dr. Martin Luther King, Jr. Street, Indianapolis

Willard Park

ID 49.1993.2

CL Erected 1993 Indiana Historical Bureau and Ind. School for the Deaf and the Alumni Assn., PTCO of ISD, Ind. Assn. of the Deaf

D Willard Park, 1901 E. Washington Street, Indianapolis

Named for William Willard; site of Indiana School for the Deaf, 1850-1911. School founded by Willard, a deaf person, 1843; state-supported since 1844. School now at 1200 East 42nd Street. Willard, principal and teacher, was a dedicated educator of deaf people.

Indiana School for the Blind

ID 49.1994.1

CL Erected 1994 Indiana Historical Bureau

D 7725 N. College Avenue, north side of entrance, Indianapolis

Established 1847 by the General Assembly to provide education for Indiana's blind children. School on downtown site, 1848-1930. Relocated 1930 to present site on North College Avenue. Provides services to blind and visually impaired school-age children.

Indiana Avenue

Indiana Avenue, Walker Theatre, Indianapolis, Marion County.

African Americans, by the 1890s, had established a vibrant social, commerical, and economic community along Indiana Avenue. Black entertainers, entrepreneurs, politicians, and working people developed the Avenue into a thriving, widely-known neighborhood of theaters, jazz clubs, stores, offices, and residences.

ID 49.1994.2

CL Erected 1994 Indiana Historical Bureau with support from individuals and organizations dedicated to preserving the heritage of Indiana Avenue

D SE corner on traffic island, West Street & Indiana Avenue, Indianapolis

Bulgarian Orthodox Church

Original site of Saint Stephan Bulgarian Orthodox Church in 1915; relocated in 1955 to 1435 North Medford Avenue. Founded by Macedonian and Bulgarian immigrants to fulfill their religious needs and enjoyment of the traditions, customs, and fellowship of their Slavonic heritage.

ID 49.1995.1

CL Erected 1995 Indiana Historical Bureau, Ladies Auxillary of St. Stephen, and St. Stephen Church Members

D IUPUI Campus, 226 N. Blackford Street, Indianapolis.

Joseph W. Summers Memorial Bridge

ID 49.1995.2

CL Erected 1995 Indiana Historical Bureau and Friends of Joe Summers

D East side of Meridian Street on SE corner of Fall Creek bridge, Indianapolis

Joseph W. Summers Memorial Bridge, Indianapolis, Marion County.

Built in 1917, this Neo-Classical, reinforced concrete arch bridge was designed by nationally prominent landscape architect, George Kessler. In 1991 the bridge was named in honor of State Representative Joseph Summers, who served with distinction as a bridge between diverse racial and cultural groups.

Joseph W. Summers Memorial Bridge

ID 49.1995.3

CL Erected 1995 Indiana Historical Bureau and Friends of Joe Summers

D West side of Meridian Street on NW corner of Fall Creek bridge, Indianapolis

Built in 1917, this Neo-Classical, reinforced concrete arch bridge was designed by nationally prominent landscape architect, George Kessler. In 1991 the bridge was named in honor of State Representative Joseph Summers, who served with distinction as a bridge between diverse racial and cultural groups.

The Old Northside

Vibrant historic district was home to many social, political, commercial, and industrial leaders of Indianapolis during last half of nineteenth through early twentieth centuries. Revitalization of Old Northside is part of national historic preservation movement. Listed in National Register of Historic Places, 1978.

ID 49.1995.4

CL Erected 1995 Indiana Historical Bureau and Old Northside Foundation

D 1456 Central Avenue, Indianapolis

The Old Northside

Vibrant historic district was home to many social, political, commercial, and industrial leaders of Indianapolis during last half of nineteenth through early twentieth centuries. Revitalization of Old Northside is part of national historic preservation movement. Listed in National Register of Historic Places, 1978.

ID 49.1995.5

CL Erected 1995 Indiana Historical Bureau and Old Northside Foundation

D 12th & Delaware Streets, Indianapolis

Fort Benjamin Harrison

Established by Congress, 1903, as infantry post. Named for former U.S. president from Indianapolis. Became important as administration and finance training center. Historic district–listed in National Register of Historic Places, 1995--retains characteristics of turn-of-the-century military community.

ID 49.1996.1

CL Erected 1996 Indiana Historical Bureau and Fort Benjamin Harrison Historical Society

D Otis Avenue between Hess and Lawton Roads, Indianapolis. Removed for repairs.

Bates-Hendricks House

ID 49.1996.2

CL Erected 1996 Indiana Historical Bureau

D 1526 S. New Jersey Street along median, north of Lincoln Street, Indianapolis

Bates-Hendricks House, Indianapolis, Marion County.

Combines two nineteenth-century architectural styles. Built 1850s-1860 in Italianate Style. Later additions in Second Empire Style. Owners included Hervey Bates, Sr., first Marion County sheriff, Thomas A. Hendricks, U.S. vice president, and John Coburn, U.S. congressman. Listed in National Register of Historic Places, 1976.

Indiana Federation of Colored Women's Clubs

ID 49.1997.1

CL Erected 1997 Indiana Historical Bureau and Indiana Federation of Colored Women's Clubs

D 2034 N. Capitol Avenue, Indianapolis

Clubhouse of Indiana Federation of Colored Women's Clubs, Indianapolis, Marion County.

Organized 1904 by Lillian Thomas Fox with 14 clubs. Affiliated with National Association of Colored Women's Clubs, founded 1896. Objectives include improvement of education, health, living standards, inter-racial understanding. Clubhouse at 2034 N. Capitol since 1927. Listed in National Register of Historic Places, 1987.

Romanian Orthodox Church

Here, at 635 W. Market Street, original Saints Constantine and Elena Romanian Orthodox Church was dedicated in 1911; incorporated in 1916. Church has served Romanian community spiritually, culturally, and socially. Congregation built current church at 3237 W. 16th Street in 1949; consecrated in 1952.

ID 49.1998.1

CL Erected 1998 Indiana Historical Bureau and Sts. Constantine and Elena Romanian Orthodox Church

D White River State Park at the NE corner of the Central Canal and N. Blackford Street bridge, Indianapolis

Lockerbie Square

Lockerbie Square, Resident James Whitcomb Riley & Hoosier Writer Friends: Meredith Nicholson standing, George Ade & Booth Tarkington seated left to right, Picture Collection, MS. Section, Indiana State Library.

Side one: This historic neighborhood was originally platted in 1847 and 1850. Its name was derived from Lockerbie Street, which was named after George M. Lockerbie, an early Indianapolis resident. James Whitcomb Riley, who resided on Lockerbie Street 1893-1916, made it famous in an 1880 poem. Lockerbie was home to business leaders, skilled laborers, and craftsmen.

Side two: Lockerbie Square includes residential, commercial, religious, and educational structures built mainly circa 1855-1930 in a mix of architectural styles. Neighborhood revitalization begun in 1960s resulted in the first historic district preservation area in Indianapolis. Listed in National Register of Historic Places, 1973; area enlarged, 1987.

ID 49.1998.2

CL Erected 1998 Indiana Historical Bureau and Lockerbie Square People's Club

D Lockerbie & N. East Streets, Indianapolis

German Greenhouses and Truck Gardens

ID 49.1998.3

CL Erected 1998 Indiana Historical Bureau, Indpls. Gardeners Benefit Soc., Marion Co. Greenhouse Growers Assn., and Indpls. Vegetable Growers Assn.

D Bluff Road & Hanna Avenue, Bluff Park, Indianapolis

Side one: Many of Indiana's German immigrants settled in southwestern Marion County during the mid-1800s and began greenhouses and truck gardens on Bluff Road; area grew to major boundaries of Harding, Raymond, Madison, and Banta streets. Family owners formed organizations for collective bargaining power, uniform product quality, and members' health and death benefits.

Side two: German Gardeners Benefit Society founded 1867. "Hoosier Boy" trade name used by 87 businesses of Marion County Greenhouse Growers Association, founded 1920. Area was one of the largest concentrations of winter tomato and lettuce production under glass in U.S. Refrigerated transportation contributed to closure of many growers' businesses. Greenhouses still a part of the economic life of this area.

Indianapolis Fire Department / Bowen-Merrill Fire

ID 49.1999.1

CL Erected 1999 Indiana Historical Bureau and Indianapolis Firefighters Local 416

D North side of street, 2 W. Washington Street, Indianapolis

Side one: Volunteer force founded 1826; established as Indianapolis Fire Department with paid force 1859. Bowen-Merrill disaster 1890 led to reorganization and city Board of Public Safety. Indiana General Assembly enabled Fireman's Pension Funds 1891. Improvements in training, equipment, and water access came by early 1900s.

Side two: On March 17, 1890 the Bowen-Merrill Company stationery and book store at 16-18 West Washington Street caught fire. Eighty-six firemen fought the blaze. The woodframed roof and floors collapsed, dropping many men into the fire. Thirteen deaths resulted, the deadliest fire for firefighters in Indianapolis history.

Athenaeum

Side one: Built for German societies of Indianapolis including Socialer Turnverein: east wing 1893-1894, west wing 1897-1898. Designed in German Renaissance Revival Style by Indianapolis firm of Vonnegut and Bohn. Sculpted terra cotta and limestone by local artist Alexander Sangernebo. Major renovation 1990s. Listed in National Register of Historic Places 1973.
Side two: Originally called Das Deutsche Haus; name changed to Athenaeum during World War I because of anti-German sentiment. Facilities included gymnasium, auditorium, restaurant, concert-ballroom, bowling alleys, and beer garden with concert pavilion. Home of Normal College of the North American Gymnastic Union 1907-1970. Has continued as vital social and cultural center.

ID 49.1999.2

CL Erected 1999 Indiana Historical Bureau and Athenaeum Foundation

D 401 E. Michigan Street, Indianapolis

Market Street Temple

Side one: Indianapolis Hebrew Congregation (Reform) founded 1856 as state's fourth Jewish congregation. Its temple, first in the city, built here 1865-1868 to serve members in area's German Jewish neighborhood. As membership grew and moved northward, congregation built new temple at Delaware and Tenth streets 1899 and at 6501 North Meridian Street 1958.
Side two: Hungarian Jews were replacing German Jews in Market Street neighborhood in late 1800s. Hungarian Ohev Zedeck Congregation (founded 1884) purchased Market Street Temple and occupied it 1899-1927. Ohev Zedeck merged 1927 with Congregation Beth El (founded 1915), forming Beth El Zedeck. Vacant Market Street Temple, landmark of Indianapolis and Reform Judaism, demolished 1933.

D 49.1999.3

ID Erected 1999 Indiana Historical Bureau, Indianapolis Hebrew Congregation, and Charles B. Feibleman Fund

CL 435 E. Market Street, Indianapolis

Holy Rosary - Danish Church Historic District

ID 49.2000.1

CL Installed 2000 Indiana Historical Bureau and Italian Heritage Society of Indiana

D SE corner of S. East Street & S. Stevens Street, Indianapolis

Holy Rosary Catholic Church, Indianapolis, Marion County.

Side one:
Platted 1854; now bounded by South East Street, Virginia Avenue, and interstates 65/70. Early residents were Germans, Irish, Scots, and Welsh. Danes resided in area circa 1870-1890. By 1910, ninety percent of area residents were Italian immigrants.
Side two:
Area became Indiana's largest continuously occupied Italian neighborhood. Sicilians opened nearby produce businesses. District, containing mainly working-class cottages, includes Trinity Danish Evangelical Lutheran Church built 1872, Horace Mann Public School built 1873, and Holy Rosary Catholic Church built 1911-1925. District listed in National Register of Historic Places 1986.

Widows and Orphans Friends' Society

Side one:
Society created by Indianapolis Benevolent Society 1849 to provide relief for indigent widows and orphans; incorporated 1851 by Indiana General Assembly. Opened its first orphanage on this site 1855. White House Conference in 1909 focused attention on, and led to federal legislation and grants for, dependent children.
Side two:
As public policy and funding evolved in the twentieth century, the Society changed its name, location, and specific functions as it strove to address the needs of children and families. Since 1961, organization has offered services as the Children's Bureau of Indianapolis, Inc.

ID 49.2003.1

CL Installed 2003 Indiana Historical Bureau and Children's Bureau of Indianapolis, Inc.

D East side of Capitol Avenue, 1/2 block South of the 14th Street intersection, Indianapolis

Greek Orthodox Church

Holy Trinity Greek Orthodox Church of Indianapolis was located here at 231 North West Street from 1919-1959. The Church, incorporated 1910, now located at 4011 North Pennsylvania Street, has also preserved customs and language of extensive Greek community.

ID 49.2003.2

CL Installed 2003 Indiana Historical Bureau, AHEPA Chapter #232, and Parish Council of Holy Trinity Church

D West Street beside Indiana Historical Society located at 450 W. Ohio Street, Indianapolis

Brookville Road

ID 49.2004.1

CL Installed 2004 Indiana Historical Bureau, Environmental Law & Policy Center of the Midwest, and Southeast Civic Association

D 10622 Brookville Road, Indianapolis

Side one: On December 31, 1821, a 78-mile state road was authorized from the Ohio border to Indianapolis through Brookville, to be built with required citizen labor. Commissioners filed a survey report June 24, 1822 for the Brookville State Road. On January 24, 1828, a turnpike company was authorized to build an improved road by bidding out sections.
Side two: Brookville Road was the principal route for goods and people from here to Cincinnati. Road travel was difficult in the 1800s, taking days to reach destinations. Taverns provided shelter and food for travelers. Along the road in Warren Township, Marion County, taverns were kept by David Woods in the 1820s and Nathan Harlan in the 1830s - 1840s.

John Muir in Indianapolis

ID 49.2004.2

CL Installed 2004 Indiana Historical Bureau, Sierra Club Hoosier Chapter, and Various Donors

D Former site of Osgood, Smith & Co., Illinois & Merrill Streets on grassy triangle, Indianapolis

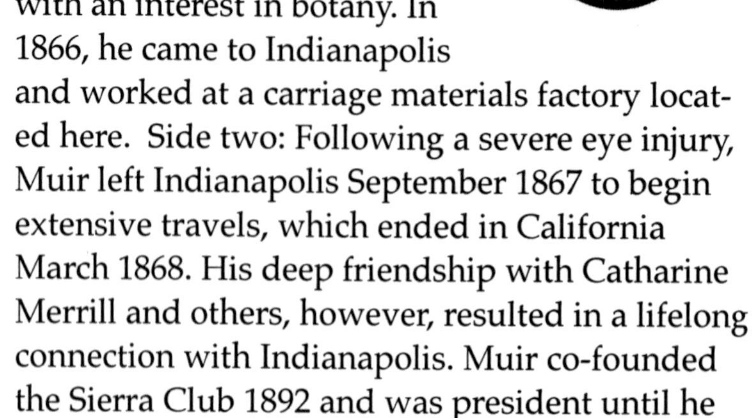

Portrait of John Muir, by Photographer William E. Dassonville, San Francisco, 1909.

Side one: Born 1838 in Dunbar, Scotland, Muir moved to the U.S. with his family, settling in Wisconsin 1849. As a youth, he became interested in nature and mechanical inventions. He attended the University of Wisconsin and was consumed with an interest in botany. In 1866, he came to Indianapolis and worked at a carriage materials factory located here. Side two: Following a severe eye injury, Muir left Indianapolis September 1867 to begin extensive travels, which ended in California March 1868. His deep friendship with Catharine Merrill and others, however, resulted in a lifelong connection with Indianapolis. Muir co-founded the Sierra Club 1892 and was president until he died December 24, 1914.

Marion County Girl Scouts

Side one: In 1917, Anna Marie Ridge founded in Irvington the first troop in Marion County; it was registered in July as Indianapolis Troop 1 by Girl Scouts, Incorporated. In 1937, Troop 1 was meeting here at Irvington Presbyterian Church. India J. Wilson began a second troop in Irvington in fall of 1917; registered as Troop 2 in 1918.
Side two: Indianapolis Marion County Girl Scout Council chartered 1921 by Girl Scouts, Incorporated. Marion County now part of Girl Scouts of Hoosier Capital Council. Basic goals--including community service, ideals of conduct, patriotism, diversity in membership--have remained; badges and programs have changed with society.

ID 49.2004.3

CL Installed 2004 Indiana Historical Bureau and Girl Scouts of Hoosier Capital Council, Inc.

D Irvington Presbyterian Church, 55 Johnson Avenue, Indianapolis

Zerelda G. Wallace

Portrait of Mrs. Zerelda G. Wallace, pg. 871, History of Indiana, Vol. II, by Wm. H. Smith, 1897.

Side one: Born August 6, 1817 in Kentucky and came to Indianapolis with her family in the early 1830s. Was a charter member of the Church of Christ (later Central Christian Church) 1833. Married David Wallace (later governor) 1836. Was first president of Woman's Christian Temperance Union in Indiana 1874 and member of the Equal Suffrage Society of Indianapolis.
Side two: She spoke nationally on temperance and suffrage. On January 21, 1875, she testified before Indiana General Assembly, presenting 21,050 signatures on temperance petitions from 47 counties. On January 23, 1880, she testified before U.S. Senate, Judiciary Committee on woman's right to vote. Died March 19, 1901; buried in Crown Hill Cemetery.

ID 49.2004.4

CL Installed 2004 Indiana Historical Bureau, Indiana Commission for Women, Indiana Women's History Association, and Central Christian Church

D Central Christian Church, 701 North Delaware Street, Indianapolis

28th Regiment USCT

ID 49.2004.5

CL Installed 2004 Indiana Historical Bureau, Indiana War Memorials Commission, Andrew & Esther Bowman, and African American Landmarks Committee of Historic Landmarks Foundation of Indiana, Inc.

D Virginia Avenue & McCarty Street, Indianapolis

Side one: Indiana's only African-American Civil War regiment served as part of the 28th Regiment of U.S. Colored Troops. African-American infantry was authorized in 1863 to help fill federal quota for soldiers. The Reverend Willis Revels was recruiting officer. Recruits trained at Camp Fremont, established on land near here owned by Calvin Fletcher. Side two: In April 1864, six companies were organized and activated. The 28th regiment served valiantly in the Battle of the Crater at Petersburg, Virginia on July 30, 1864, when nearly half of the men were killed or wounded. The 28th returned to Indianapolis January 6, 1866 to a reception in its honor; officers and men were discharged January 9.

Robert F. Kennedy on Death of Martin L. King

ID 49.2005.1

CL Installed 2005 Indiana Historical Bureau and City of Indianapolis, Mayor Bart Peterson

D King Park, 17th Street and Broadway, Indianapolis

Robert F. Kennedy. Illustration by Lowell Hildebrandt.

Side one: Here on the evening of April 4, 1968, Kennedy came to address a large crowd of mostly African Americans in his bid for Democratic Party nomination for president of U.S. Instead, visibly shaken, he gave an impromptu speech about the assassination of Martin Luther King, Jr. that day in Memphis, Tenn.Side two: Kennedy urged the crowd to follow Rev. King's lead and respond with understanding and prayer. Citing the need to avoid division, hatred, and violence, he called for love, wisdom, compassion, and justice. The speech is credited with keeping Indianapolis calm, while other cities reacted with violence.

Calvin Fletcher

Calvin Fletcher. Illustration by Lowell Hildebrandt.

Side one: Born 1798 in Ludlow, Vermont, Fletcher and his wife Sarah came to this newly-named state capital 1821. They lived here 1839-1855 on a 269-acre farm, Wood Lawn, which encompassed most of today's Fletcher Place Historic District. He was active and influential in most aspects of life and culture in Indianapolis and in development of the state.
Side two: Fletcher opposed slavery and promoted organization of U.S. colored troops in Indiana in Civil War. He died 1866 and is buried in Crown Hill Cemetery. He firmly established the Fletcher name in Indianapolis history; some of his children continued the legacy. His extensive diaries and letters remain essential sources for study of early Indiana.

ID 49.2006.1

CL Installed 2006 Indiana Historical Bureau, Fletcher Place Neighborhood Association, and Flanner and Buchanan Funeral Centers

D Virginia Avenue and East Street, Indianapolis.

John Freeman

Side one: In 1844, John Freeman, a free black, purchased land in Indianapolis. By 1853, he owned land in this area worth $6,000. In June 1853, a slaveholder claimed Freeman was his runaway slave. Freeman spent nine weeks in jail; he hired lawyers; claim was dismissed. Black citizens held public meeting August 29 at Masonic Hall to congratulate Freeman.
Side two: Under Fugitive Slave Law of 1850, seizure of free blacks and freedom seekers in the north was common. The Underground Railroad refers to a widespread network of diverse people in the nineteenth century who aided slaves escaping to freedom from the southern U.S.

ID 49.2006.2

CL Installed 2005 Indiana Historical Bureau, Division of Historic Preservation & Archaeology, IDNR; African American Landmarks Committee of Historic Landmarks Foundation of Indiana, Inc.; Fred A. Taylor, and Gwen Crenshaw

D On the west side of Pennsylvania Street between 10th and 11th streets, in green space next to the Landmark Center, located at 1099 N. Meridian St., Indianapolis

1907 Indiana Eugenics Law

ID 49.2007.1

CL Installed 2007 Indiana Historical Bureau, Indiana University, and Indiana University Foundation

D Indiana Library and Historical Building, 140 North Senate Avenue, Indianapolis.

Side one: By late 1800s, Indiana authorities believed criminality, mental problems, and pauperism were hereditary. Various laws were enacted based on this belief. In 1907, Governor J. Frank Hanly approved first state eugenics law making sterilization mandatory for certain individuals in state custody. Sterilizations halted 1909 by Governor Thomas R. Marshall.
Side two: Indiana Supreme Court ruled 1907 law unconstitutional 1921, citing denial of due process under Fourteenth Amendment. 1927 law reinstated sterilization, adding court appeals. Approximately 2,500 total in state custody were sterilized. Governor Otis R. Bowen approved repeal of all sterilization laws 1974; by 19977, related restrictive marriage laws repealed.

Ovid Butler, Sr.

ID 49.2007.2

CL Installed 2007 Indiana Historical Bureau, Division of Historic Preservation & Archaeology, IDNR; and Old Northside Foundation

D 1306 North Park Avenue, Indianapolis.

Side one: Born 1801 in New York; moved to Indiana 1817. Admitted to bar 1825; became influential lawyer. Settled in Indianapolis 1836. His opposition to slavery on moral and religious grounds was reflected in his political affiliations and support of anti-slavery newspapers; his writings publicly condemned slavery and the Fugitive Slave Law of 1850.
Side two: Butler wrote North Western Christian University charter 1849; founders wanted to provide "liberal and Christian education" away from slavery influences. Indiana General Assembly passed charter 1850; university opened 1855 at 13th Street and College Avenue; renamed to honor Butler 1877. He resided here in "Forest Home" until his death in 1881.

St. Vincent's Infirmary

Side one: Bishop Francis Silas Chatard began work to open an infirmary here in St. Joseph's Seminary by 1878. Many local residents and physicians opposed the infirmary, fearing the spread of disease. The Daughters of Charity of St. Vincent de Paul in Maryland sent sisters to take charge of the infirmary 1881. It was incorporated as St. Vincent's Infirmary 1884.
Side two: Overcrowding required new infirmary, built 1889 at South and Delaware Streets. By 1899, new infirmary added 19 private rooms, an operating room, and an operating theater used for teaching. Industrialization of city and continuous influx of patients created safety problems; building damaged by gas explosion 1908. Moved to Fall Creek Boulevard 1913.

ID 49.2007.3

CL Installed 2007 Indiana Historical Bureau and St.Vincent Indanapolis Hospital.

D 536 E.Vermont Street, Indianapolis.

Marion

Trail of Death

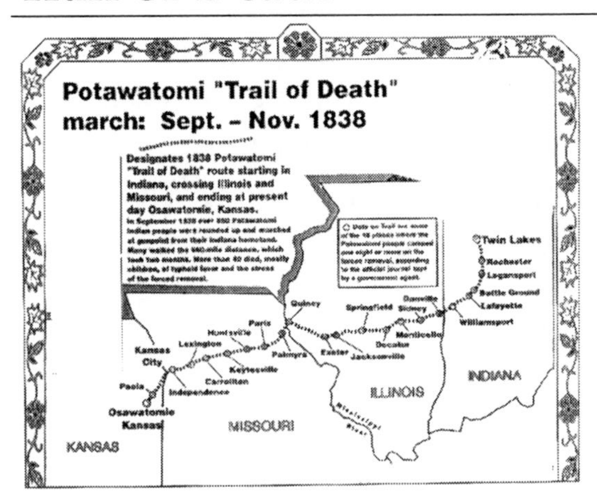

Potawatomi "Trail of Death" March, map by Tom Hamilton, Fulton County Historical Society.

Two miles east, on north bank of Twin Lakes, some 800 Potawatomi Indians were collected in August 1838 and forced to begin their long march to new homes in the West. Many perished on the way.

ID 50.1949.1

CL Indiana Historical Bureau

D SR 17 & CR 12, 1.3 miles NE of junction of SR 8 & SR 17, 2 miles west of Twin Lakes

Marshall

Marshall

Second Principal Meridian

ID 50.1966.1

CL Erected by Indiana Sesquicentennial Commission 1966

D 1.6 miles west of junction of SR 110 and SR 17 on north side of Marshall County Line Road/ Fulton CR 1200 W/Pulaski CR 800 N/ and Starke CR 900 S

This marker is on the corner of Starke, Marshall, Pulaski and Fulton counties and on the Second Principal Meridian. This Meridian is the line from which all east-west land descriptions and measurements are made. {State map}

Martin

Site of Hindostan (0.6 mile south)

ID 51.1966.1

CL Erected by Indiana Sesquicentennial Commission, 1966

D SE corner of SR 550 & CR 55, near Hindostan Falls, Loogootee

First settled in 1818, Hindostan became county seat of Martin County, boasting a population of approximately 1,200. A "Great Sickness" struck in 1828 bringing death to the inhabitants. The town was never occupied again.

Burial Place of Francis Godfroy

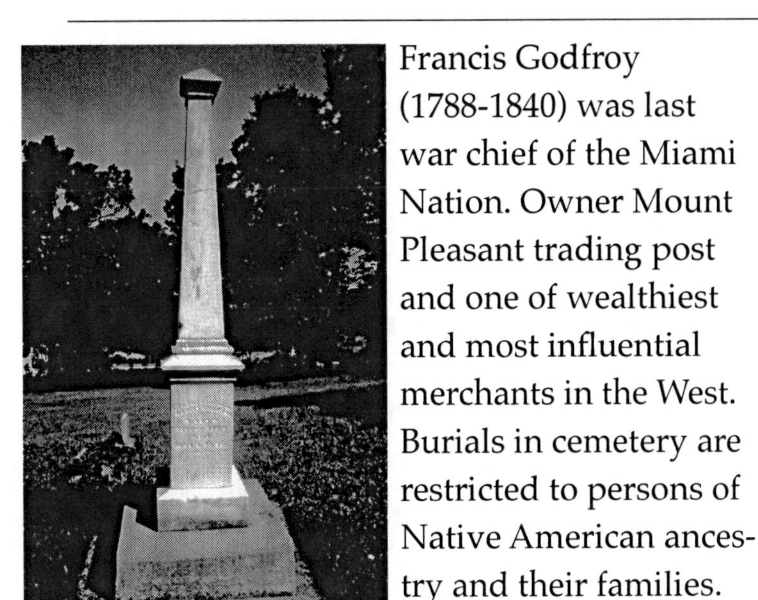

Grave Site of Francis Godfroy, Peru, Miami County.

Francis Godfroy (1788-1840) was last war chief of the Miami Nation. Owner Mount Pleasant trading post and one of wealthiest and most influential merchants in the West. Burials in cemetery are restricted to persons of Native American ancestry and their families.

ID 52.1992.1

CL Erected 1992 by Indiana Historical Bureau

D Chief Francis Godfroy Cemetery, SR 124, 4 miles east of Peru

House of Chief Richardville

Home of Chief Richardville, Peru, Miami County.

ID 52.1992.2

CL Erected 1992 by Indiana Historical Bureau

D CR 300 E/Mississinewa Road, 3 miles east of Peru

Jean Baptiste Richardville (1761-1841) was principal chief of the Miami Tribe from 1812 to 1841. He signed six treaties with the United States ceding Miami land in Indiana. This house was built for him under one of the treaties.

Stinesville Limestone Industry

ID 53.1996.1

CL Erected 1996 Indiana Historical Bureau and Danny Phelix Jacobs

D McGlocklin Memorial/ Victor Oolitic Park near Jacks Defeat Creek, Stinesville

Stinesville Limestone Industry, Limestone Carved Sign, Monroe County.

In 1827, Richard Gilbert opened a commercial limestone quarry three quarters of a mile south on Jack's Defeat Creek. Stinesville's oolitic limestone, desirable as building stone, was used in several Indiana courthouses and Soldiers' and Sailors' Monument, Indianapolis. Limestone industry has been major economic factor in area.

Ferry Bridge

ID 53.2000.1

CL Installed 2000 Indiana Historical Bureau, Jane Wampler Stouder and Mary Asher Wampler

D CR 450 W over West Fork of White River, 2 miles south of Gosport. In storage.

Ferry Bridge Over White River West Fork, near Gosport, Monroe County.

Side one: Pennsylvania through truss iron bridge built 1903 by Lafayette Engineering Co.; crosses West Fork of White River, spans 316 feet, and rests on concrete and stone abutments. One of longest single-span iron bridges in Indiana; longest highway bridge of its type. Has unique iron framework, original lattice railing. Replaced Secrest's Ferry.

Side two: Commissioners from Owen and Monroe counties met 1901 to plan for a bridge. Owen paid two-thirds of cost, Monroe one-third. Served as vital link between Gosport and Spencer and Bloomington. Closed to vehicles and bypassed by the modern bridge to the west 1990. Listed in National Register of Historic Places 1996.

Monroe County Courthouse

Monroe County Courthouse, Bloomington.

ID 53.2001.1

CL 2001 Indiana Historical Bureau and Monroe County Government

D Courthouse Square, south entrance, Bloomington

Side one:
County formed by Indiana General Assembly and Bloomington selected as county seat 1818. One-story, two-room log cabin built 1818 as first courthouse and school. Second courthouse, built here 1819-1826, was two stories, brick with stone foundation; expanded 1856-1857, 1875; demolished 1906 for construction of new courthouse.
Side two:
Present courthouse completed 1908; designed by Wing and Mahurin of Fort Wayne in Beaux Arts style; built of locally quarried limestone. Features original fish-shaped weather vane from 1826 courthouse, carved classical figures, Ionic and Egyptian columns, stained glass; completely restored 1983-1984. Listed in National Register of Historic Places 1976.

The Colored School

ID 53.2005.1

CL Installed 2005 Indiana Historical Bureau and Bloomington Black Business & Professional Association, and Unitarian Universalist Church of Bloomington

D Sixth and Washington Streets, Bloomington

Side one:
By 1874, what has been known as the Colored School opened in Center School here at Sixth and Washington Streets to serve African-American elementary students of Bloomington. An 1869 law had mandated education of colored children, with a separate enumeration and separate schools supported with tax revenue within the common school system.
Side two:
Before 1869, education of African-Americans was generally not within the common school system. The school building on this site was used until 1915, when it was replaced by the Carnegie library. Students attended classes at another site until the new Banneker School opened on the west side December 1915; the school remained segregated until 1951.

Monroe's Carnegie Library

ID 53.2007.1

CL Installed 2007 Indiana Historical Bureau and Monroe County Public Library Foundation

D 202 East 6th St., Bloomington.

Side one: County's only Carnegie Library dedicated 1918 as Bloomington Public Library with 6, 439 volumes; built with local support and $31,000 from Carnegie Corporation. Replaced Colored School, at this site circa 18974-1915. Addition built at southeast corner 1955. Library moved to new building nearby 1970.
Side two: One of 1, 679 libraries built in U.S. with funds from philanthropist Andrew Carnegie. Indiana built more Carnegie libraries than any other state. Building listed in National Register of Historic Places 1978. Monroe County Historical Society and Museum refurbished and occupied building 1980.

Monroe

Hoagy Carmichael

Side one: Born and reared in Bloomington, he is considered one of the most important American songwriters of the twentieth century. Began attending Indiana University 1920; graduated with a law degree 1926. Tried law as a career, but returned to music. Inducted into Songwriters Hall of Fame 1971. Died on December 27, 1981 in California; buried in Bloomington.
Side two: Hoagy wrote that he composed "Stardust" in part on the piano of the Book Nook located here. Among his other popular songs were, "Heart and Soul," "Georgia on My Mind," "Lazybones," and "Ole Buttermilk Sky," which was nominated for an Academy Award 1946. Won an Academy Award 1951 for "In the Cool, Cool, Cool of the Evening" from Here Comes the Groom.

ID 53.2007.2

CL Installed 2007 Indiana Historical Bureau and City of Bloomington

D In front of the Gables (formerly the Book Nook). 114 South Indiana Avenue, Bloomington

Benjamin Banneker School

Side one: African-American students went to "Colored School" on 6th Street, circa 1874-1915, under 1869 law. New elementary school for black students opened here December 7, 1915 with 93 students and 3 teachers. Gymnasium added 1941-1942. Schools integrated under 1949 Indiana law. Segregation at Banneker ended in 1951 despite protests from some citizens.
Side two: Renamed Fairview Annex, integrated sixth grade classes with Banneker and Fairview students met here 1951-1954, until new integrated Fairview School was completed. By 1955, this building became Westside Community Center. In 1994, after major renovation, it was renamed Benjamin Banneker Communithy Center to commemorate its history as segregsated school.

ID 2008

CL Installed 2008 Indiana Historical Bureau, Bloomington's Black Business & Professional Association, Repairing the Breach Committee, and City of Bloomington.

D Benjamin Banneker Community Center, 730 West 7th Street, Bloomington.

Lane Place

ID 54.1962.1

CL Erected by the Indiana Civil War Centennial Commission, 1962

D 212 S. Water Street at Wabash Avenue, Crawfordsville

Lane Place, Crawfordsville, Montgomery County.

Home of Henry S. Lane (1811-81), congressman, governor and Civil War senator. Chairman of the first Republican National Convention, 1856, he was a strong supporter of Lincoln and the Union.

Major General Lew Wallace 1827-1905

ID 54.1963.1

CL Erected by the Indiana Civil War Centennial Commission, 1963

D 501 Pike Street & Wallace Avenue, Crawfordsville

Major General Lew Wallace (1827-1905) Study, Ben-Hur Museum, Crawfordsville, Montgomery County.

As Indiana's adjutant general he organized the state for war. He saw action at Ft. Donelson, Shiloh and Monocacy. Later served as governor of New Mexico Territory and minister to Turkey. Author of Ben Hur.

Chief Cornstalk's Village

Chief Peter Cornstalk's village of Snakefish (Eel River) tribe of Miami Indians was located three miles from here along Cornstalk Creek. Wigwams and Indian burial ground were near the little Harshbarger family cemetery. The Indians lived at peace with settlers moving here in the 1800s.

ID 54.1981.1

CL Erected by Montgomery County Historical Society, 1982

D US 231 & CR 1150 S adjacent to Parkersburg Spring, Parkersburg

Darlington Covered Bridge

Darlington Covered Bridge, Montgomery County.

Local donations helped build this important transportation link. Completed 1868; closed to vehicular traffic, 1976. Listed in National Register of Historic Places 1990. Approximately 166 feet long; Howe Truss design; built of oak and poplar with limestone abutments. Construction superintendent, Richard M. Epperson; builder, Joseph Kress.

ID 54.1993.1

CL Erected 1992 Indiana Historical Bureau and Darlington Community Association, Inc.

D CRs 500 N & 600 E at SW corner of Sugar Creek bridge, Darlington

Montgomery

Speed Cabin

ID 54.1995.1

CL Erected 1995 Indiana Historical Bureau and Montgomery County Community Foundation

D 310 N. Grant St., Crawfordsville

Speed Cabin, Lane Place, Crawfordsville, Montgomery County.

Site of house reputed to be a stop on the "Underground Railroad." Reconstructed cabin, which was portion of house owned by John Allen Speed, now located on grounds of Lane mansion. Speed, active in abolitionist movement, was mayor of Crawfordsville, 1868-1869.

Montgomery County Rotary Jail

ID 54.2000.1

CL Installed 2000 Indiana Historical Bureau and Montgomery County Cultural Foundation, Inc.

D Old Jail Museum, 225 N. Washington Street/US 231 & Spring Street, Crawfordsville

Montgomery County Rotary Jail, Crawfordsville, Montgomery County.

Side one: This jail and sheriff's residence built 1882. First rotary jail built in U.S. Constructed to plans based on patented design of William H. Brown and Benjamin F. Haugh of Indianapolis. In use until 1973. Opened as museum and restoration begun 1975. Listed in National Register of Historic Places 1975.

Side two: Circular cell block has sixteen wedge-shaped cells on a two-story turntable around a central shaft. Design promised better prisoner security and jailer safety. Cell block immobilized 1930s as hazard to prisoners. County jails first established 1792 under laws of Northwest Territory; continued under laws of Indiana Territory and state constitutions of 1816 and 1851.

William Bratton, Lewis and Clark Expedition Member

Side one:
Bratton (1778-1841) is buried in this cemetery. With U.S. Army rank of private, he joined Lewis and Clark Expedition's Corps of Discovery near Clarksville, Indiana 1803. Corps explored lands of Louisiana Purchase and Pacific Northwest.
Side two:
Bratton's duties included hunter, blacksmith, saltmaker. He completed entire journey; discharged October 10, 1806. Settled on farm in Wayne Township 1822; held various county and township offices, including Justice of the Peace.

ID 54.2002.1

CL Installed 2002 Indiana Historical Bureau and Ohio River Chapter of Lewis & Clark Trail Heritage Foundation, Fountain Co. DAR, Fountain Co. Hist. Soc., Pine Village Literary Club, John Culver, Barbara Haniford, Louis & Pauline McKee

D East junction of US 136 & SR 25, Old Pioneer Cemetery, east edge of Waynetown

Whetzel Trace

Jacob Whetzel Gravesite, Waverly, Morgan County.

A Trail from Whitewater River at Laurel terminated here at the Bluffs of White River. Cut in 1818 by Jacob Whetzel, it was the first east-west road into central Indiana.

ID 55.1957.1

CL Erected by the National Society of the Colonial Dames of America in the State of Indiana, September 28, 1957

D 8465 Old SR 37 south of Central Avenue & Waverly Road, 1.5 miles south of SR 144 intersection, Whetzel Cemetery, east side of highway, Waverly

Newton

State Line Survey

ID 56.1966.1

CL Erected by Indiana Sesquicentennial Commission, 1966

D US 24 at state line, west of Kentland. Missing

In 1821 the Indiana-Illinois state line was surveyed by General John Tipton for Indiana and Samuel McClintoc for Illinois. They ran the line and marked each mile of it from Vincennes to Lake Michigan.

Noble

Camp Mitchell

ID 57.1963.1

CL Erected by the Indiana Civil War Centennial Commission, 1963

D Orchard & Rush Streets, Kendallville. Redone 1999

Civil War training camp for the then 10th Congressional District was located at Kendallville. The 12th Indiana Cavalry and the 129th Volunteer Infantry were organized and trained here.

Chief Papakeecha's House (one quarter mile south)

ID 57.1967.1

CL Erected 1967 by Noble County Historical Society

D CRs 200 N & 1150 W, 0.8 mile west of SR 5 on CR 200 N, 2.4 miles SW of Cromwell

Built in 1827 by Federal Government on 36-section reservation for $562; later destroyed by "great wind". Papakeecha (Flat Belly) was a Miami leader, 1820 to his death in 1837, shortly before the Miami removal.

Indian Oven (80 rods east)

Here at a fireplace or oven on the east shore of Indian Village Lake those Miamis that had comprised Papakeecha's Band prepared their last meal before leaving tribal lands c. 1839.

ID 57.1967.2

CL Erected by Noble County Historical Society

D SR 5 at public access site entrance to Indian Village Lake, Indian Village

Sylvan Lake

Sylvan Lake, Rome City, Noble County.

Created 1837-1838 as reservoir for proposed canal link between Fort Wayne and Lake Michigan. Part of 1836 internal improvements program. Popular resort area; site of Chautauqua, 1878-1906. Provided hydraulic power. Earthen dam on Elkhart River impounds 630 acres of water.

ID 57.1992.1

CL Erected 1992 Indiana Historical Bureau and Rome City Chautauqua Committee

D SR 9, Sycamore Park, Sylvan Lake dam & outlet site, Rome City

Noble

Noble County Seat/Noble County Courthouse

ID 57.1999.1

CL Erected 1999 Indiana Historical Bureau and Courthouse Square Preservation Society, Inc.

D Courthouse Square, Albion

Noble County Courthouse, Albion.

Side one:
Noble County formed by General Assembly 1836; named after James Noble, first U.S. Senator from Indiana. County seats Sparta 1836, Augusta 1837, Port Mitchell 1844, Center, later named Albion, selected 1846 as county seat in runoff election. Arrival of railroad in 1874 brought prosperity and major construction on courthouse square circa 1880-1890.
Side two:
First courthouse (1847) destroyed by fire; replaced by two-story brick structure 1860. This courthouse, third on the site, built 1887-1889 in Richardsonian Romanesque Style of brick and limestone. Designed by E. O. Fallis & Co., Toledo, Ohio. Listed in National Register of Historic Places 1981.

Ohio

Lochry's Defeat

ID 58.1961.1

CL Erected by the Sons of the American Revolution, 1961

D SR 56 at Ohio-Dearborn County line, 200 feet south of Laughery Creek, north of French

On Aug. 24, 1781, Col. Archibald Lochry and 107 recruits for Gen. Clark were ambushed at Lochry Creek by Joseph Brant's raiders. One-third were killed, the rest captured. Lochry and the wounded were later murdered.

Pivot Point

600 yards west, intersection of the baseline and the second principal meridian, the lines fixed in 1805 by Ebenezer Buckingham, to govern land survey in Indiana under the Ordinance of 1785.

ID 59.1961.1

CL Erected by the Society of Indiana Pioneers, 1961

D SR 37 & Pivot Point Road, 6.5 miles south of Paoli, 0.5 mile south of Pine Valley & CR 550 S

Orange

Freeman's Corner (250 feet east)

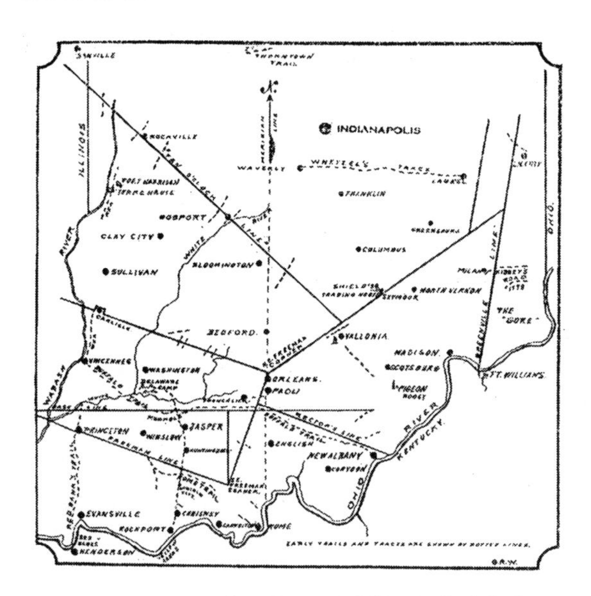

Freeman's Corner, map from George R. Wilson's, Early Indiana Trails & Surveys, Indiana Historical Society Publications, Vol. 6, no. 3, Indianapolis, 1919.

This point marks the junction of three important Indian land cessions. Treaty of Fort Wayne, 1803 Treaty of Grouseland, 1805 Treaty of Fort Wayne, 1809 The corner was established by Surveyor Thomas Freeman in 1803. [State map]

ID 59.1966.1

CL Erected by Indiana Sesquicentennial Commission, 1966

D SR 37, east side of highway north of water works facility, north edge of Orleans

Orange

Orleans Congress Square

ID 59.2004.1

CL Installed 2004 Indiana Historical Bureau and Town of Orleans

D East side of Congress Square, Veterans Way Street, Orleans

Side one:
Orleans was platted March 11, 1815. This town square, called Congress Square, was part of the plat. Orleans Academy was built here 1866, in operation by 1867. In 1870s, the Academy was purchased, and its building was made part of the public schools. The building remained in use until razed October 7, 1963. After 1963, a park was built here.
Side two:
Orleans Town Park was rededicated June 7, 2001 as part of a downtown revitalization. The restored bandstand nearby was built in 1926. As in many other towns and cities, Congress Square has been the center of educational, social, political, and business activity, creating a strong sense of community throughout Orleans' history.

Owen

Camp Hughes

ID 60.1966.1

CL Erected by the Indiana Civil War Centennial Commission, 1963

D SR 67 & 7th Street at roadside park, Gosport

Civil War training camp for the 59th Indiana Volunteer Infantry in 1861-62 was located one-half mile southwest of Gosport on White River. Named for former Indiana Congressman James Hughes.

Owen County Courthouse

Owen County formed by General Assembly, 1819. Spencer selected county seat, 1820. Neoclassical building, designed by Jesse T. Johnson, Indianapolis and built by Christian Kanzler & Son, Evansville (1910-1911), was second courthouse on land donated by Daniel Beem. Listed in National Register of Historic Places, 1994.

ID 60.1997.1

CL Erected 1997 Indiana Historical Bureau and Owen County Preservations, Inc.

D SW corner of courthouse lawn, Spencer

Wabash & Erie Canal

The Wabash & Erie was the longest canal built in North America, running from Toledo to Evansville. Montezuma was the main port of Parke County. This portion was abandoned about 1865.

ID 61.1966.1

CL Erected by Indiana Sesquicentennial Commission, 1966

D Median between US 36 & Crawford Street near Wabash River bridge, Montezuma

Armiesburg

So named because armies of Gen. Wm. H. Harrison (1811) and Gen. Saml. Hopkins (1812) bivouacked nearby. A busy village during waterpower days, court was held here before the county was judically organized.

ID 61.1966.2

CL Erected by Parke County Historical Society, 1966

D Lafayette Road / CR 600 W, (west side of road) south of US 36, north of Armiesburg. Reinstallation pending

Roseville

ID 61.1966.3

CL Erected by Parke County Historical Society, 1966

D Mecca-Roseville Road, Roseville Covered Bridge, Coxville

Roseville Covered Bridge, Coxville, Parke County.

The first business in Parke County was a grist mill built near here by Chauncey Rose and associates in 1819. This was the first flatboat landing in the county; territorial court was held here and this was a stop for stagecoaches.

Boyhood home of J.G. "Uncle Joe" Cannon

ID 61.1966.4

CL Erected by Parke County Historical Society, 1966

D CR 50 W at south edge of Annapolis, 1 mile north of Bloomingdale

From about 1835 to 1880 Annapolis was a thriving town with many factories, stores and potteries.

10 O'Clock Line

ID 61.1968.1

CL Erected by the Parke County Historical Society 1968

D US 41, 4 miles south of Rockville at church & junction of W. Mecca Road & CR 325 West

The famous Indian Reserve Line of 1809 which began at the mouth of Big Raccoon Creek and ended on the Ohio boundary crossed this point.

10 O'Clock Line

The famous Indian Reserve Line of 1809 which began at the mouth of Big Raccoon Creek and ended on the Ohio boundary crossed this point.

ID 61.1968.2

CL Erected by the Parke County Historical Society 1968

D North side of covered bridge & dam, north Bridgeton

Mansfield circa 1820

First named New Dublin. Later called Strain's Mills before being named Mansfield during the 1830s.

ID 61.1968.3

CL Erected by the Parke County Historical Society 1968

D West of the covered bridge, Mansfield

Turkey Run

Little Ned Garland, son of the first family to settle in Indiana north of the 10 O'clock Line, is said to have named the stream below the cliff because wild turkeys roosted in trees within the chasm.

ID 61.1968.4

CL Erected by the Parke County Historical Society 1968

D South side of SR 47 at Turkey Run State Park entrance

Dennis Hall

ID 61.1970.1

CL Erected by Parke County Historical Society, 1970

D Across from Quaker Church, south edge of Bloomingdale

An 1860 addition to Western Manual Labor School. The school was operated by Quakers from 1846 to 1916. The name was changed to Friends Bloomingdale Academy in 1862.

[Parke County Museum]

ID 61.1975.1

CL Purchased in 1975 by Parke Co. Historical Society

D South side of Ohio Street, 2 blocks east of the intersection of US 41 & US 36, Historical Museum, Rockville

This Museum Building built in 1839 first used as a seminary; an armory during the Civil War, a school for negro children from 1873-1924, later a gas station, a restaurant, and gift shop.

Portland Mills Covered Bridge

ID 61.1998.1

CL Erected 1998 Indiana Historical Bureau and Portland Mills Homecoming Association

D CR 650 N, gravel road, Portland Mills Covered Bridge, SW of Waveland

Portland Mills Covered Bridge, Waveland, Parke County.

Built 1856 by Henry Wolfe to Burr arch truss design. Moved here 1961 to replace Dooley Station Bridge. Restored and reopened 1996. Horizontal yellow poplar siding replaced with pine; oak arches; new cedar shingles; concrete abutments. Listed in National Register of Historic Places with Parke County covered bridges 1978.

Rockville Chautauqua Pavilion

Rockville Chautauqua Pavilion, Beechwood Park, Parke County.

ID 61.2001.1

CL Installed 2001 Indiana Historical Bureau and Parke County Historical Society

D Beechwood Park, W. Pennsylvania & S. College Streets, in SW Rockville

Side one:
Pavilion was built 1913 by Edgar Jerome (1862-1942) of Rockville. He used wooden bridge building techniques in timber framing which supports entire structure. It was designed to seat 3,000 people under its roof. Repairs made 1976-1978 and 1992. Listed in National Register of Historic Places 1999.
Side two:
Chautauquas held here 1911-1930; largest crowd estimated at 8,000 in 1915 when former President William H. Taft spoke. Popularized in late nineteenth century at Chautauqua, New York, chautauquas were significant social and educational events, bringing speakers, music, and ideas to towns across the U.S.

Parke

Christmas (Noel) Dagenet

ID 61.2004.1

CL Installed 2004 Indiana Historical Bureau and The Dagenett Family

D West side of Lafayette Road/CR 600 W, 0.25 mile north of Armiesburg

Side one:
Born December 25, 1799 near Terre Haute; baptised by Father Rivet, missionary at Vincennes. Son of French fur trader Ambrose Dagenet and Mechinquamesha, sister of Wea chief Jacco. Served Wea nation and U.S. government at Treaty of St. Mary's signed 1818. Married to Mary Ann Isaacs 1819 by Isaac McCoy at his Baptist Indian mission near here.
Side two:
Recommended by William Clark to work for U.S. government as Interpreter, receiving $400 per year, June 1824 through 1827. He selected land here to fulfill grant in Treaty of St. Mary's; land recorded 1824. Family moved west 1847. Dagenet employed in the last removal of Miamis from Indiana beginning 1846. He died before April 10 in 1848.

Perry

Abraham S. Fulton

ID 62.1961.1

CL The Perry County Historical Society, 1961

D SW corner of Washington Street & Franklin/SR 66, near Ohio River, Troy

Brother of Robert Fulton, inventor of the steamboat, is buried in Troy Cemetery near this spot. He was fatally injured while felling trees to build the family home on the site called Fulton Hill. The Fulton family owned extensive acreage in Perry County. They had bought the land from Nicholas J. Roosevelt, great-uncle of Theodore and Franklin D. Roosevelt about 1811. Nicholas J. Roosevelt commanded the first craft propelled by steam upon Western waters --the New Orleans -- built after Fulton's model. This boat stopped at Troy, one of the few fueling sites along the Ohio.

Perry

Hines Raid 1862

Captain Thomas H. Hines with 62 Confederate cavalrymen entered Perry County between Rome and Derby, June 17. Ambushed near Leavenworth, June 19, most of his command were captured.

ID 62.1963.1

CL Erected by the Indiana Civil War Centennial Commission, 1963

D SR 66, west side of highway just north of CR 104 & Poison Creek bridge, 4 miles south of Derby

Civil War Memorial Grave 1865

Civil War Memorial Graves, 1865, Magnet, Perry County.

On August 21,1865, the steamer, U.S.S. Argosy, (Number 3), was caught in a storm, blown aground and her boilers exploded. Ten fatalities occurred among Union soldiers returning home from war service. They were buried in a mass grave one half mile from Magnet (Rono) where memorial markers perpetuate this burial ground.

ID 62.1965.1

CL Erected by Indiana Civil War Centennial Commission, 1965

D CR 36 next to Ohio River and right before paved road turns to gravel, 0.5 mile south of Magnet

Perry

Indiana Cotton Mill

ID 62.1966.1

CL Erected by Indiana Sesquicentennial Commission, 1966

D Washington Street at 3rd, Cannelton

Indiana Cotton Mill, Cannelton, Perry County.

Built of native sandstone, 1847-1849. It began operating in 1850 and employed 400 people on 372 looms. Indiana's largest industry in its early years, it was in continuous operation until 1954.

Pike

The Buffalo Trace

ID 63.1966.1

CL Erected by Indiana Sesquicentennial Commission, 1966

D SR 61, SE corner of Gray Memorial Bridge over White River, Petersburg

Crossed White River at a nearby ford. It was made by migrating buffalo herds. The trace ran from Vincennes to Louisville and was the only through trail in pioneer days.

Wabash and Erie Canal Completed 1853

Wabash & Erie Canal, Pike-Gibson County Line, Pike County.

ID 63.1976.1

CL Bicentennial Project Wood Memorial U. S. History Students-Kiwanis Club, Oakland City

D SR 57, west side of highway between Patoka River & South Fork of Patoka River bridges, 3.5 miles north of Oakland City. Formerly listed as being in Gibson County (26.1976.1)

The approximately 460 mile canal from Toledo, Ohio, to Evansville, Indiana, was the longest canal built in the United States. Here a section constructed above the natural land surface to prevent flooding and erosion, remains intact.

Wabash and Erie Canal

Site of depot for canal which passed through town at foot of Main Street. Operations through Petersburg ceased 1860. Constructed 1832-1853, canal was nation's longest, connecting Lake Erie at Toledo with Ohio River at Evansville, through Fort Wayne, Lafayette, and Terre Haute.

ID 63.1992.1

CL Erected 1992 Indiana Historical Bureau

D North side, 108 W. Main Street, Petersburg

Iron Brigade

ID 64.1995.1

CL Erected 1995 Indiana Historical Bureau, Porter Co. Tour. Com., Indpls. Civil War Rnd. Tbl., Porter Cmp. 116, Dept. of Ind., Sons of Un. Vets. of Civil War

D Eastbound US 20 at SE corner of SR 49 overpass, Chesterton

Composed of infantry regiments from Indiana, Wisconsin, and Michigan, the Iron Brigade fought with Army of the Potomac during the Civil War (1861-1865). Received name for valor at battle of South Mountain, Maryland (1862). Sustained combat fatalities among the highest in the Union armies.

Willow Creek Confrontation

ID 64.1995.2

CL Erected 1995 Indiana Historical Bureau

D SE corner of Woodland Park, 2100 Willow Creek Road, Portage

As railroad lines expanded through U.S., conflict occurred between competing lines. Michigan Central Railroad, with track in Porter County since 1851, briefly defied state militia and court orders (1874) to allow Baltimore and Ohio Railroad to cross its track. Crossing was built at Willow Creek Station.

Ogden Dunes Ski Jump

Porter

Steel and wood ski jump with adjustable height and length was built here for Ogden Dunes Ski Club, incorporated in 1927 to promote winter sports. Five annual events with international competitors were held 1928-1932, with 7,000 to 20,000 spectators. Reputed to be the largest artificial ski jump at the time. Dismantled after 1932 event.

ID 64.1997.1

CL Erected 1997 Indiana Historical Bureau and Historical Society of Ogden Dunes

D Kratz Field, 82 Hillcrest Road at Boat Club Road, Ogden Dunes

New Harmony

Posey

Location of two attempts at communal living: The Harmonists under Reverend George Rapp, 1814-1825, and the Owenites under philanthropist Robert Owen, 1825-1826. New Harmony remained, an important cultural center for many, years thereafter.

ID 65.1966.1

CL Erected by Indiana Sesquicentennial Commission, 1966

D Near 513 E. Church Street across from post office, New Harmony

Alvin P. Hovey 1821-1891

ID 65.1966.2

CL Erected by the Indiana Historical Bureau, 1966

D East side of SR 69/5500 Industrial Road, Bellefontaine Cemetery entrance, north of Mt. Vernon

Alvin P. Hovey (1821-1891), Indiana Governor (1889-1891), Mt. Vernon, Posey County, Indiana Governors' Portraits Collection, Indiana Historical Bureau.

Governor of Indiana, 1889 to death, November 23, 1891. Born and educated in Mt. Vernon, he attained distinction as a lawyer, judge, Civil War general, diplomat and congressman. Buried in Bellefontaine Cemetery.

New Harmony Workingmen's Institute

New Harmony Workingmen's Institute, Museum, Upper Floor, New Harmony, Posey County.

ID 65.2001.1

CL Installed 2001 Indiana Historical Bureau and Workingmen's Institute

D Workingmen's Institute, 407 W. Tavern Street in front of library, New Harmony

Side one:
William Maclure and other intellectuals came to New Harmony 1826 to join Robert Owen's utopian experiment. Maclure established the Workingmen's Institute 1838 to serve as model of self-education for laborers. Operated in various New Harmony sites until construction of this Romanesque style building 1894.
Side two:
This is the last remaining workingmen's library of 144 in 89 Indiana counties sponsored by Maclure's bequest. It still serves as library, archives, and museum and is oldest continuously operating public library in the state. Part of National Historic Landmark Historic District designated 1966.

Tri-State Tornado

ID 65.2004.1

CL Installed 2004 Indiana Historical Bureau and Griffin High School Alumni Association and Friends

D SE corner of Main & First Streets, Griffin

Side one:
At 4:00 p.m. on March 18, 1925, a tornado arrived in Indiana after devastating parts of Missouri and Illinois. The town of Griffin was destroyed; the Owensville area and Princeton suffered heavy losses. Hundreds were injured; 76 were killed. Within hours, help came from nearby towns, the American Red Cross, and the Indiana National Guard.
Side two:
Heavy rains caused the Wabash River to flood, and by March 23, 1925 the only way to reach Griffin was by boat or railroad. Within weeks, Griffin was slowly being rebuilt. After a year, much of the town was rebuilt, including a schoolhouse, one church, and a grain elevator. This tornado is still rated the deadliest in U.S. weather history.

Griffin Oil Discovery

ID 65.2006.1

CL Installed 2005 Indiana Historical Bureau, Town of Griffin, Griffin Alumni Association, and Friends

D Main and First Streets, Griffin

Side one:
On December 14, 1938, at 8:20 p.m. oil was struck north of here at Fitzpatrick and Hayes #1 Cooper well. A gusher, it produced an estimated 1,000 barrels a day and began an oil boom in Griffin and the surrounding area. By 1941, 120 oil wells in this area were producing oil. Annual oil production in Indiana peaked 1956 at over 12 million barrels.
Side two:
Oil brought economic and social change to Griffin and surrounding area. Oilmen and their families moved in, businesses flourished, and land was leased to oil companies. Oil production has continued in the Griffin Oil Field—roughly 25 square miles in Gibson and Posey counties; through 2003, it had produced a cumulative 84,412,739 barrels of oil.

Pulaski

First Indiana Natural Gas Well

One mile southwest of this marker gas was discovered in 1867 by G. Bates while drilling for oil at a depth of 500 feet. Gas wells were drilled in 1887-1888; gas piped into Francesville lasted only four years.

ID 66.1988.1

CL Erected 1988 by the Pulaski County Historical Society

D South 1.5 miles on US 421, west side of road across from quarry entrance, Francesville

Putnam

10 O'Clock Treaty Line

Runs northwest-southeast through this point. On September 30, 1809, Indiana Territorial Governor, William Henry Harrison, obtained for the United States almost three million acres from the Potawatomi, Delaware and Miami tribes.

ID 67.1966.1

CL Erected by Indiana Sesquicentennial Commission, 1966

D US 40 westbound, 0.5 mile east of Putnam-Clay County line

Portland Mills

This marker stands on the corner of four Townships on the Parke and Putnam Co. line, once the center of the thriving rural town of Portland Mills Settled in the early 1800's
CHRISTIAN CHURCH
Established 1838–Relocated 1959
WATER POWERED MILL
Built 1822–Destroyed by fire 1960

ID 67.1972.1

CL Erected by Clinton, Greene, Russell, and Union Twps 1972

D CR 900 W and CR 800 N, Portland Mills Picnic Area (Raccoon SRA, Calvert Shelter)

Putnam

Kappa Alpha Theta

ID 67.2006.1

CL Installed 2006 Indiana Historical Bureau, Alph Chapter of Kappa Alpha Theta Facility Corporation

D 904 College Road, Greencastle

Side one: On January 27, 1870, Bettie Locke, Alice Allen, Hannah Fitch, and Bettie Tipton established first female Greek-letter college fraternity, Kappa Alpha Theta, at Indiana Asbury University. Fraternity fostered unity, promoted scholastic achievement, and provided social outlet. House built after 1940, when prior chapter house on site demolished.
Side two: Indiana Asbury University founded 1937. Locke and Allen were two of first women enrolled on limited basis 1867. Women were opposed and ostracized by many male students, faculty, citizens of town, and students at local female seminary. Based on success of these early women, university allowed women to take classes "on the same terms as" men 1871.

Randolph

Farmland Downtown Historic District

ID 68.2005.1

CL Installed 2005 Indiana Historical Bureau and Farmland History Book Committee of Historic Farmland USA, Inc.

D 106 North Main Street, Farmland.

Farmland Downtown Historic District, Indiana Historical Bureau Photo, Randolph County.

Side one: Farmland platted 1852 in Randolph County and listed as station on Indianapolis and Bellfontaine Railroad. Town incorporated 1867. Commerce based on agriculture and, by late 1880s, gas and oil production nearby. Responding to 1897 fire, community built six major buildings within two years of disaster. Side two: Historic district boundaries include parts of Main, Henry, and William streets, on original plat. Buildings were built circa 1867-1929 and are close to original condition. District demonstrates growth of railroad-based rural agricultural community. Listed in National Register of Historic Places 1994.

Michigan Road

Extending from Michigan City to the Ohio River at Madison. Begun by the state in 1832 with funds obtained from sale of land granted by the Potawatomi Indians. Opened northern part of state to settlers.

ID 69.1949.1

CL Indiana Historical Bureau 1949

D US 50 and N. Old Michigan Road, 2 miles east of Holton.

Morgan's Raid July 8-13, 1863

General John Hunt Morgan, Confederate cavalry commander, occupied Versailles on Sunday afternoon, July 12. Having seized county treasury he moved North at 4:00 P.M. as Union forces began to close in upon him.

ID 69.1963.1

CL Erected by the Indiana Civil War Centennial Commission 1963

D East entrance of courthouse, Versailles

Morgan's Raid, July 8-13, 1863, Map Route Through Southern Indiana.

Berry's Trace

This trail was cut about 1808, by John Berry (1777-1835). It began at Napoleon, ran west to Flat Rock and Blue Rivers, and thence northward into central Indiana. The Trace branched off the Brownstown-Brookville Road.

ID 69.1972.1

CL Erected by the Society of Indiana Pioneers, 1972

D US 421/ Madison & Wilson Streets, Napoleon

Union Church

ID 69.2004.1

CL Installed 2004 Indiana Historical Bureau, Rising Sun Regional Foundation, and Division of Historic Preservation & Archaeology, IDNR

D Union Flat Rock Baptist Church, CR 975 W and Flat Rock Road/CR 650 N, Flat Rock

Union Church, Flat Rock, Indiana. Historical Bureau Photo, Ripley County.

Side one: August 12, 1843 Union Church organized as Freewill Baptist church at home of Harvey Marshall. Church covenant states: "We cannot receive slaveholders into the church nor those who believe that slavery is right." First church building completed 1859 near here. In 1914, members changed denomination and name of church. New church built here 1921. Side two: Strong anti-slavery stance of Freewill Baptist churches contributed to end of slavery and freedom for those enslaved. The Underground Railroad refers to a widespread network of diverse people in the nineteenth century who aided slaves escaping to freedom from the southern U.S.

Stephen S. Harding

ID 69.2004.2

CL Installed 2004 Indiana Historical Bureau, Rising Sun Regional Foundation, and Division of Historic Preservation & Archaeology, IDNR

D Washington and Tyson Streets, SW corner of Courthouse Square, Versailles

Side one: Born 1808 Ontario County, New York. Moved with family to Ripley County, 1820. Prominent abolitionist and orator, delivering powerful anti-slavery speeches throughout the area, often against public sentiment. Was active in Liberty Party and Republican Party. Received several appointments from President Abraham Lincoln. Died February 12, 1891.
Side two: Harding was an early leader in the opposition to slavery, helping to bring freedom to enslaved people in U.S. The Underground Railroad refers to a widespread network of diverse people in the nineteenth century who aided slaves escaping to freedom from the southern U.S.

O & M Railroad

Side one: Chartered in Indiana 1848 by the General Assembly. The people of Ripley County voted March 1849 to provide local financial support for building the railroad. Surveys of the Eastern Division (Cincinnati to Vincennes) began 1852. The town of Osgood was named to honor O & M division engineer, A. L. Osgood.
Side two: Railroad was completed from Cincinnati to East St. Louis 1857. Depot, freight house, engine house, turntable, stock pens, and sidings were built at Osgood, which was considered the center of transport and commerce for Ripley County. Company was taken over by Baltimore and Ohio Railroad 1899-1900.

ID 69.2006.1

CL Installed 2006 Indiana Historical Bureau, Ripley County Historical Society, and Rising Sun Regional Foundation

D O&M Avenue, between Buckeye and Walnut Streets, Osgood

James Harrison Cravens

Side one: Born 1802 in Virginia; admitted to the bar 1823. Moved to Jefferson County, Indiana 1829. Established law office in Versailles, Ripley County 1833. Served four terms in Indiana General Assembly. Elected as Whig to U.S. Congress 1841. Lost as Free Soil party candidate for Indiana governor 1849 and as Republican candidate for attorney general 1856.
Side two: A well-known debater, he opposed extension of slavery, 1850 Fugitive Slave Act requiring citizens to return escaping slaves to their owners, and Article 13 of 1851 Constitution prohibiting blacks from moving into Indiana. Served briefly in Civil War. Moved to Osgood area before 1860; built home here circa 1865. Died at Osgood December 4, 1876.

ID 69.2006.2

CL Installed 2006 Indiana Historical Bureau, Ripley County Historical Society, and Rising Sun Regional Foundation

D 321 E. Fairground Avenue, Osgood

Wendell L. Willkie 1892-1944

ID 70.1969.1

CL Erected by Indiana Historical Society, 1969

D SR 44, East Hill Cemetery entrance, east of Flat Rock River Bridge, Rushville

Portrait of Wendell L. Willkie (1892-1944), Indiana Picture Collection, MS. Section, Indiana State Library.

Lawyer and business leader - Republican presidential nominee, 1940 - the only native Hoosier to be nominated for the Presidency by a major political party - author of *One World* - grave and memorial in East Hill Cemetery, Rushville.

Wendell L. Willkie 1892-1944

ID 70.1969.2

CL Erected by Indiana Historical Society, 1969.

D Rush County Courthouse, 101 E. 2nd Street, north lawn, Rushville

Wendell L. Willkie, On The Campaign Trail, Indiana Picture Collection, MS. Section, Indiana State Library.

Lawyer and business leader - Republican presidential nominee, 1940 - the only native Hoosier to be nominated for the Presidency by a major political party - author of *One World* - grave and memorial in East Hill Cemetery, Rushville.

Rush

Wendell L. Willkie 1892-1944

Lawyer and business leader - Republican presidential nominee, 1940 - the only native Hoosier to be nominated for the Presidency by a major political party - author of *One World* - grave and memorial in East Hill Cemetery, Rushville.

ID 70.1969.3

CL Erected by Indiana Historical Society, 1969.

D N. Main Street/ SR 3 & Park Boulevard, NW side of street, Rushville

Wendell L. Willkie 1892-1944

Lawyer and business leader - Republican presidential nominee, 1940 - the only native Hoosier to be nominated for the Presidency by a major political party - author of *One World* - grave and memorial in East Hill Cemetery, Rushville.

ID 70.1969.4

CL Erected by Indiana Historical Society, 1969.

D East side of 221 N. Main Street/ SR 3 in downtown pocket park, Rushville

St. Joseph

La Salle's Camp 1 Mile West

La Salle, "The Miami Treaty", Portage Prairie, May, 1681, Indiana Picture Collection, MS. Section, Indiana State Library.

Site of La Salle's camp, 1679, on portage between St. Joseph and Kankakee rivers. La Salle was the first white man to enter Indiana, passing here again in 1681.

ID 71.19??.1

CL National Society of the Colonial Dames of America in the State of Indiana

D SR 933/Dixie Highway & Darden Road, South Bend

Camp Rose

ID 71.1963.1

CL Erected by the Indiana Civil War Centennial Commission 1963

D Leland & Portage & Notre Dame Avenues, South Bend.

Civil War Training camp for then 9th Congressional District was located at the old fairgrounds. The 99th, 73rd and 87th Indiana Volunteer infantry regiments were organized and trained here in 1802.

Sisters of the Holy Cross, Civil War Nurses, 1861-1865

ID 71.1965.1

CL Erected by the Indiana Civil War Centennial Commission 1963

D Madison Street & Notre Dame Avenue, South Bend

In response to Governor Morton's call of October 1861, eighty Sisters of the Holy Cross under the leadership of Mother Angela served as military nurses. The Sisters became the forerunners of the Navy Nurse Corps in 1862 when they boarded the Red Rover, the navy's first hospital ship.

Indiana Territorial Line

ID 71.1966.1

CL Erected by Indiana Sesquicentennial Commission, 1966

D US 31 & Johnson Road, south edge of South Bend

(east~west boundary at this point)
The boundaries between Indiana and Michigan territories was established on June 30, 1805. Just before Indiana became a state in 1816, the line was moved ten miles north to provide frontage on Lake Michigan.

Site of Home of Schuyler Colfax March 23, 1823–January 1, 1885

Portrait of Schuyler Colfax, South Bend, St. Joseph County, Indiana Picture Collection, MS. Section, Indiana State Library.

Prominent newspaperman and political leader; member of Congress, 1855-1869; Speaker, House of Representatives, 1863-1869; and Vice-President of the United States, 1869-1873.

ID 71.1966.2

CL Erected by Indiana Sesquicentennial Commission, 1966

D Colfax & Taylor Streets, South Bend

First Dam Across the St. Joseph River/ Power Race

First Dam Across The St. Joseph River, Mishawaka, St. Joseph County.

The original dam, providing power for which Mishawaka was noted, was completed in 1837. It was 577 feet long, 24 feet thick and cost $38,000.00.

Along this race, providing water power, and along its counterpart across the river, early Mishawaka factories were located. These industries produced flour, lumber, woolen goods, iron, boots, shoes, furniture, coffins, barrel staves, saddles and harness, and wagons, valued at many hundreds of thousands of dollars each year.

ID 71.1968.1

CL none

D Race & First Streets, Mishawaka

First Bridge

ID 71.1968.2

CL none

D 300 block of N. Main Street at St. Joseph River, Mishawaka.

The first bridge across the St. Joseph River was built at this place in 1837 at a cost of $2499 and was paid for by popular subscription. The bridge replaced a ferry which had operated here from 1834. First bridge replaced by the red, covered bridge in 1846, an iron truss bridge in 1874, and the present concrete bridge in 1907.

The Mishawaka Academic and Normal Institute 1846-1868

ID 71.1968.3

CL none

D 303 S. Main at 4th Street, Mishawaka

Opposite the south end of Main Street at 4th Street stood the two-storied, red brick Institute Building, where the Mishawaka Academic and Normal Institute classes were held. This was a Free school for Mishawaka children and a Select school for advanced study and teacher training, supported by the village, with an enrollment of over two hundred students from the town and surrounding area.

St. Joseph Iron Works

ID 71.1968.4

CL none

D 300 block of N. Main Street, Mishawaka.

At this site Alanson M. Hurd, a Detroit, Michigan, businessman, built the first successful iron blast furnace in Indiana. The town he platted in 1833 on the south bank of the river was called the St. Joseph Iron Company. On February 17, 1838, the General Assembly incorporated Indiana City on the north side of the river and the St. Joseph Iron Company, with all additions, into one town, Mishawaka.

Mishawaka High School

Mishawaka's first public high school was opened in 1874 with an enrollment of sixty students. Accredited in 1876, the school graduated its first class in June, 1878. The original building was a three-story red brick structure at First and Hill streets. In 1911 a new building was erected one block further south on Hill and facing what is now Lincoln Way West. This present Mishawaka High School was dedicated in the fall of 1924.

ID 71.1976.1

CL none

D Mishawaka High School, 1202 Lincoln Way East, Mishawaka

Kamm & Schellinger Brewery

Kamm & Schellinger Brewery, Mishawaka, St. Joseph County.

Kamm and Schellinger Brewery is significant in the industrial heritage of Mishawaka and Indiana. First structures built 1853; expansions in late nineteenth and early twentieth centuries. Incorporated in 1883; beer production ended in 1951. Listed in National Register of Historic Places, 1979.

ID 71.1995.1

CL Erected 1995 Indiana Historical Bureau and 100 Center Property Owners Association

D 100 Center Street Complex & Lincoln Way, south bank of St. Joseph River, Mishawaka

Normain Heights Subdivision

ID 71.1997.1

CL Erected 1997 Indiana Historical Bureau and Beiger Heritage Corporation

D Local fire station lawn, 2332 N. Main Street & McKinley Highway/US 20, Mishawaka

Veterans' Homes of Mishawaka, Inc., founded by veterans, 1946, built (1947-1949) to counter housing shortage after World War II. 315 houses built on battle-named streets to seven designs; innovative features: aluminum siding, complete kitchen and bath, central heating, landscaping. Part of national trend for planned suburban communities.

Battell Park

ID 71.1997.2

CL Erected 1997 Indiana Historical Bureau, Citizens of Mishawaka and Beiger Heritage Corporation

D 400 W. Mishawaka & Charlotte Avenues, Mishawaka

Battell Park, Bandshell, Mishawaka, St. Joseph County.

Mishawaka's oldest park, circa 1860s; given to city (1881) by members of Battell family. Features include Civil War soldiers monument (1884); neoclassical copperdomed, brick and limestone bandshell commemorating WW I (1927): exceptional Works Progress Administration rock garden (1937). Listed in National Register of Historic Places, 1996.

Huggart Settlement

First land purchased by Huggart brothers in 1834; area settled and farmed by their families and several other African-American households circa 1850-1890s. Settlement families attended nearby schools and churches and worked with neighbors in surrounding areas. Many residents were buried in nearby Porter-Rea Cemetery now in Potato Creek State Park.

ID 71.1998.1

CL Erected 1998 Indiana Historical Bureau and Huggart Settlement Task Force

D NW corner at junction of SR 4 & Mulberry Road east of Potato Creek State Park, Union Township

Dodge Manufacturing Company

Wallace H. Dodge (1849-1894) founded company 1878; made wood products; moved to this site 1880. Patented wood split pulley 1882, revolutionary for standardized, interchangeable parts. Its innovative products have led to advances in power transmission and conveyor technologies.

ID 71.1999.1

CL Erected 1999 Indiana Historical Bureau and Dodge

D 500 S. Union Street at parking lot & entrance to RMG foundry of the Troyer Group, Mishawaka

Jewish Cemetery Site

Side one:
Hebrew Society of Brotherly Love of South Bend established Jewish cemetery on this site 1859. First Jewish families settling in a new community typically organized a burial society before establishing a formal congregation. Before Civil War era, such organizations helped widely scattered Jews in Indiana maintain Jewish identity and traditions.
Side two:
Hebrew Society purchased larger tract of land 1883; bodies from original cemetery reinterred at new site 1884; later named Rose Hill Cemetery. Many society members were part of migration starting in 1820s of German-speaking Jews seeking civil liberties. During twentieth century, Jewish population in area was second or third largest in state.

ID 71.2002.1

CL Installed 2002 Indiana Historical Bureau and Michiana Jewish Historical Society

D 500 block on west side of N. Niles Avenue, South Bend

Porter (Rea) Cemetery

ID 71.2003.1

CL Installed 2003 Indiana Historical Bureau, Friends of Porter Rea, and Historic Landmarks Foundation of Indiana

D Cemetery located in Potato Creek State Park, North Liberty

Porter-Rea Cemetery, Potato Creek State Park, St. Joseph County.

Side one:
This cemetery was officially created September 6, 1854 when Samuel Gard deeded land to trustees for a burial ground. Free African-American settlers from Huggart Settlement were buried here alongside their white neighbors, not segregated. Porter Cemetery Association was formed May 9, 1884 with both white and African-American charter members.
Side two:
Cemetery has always been a neighborhood burial ground for members from churches of various denominations. It has been called Porter Rea for decades perhaps because both Porter and Rea families owned adjacent land. Although enclosed in Potato Creek State Park, it remains an active independent cemetery managed by Porter Cemetery Association.

Scott

Morgan's Raid July 8-13, 1863

Confederate Gen. John Hunt Morgan and his staff spent the night of July 10, 1863, in Lexington. He left for Vernon on the morning of July 11, 1863.

ID 72.1963.1

CL Erected by the Indiana Civil War Centennial Commission 1963

D SR 203, town square, east edge of school, Lexington

Site of William Hayden English Home

Portrait of William H. English, Lexington, Scott County, Indiana Picture Collection, MS. Section, Indiana State Library.

English (1822-1896), politician, banker, and historian, served as secretary of 1850 Indiana Constitutional Convention, as Speaker of Indiana House, and in U.S. House. Candidate for U.S. Vice President, 1880; President, Indiana Historical Society. Town of English named for him.

ID 72.1992.1

CL Erected 1992 by Indiana Historical Bureau

D SR 203, north edge of Lexington, west side of highway at drive entrance, Englishton Park, Lexington

Site of Western Eagle

ID 72.1992.2

CL Erected 1992 by Indiana Historical Bureau

D SR 356/Main & Mulberry Streets, Lexington

Western Eagle was second newspaper in Indiana Territory. Founded in Madison 1813, moved to Lexington July 8, 1815 and to this site October 1815. Jacob Rhoads, publisher after 1814, terminated publication January 6, 1816 for financial reasons. Rhoads was printer for Indiana Territory 1814-1816.

Scott County Courthouse

ID 72.2001.1

CL Installed 2001 Indiana Historical Bureau, Preservation Alliance, Inc., and Scott County Community Foundation

D 1 E. McClain Avenue, Scottsburg

Scott County Courthouse, Scottsburg.

Side one:
County formed by Indiana General Assembly 1820. First county seat located at Lexington; first courthouse built 1821. Several attempts made 1822-1870 to move county seat to more central location, creating animosity among citizens. Scottsburg designated second county seat and plat recorded 1871; second county courthouse built here 1873-1874.
Side two:
Courthouse designed in Italianate style by Andrew R. Baty 1871. Cornerstone not laid until 1873 because injunction stopped county seat relocation proceedings. Structure renovated 1979. Addition in 1997 tripled courthouse space; 1874 courthouse remains as west wing.

John Kimberlin Farm

Side one: Kimberlin, a Revolutionary War veteran, was first person to purchase land in what is now Scott County. In 1804 he bought Tract 264 of land grant to soldiers of George Rogers Clark. His family settled 1805 in well-built cabin northwest of here, cleared land, built fences, and farmed. He and his wife are buried in the cemetery southwest of here.
Side two: After Pigeon Roost Massacre in September 1812, his cabin was converted to fortified blockhouse and sheltered area settlers. Nearly 600 mounted volunteers from Kentucky and Indiana Territory came to protect the area, encamped on his land, and used his supplies. He petitioned the U.S. Congress in 1832 for payment and received $150 in 1834.

ID 72.2001.2

CL Installed 2001 Indiana Historical Bureau, Preservation Alliance, Inc., and Scott County Community Foundation.

D 5765 S. Westport Road, 0.2 mile northwest of SR 362, Nabb

Scott County's Carnegie Library

Side one: Scott County Board of Commissioners appointed a library board 1917 in response to citizen petitions for a public library. Library board sought Carnegie grant for funding assistance. Locally $7,500 was raised; Carnegie grant of $12,500 was added. Library opened and had 4,453 volumes in 1921.

Scott County Carnegie Library, Scottsburg.

Side two: Structure of brick and limestone designed by Clifford Shopbell & Co. in Renaissance Revival style; 1986 addition designed by Pecsok, Jelliffe, Randall & Nice. One of 1,679 libraries built in U.S. with funds from philanthropist Andrew Carnegie. Indiana built more Carnegie libraries than any other state.

ID 72.2002.1

CL Installed 2002 Indiana Historical Bureau, Preservation Alliance, Inc., and Scott County Community Foundation

D 108 S. Main Street, Scottsburg

Scott County Home

ID 72.2002.2

CL Installed 2002 Indiana Historical Bureau, Preservation Alliance, Inc., and Scott County Community Foundation

D 1050 S. Main Street, Scottsburg

Scott County Home, Scottsburg.

Side one:
Indiana law in 1831 authorized counties to establish institutions to support and accommodate the poor, carrying out 1816 Constitution provision. First Scott County home built 1861 north of Lexington; closed 1879. County home moved here to frame house on 180 acres. Residents of such asylums could farm and help support the facilities.
Side two:
This brick structure replaced the frame house in 1892. Over time, acreage was reduced. Structure ceased to function as county home 1973. Scott County public services and government offices located here until 1995. Listed in National Register of Historic Places 2000. Property named home of Scott County Heritage Center and Museum 2001.

Lexington First County Seat

Side one: Scott County formed by Indiana General Assembly 1820; Lexington selected county seat. Attempts made 1823, 1839, 1840 to relocate county seat to more central location. Petition to County Commissioners 1870 was successful; town of Scottsburg platted 1871 as new county seat; actual move occurred 1874.
Side two: Lexington laid out 1810; plat recorded 1813; town incorporated 1816. First Scott County courthouse built here 1821 by Daniel P. Faulkner. Specifications called for brick construction and a hipped roof with poplar shingles and a twenty-foot cupola. Structure served as school 1874-1889, then was demolished.

ID 72.2002.3

CL Installed 2002 Indiana Historical Bureau, Preservation Alliance, Inc., and Scott County Community Foundation

D SR 356/Main Street, south edge of school, Lexington

Scottsburg Depot

Scottsburg Depot, Scott County.

Side one: Built 1872. One of the classic "combination" depots for passengers and freight, with board and batten siding, wide overhanging roof, and agent's bay window. Interior included separate waiting rooms for men and women. Served as depot until early 1950s. Listed in National Register of Historic Places 1991 and moved one block north to preserve it.
Side two: Jeffersonville Railroad came through this area by 1852; when platted as new county seat 1871, Scottsburg was located on this line. Railroad was important in subsequent economic development of town and area. Depot was restored, assisted by federal transportation funds, for reuse as Scottsburg Heritage Station; it was dedicated 1996.

ID 72.2002.4

CL Installed 2002 Indiana Historical Bureau, Preservation Alliance, Inc., and Scott County Community Foundation

D 90 N. Main Street, Scottsburg

Northern Boundary of Clark's Grant

ID 72.2002.5

CL Installed 2002 Indiana Historical Bureau, Preservation Alliance, Inc., and Scott County Community Foundation

D NW corner SR 3 junction with Kinderhook Road (Section 296 Clark's Grant), 3 miles NW of Nabb. Replaces 72.1967.1

Northern Boundary of Clark's Grant, marker, near Nabb, Scott County.

Side one:
Northern boundary of Clark's Grant near here. Land grant provided by Virginia 1781 to General George Rogers Clark and his men for American Revolutionary War service against British in Illinois country. Grant was 150,000 acres divided into 298 lots of approximately 500 acres, with 1,000 acres reserved for town.
Side two:
Clarksville, first American settlement northwest of the Ohio River (1784), located at southwestern corner of grant. This marker (*) is located in Tract No. 296. [Map on side two with grant boundaries over current county boundaries]

Lake Iola Interurban Site

Lake Iola Interurban Site, Interurban Car, Scottsburg, Scott County.

ID 72.2002.6

CL Installed 2002 Indiana Historical Bureau, Preservation Alliance, Inc., and Scott County Community Foundation

D East shore of Lake Iola, William H. Graham Park, N. Bond Street, Scottsburg

Side one:
Indianapolis and Louisville Traction Company organized to build track between Seymour and Sellersburg as part of the interurban line which extended from Indianapolis to Louisville; track completed 1907. First railway in the country to operate on 1200 volt high tension, direct current system powered by generators at this site.
Side two:
Car barn and water tower also built on site. Artificial lake--later named Lake Iola--created as water source for power equipment. Indiana Railroad abandoned operation; last train October 31, 1939. Building foundations and some track remain. Land around Lake Iola is now property of Scottsburg, serving the city as park and interpretive center.

Morgan's Raid, July 1863

ID 72.2002.7

CL Installed 2002 Indiana Historical Bureau, Preservation Alliance, Inc., and Scott County Community Foundation

D 0.2 mile east of junction US 31 & SR 356 at Louisville & Indiana Railroad, south side of highway, Vienna. Replaces 72.1963.2

Side one: During the Civil War, Confederate General John Hunt Morgan (1825-1864) led a raid through southern Indiana July 8-13, 1863. Crossed Ohio River at Brandenburg, Kentucky on two commandeered steamboats with over 2,000 cavalrymen and entered Indiana near Mauckport. Following a battle at Corydon, they traveled north to Salem.
Side two: Morgan's soldiers then traveled east and reached Vienna July 10; they burned railroad bridge and depot and tapped telegraph line. Spent night in Lexington. Moving northeast, they interacted with towns including Vernon, Dupont, and Versailles. Left Indiana at Harrison (now West Harrison). Morgan and part of force were captured in eastern Ohio.

Marshfield Train Robbery

ID 72.2002.8

CL Installed 2002 Indiana Historical Bureau, Preservation Alliance, Inc., and Scott County Community Foundation

D US 31 & Terrell Road, south of the overspan railroad bridge & W. Morgan, north city limits of Scottsburg

Side one: One of earliest U.S. train robberies occurred May 22, 1868 at nearby Marshfield, a refueling and watering stop. Engine and express car were detached from Jeffersonville, Madison, and Indianapolis Railroad train and abandoned near Seymour. Notorious Reno Gang took U.S. treasury notes and government bonds from Adams Express Company safes in car.
Side two: Indiana-based Reno Gang operated after the Civil War during a period of unemployment and lawlessness. Vigilante organizations continued to be active. Pinkerton National Detective Agency investigated Marshfield robbery and apprehended several suspects. Before any were tried, members of Reno Gang were lynched by vigilantes.

Town of Austin

Side one: Jeffersonville Railroad construction began 1848, completed through here 1852. First station built on this site circa 1853 with two wood yards nearby for fuel. Official plat of Austin recorded 1853. Tradition is that town named by Mexican-American War veterans who used land vouchers given for service; several had served in Austin, Texas.
Side two: Early industries were timber-related with several saw and stave mills, which produced materials for ship building and made millions of barrel staves before the large trees were depleted. Food canning then became the major industry. In 1899, J.S. Morgan and others opened first cannery, which developed into national supplier of canned foods.

ID 72.2002.9

CL Installed 2002 Indiana Historical Bureau, Preservation Alliance, Inc., and Scott County Community Foundation

D SW corner US 31 & West Morgan Street, Austin

Joseph Hooker Shea

Side one: Shea was born at the home of his parents on this site 1862. Received A.B. degree from Indiana University 1889. Admitted to the bar at Scottsburg 1889; practiced law there, Seymour, and later Indianapolis. Shea began public service as prosecuting attorney 1892, served as circuit court judge twice, and was a long-time trustee of Indiana University.
Side two: Shea was a state senator 1897-1901 and a judge of the Indiana Appellate Court 1913-1916. Recommended by Hoosier Vice President Thomas R. Marshall, President Woodrow Wilson appointed Shea Ambassador to Chile. Shea served 1916-1921, during a time of continuing sensitive relations between Peru and Chile. He died 1928 and is buried in Madison.

ID 72.2003.1

CL Lexington Historical Society, Inc., Preservation Alliance, Inc., and Scott County Community Foundation

D 8060 E. Main Street/SR 356, next to fire station, Lexington (original site of family home)

Scott

Pigeon Roost

ID 72.2004.1

CL Installed 2004 Indiana Historical Bureau, Preservation Alliance, Inc., and Scott County Community Foundation

D Entrance to Pigeon Roost State Historic Site, US 31, 5 miles south of Scottsburg

1927, Pigeon Roost Memorial, Hohenberger Picture Collection, Manuscripts Section, Indiana State Library.

Side one: Pigeon Roost, settled 1809 in Clark County, was attacked on September 3, 1812. Over twenty settlers and an unknown number of Indians were killed. Clark County militia unsuccessfully pursued the remaining Indians. That same month Fort Harrison and Fort Wayne were attacked by Indians. The U.S. had declared war on Great Britain, June 18, 1812.

Side two: The Pigeon Roost raid was part of the ongoing conflict between Indians-influenced by the British-and settlers along the frontier, one of the contributing factors of the War of 1812 in the west. The State of Indiana appropriated $2,000 for construction of the memorial here, dedicated October 1, 1904. This site became a State Historic Site 1929.

Shelby

ID 73.1952.1

CL Unknown

D SR 9, 4.5 miles north of Shelbyville. Missing

Whetzel Trace

A trail from Whitewater River at Laurel to White River at Waverly crossed here. Blazed in 1818 by Jacob Whetzel. It was the first east-west road into the "New Purchase" of central Indiana.

ID 73.1959.1

CL Erected by the Shelby County Historical Society, 1959

D East side of CR 625 E, 0.5 mile north of E. Union Road, 2 miles NE of Rays Crossing & SR 44

De Witt Pioneer Home

Peter De Witt erected on this site in 1821 the first home in what is now Union Township, Shelby County.

Shelby

Site of Home of Thomas Andrews Hendricks September 7, 1819-November 25, 1885

Thomas A. Hendricks, Indiana Governor (1873-1877), Shelbyville, Shelby County, Indiana Governors' Portraits Collection, Indiana Historical Bureau.

Outstanding lawyer; member Indiana legislature; delegate, Second Constitutional Convention, 1850-1851; Indiana Congressman, 1851-1855; United States Senator, 1863-1869; Governor of Indiana, 1873-1877; and Vice-President of the United States, 1885.

ID 73.1966.1

CL Erected by Indiana Sesquicentennial Commission, 1966

D N. Harrison & E. Mechanic Streets, Shelbyville

Indiana's First Railroad

An experimental two mile road was completed to this point on July 4, 1834. A horse-drawn car carried Hoosiers on a railroad for the first time.

ID 73.1966.2

CL Erected by Indiana Sesquicentennial Commission, 1966

D SR 44 between E. Broadway & McLane Streets, east of downtown Shelbyville

Spencer

James Gentry, Sr.

Gentry (1778-1840) settled northwest of here in 1818. A farmer and merchant, Gentry employed Abraham Lincoln to help transport merchandise by flatboat to New Orleans in December, 1828. Lincoln family spent its last night at Gentry's home before leaving for Illinois in 1830.

ID 74.1992.1

CL Erected 1992 by Indiana Historical Bureau

D SR 162, Lincoln State Park, 0.5 mile east of Gentryville & junction of SR 62/US 231, north side of highway

Site of Rockport Tavern

ID 74.1992.2

CL Erected 1992 by Indiana Historical Bureau, Spencer County Historical Society, and Friends of Southern Hills, Inc.

D SE corner 2nd & Main Streets, across from courthouse, Rockport

In October 1844 Abraham Lincoln gave a speech at Spencer County Courthouse to promote Henry Clay, Whig presidential candidate. Lincoln, during his first trip to Indiana in 14 years, was a guest at the Tavern. Site first marked October 28, 1926.

David Turnham (1803-1884)

ID 74.1995.1

CL Erected 1995 Indiana Historical Bureau and Spencer County Historical Society

D SR 162 & CR 1625 N, in front of Heritage Hills High School, Lincoln City

In 1819, Turnham family settled less than one mile northeast of Thomas Lincoln's farm. Turnham was a friend of Abraham Lincoln. Turnham loaned Lincoln *Revised Laws of Indiana* (1824) in 1827. After Lincoln's assassination, he provided information to historians about Lincoln's youth.

Abraham Lincoln Employed

Abraham Lincoln, Boyhood Home (1816-1830), Lincoln City, Spencer County.

ID 74.2001.1

CL Installed 2001 Indiana Historical Bureau and Spencer County Historical Society.

D SR 66, 1 mile west of Troy at Lincoln Ferry road side park entrance

Spencer

Side one:
Lincoln (1809-1865) lived northwest of here 1816-1830. Worked circa 1825 as hired hand for James Taylor. William Herndon, a Lincoln biographer, wrote that Lincoln told him it "was the roughest work a young man could be made to do." He butchered, did farm tasks, and operated Taylor's ferry across Anderson River, a key Ohio River transportation link.
Side two:
Lincoln built a rowboat and used it to carry people to waiting steamers on the Ohio River. On his first trip, he earned a dollar, which made the world seem "wider and fairer," according to reports of later remarks by Lincoln." He took a flatboat of goods to New Orleans 1828. His work on the Ohio and Mississippi rivers helped to broaden his horizons.

La Salle in Indiana

ID 75.2000.1

CL Installed 2000 Indiana Historical Bureau and Starke County Historical Society

D South of US 30 on CR 50 E/ N. Range Road, 0.6 mile east of the La Porte & Starke county line & Kankakee River; Turkey Foot Conservation Area parking lot, Davis Station, Hamlet area

Portrait of La Salle, Indiana Picture Collection, MS. Section, Indiana State Library.

Side one:
Rene-Robert Cavelier, Sieur de La Salle, born Rouen, France 1643; died 1687. Emigrated 1666 to New France (near present Montreal, Quebec, Canada). Led explorations 1679-1682 in search of trade, expanded empire for France, and mouth of Mississippi River. On April 9, 1682 claimed entire Mississippi River basin for France, naming it Louisiana.
Side two:
In 1679, La Salle and his men came to present Indiana traveling on St. Joseph and Kankakee rivers. They canoed down the meandering Kankakee River through vast marsh-swamp-dune ecosystems--which covered over 625 square miles and teemed with game including fish, waterfowl, and mammals. Kankakee River forms part of northern and northwestern boundary of Starke County.

Fremont Indiana

Settled in 1834 as Willow Prairie; Village of Brockville - Platted in 1837. Post Office and town changed to Fremont in 1848 in honor of John C. Fremont "the Great Pathfinder". Located on the Vistula Trail, the meeting place for people from the Detroit, Toledo, and Pittsburg areas in their westward movement. First frame building erected in 1837 near the center of the village. In 1838 the Potawatomi Tribe was removed from the area. First Church - Methodist Episcopal was organized in 1841. First frame school was built in 1845. In 1877 a brick school was erected to replace one built in 1856 which was destroyed by fire. New school was erected on Spring Street between Tolford and Coffin Streets. Electric lights were installed in 1895. Dr. Wade opened Steuben County's first hospital in 1914. First paved streets were laid in 1922. Town erected a 60,000 gallon tank and supplied water to the community in 1937. Sewer lines and disposal plant went into service in 1957. At one time Fremont boasted 2 Hotels, and was served by 6 passenger and 4 freight trains daily. [image]

ID 76.1976.1

CL This plaque dedicated July 4, 1976 at the site of the "ole town pump"

D Toledo Street/SR 120 & Wayne Street/SR 827 at old town pump site, NW corner, Fremont

Indiana's Northern Boundary Line

ID 76.2000.1

CL Installed 2000 Indiana Historical Bureau and with donations In Memory of John R. Stanley.

D 4.7 miles east of Fremont at 775 E & SR 120, Clear Lake south shore area. Replaces 76.1966.1

Indiana's Northern Boundary Line, marker, Clear Lake, Steuben County.

Side one: Indiana admitted by U.S. Congress as nineteenth state 1816. Enabling Act moved northern boundary ten miles north of southernmost tip of Lake Michigan providing direct access to the lake. Boundary first surveyed 1817 by William Harris. Boundary disputes with Michigan and Ohio continued until Michigan statehood 1837. Side two: Enabling Act of 1816 established Indiana's northern boundary (3 miles north of here) as a line "drawn through a point ten miles north of the southern extreme of Lake Michigan." [map]

Grave of Jane Todd Crawford

ID 77.1972.1

CL Erected in 1972 by the Woman's Auxiliary to the Southern Medical Association

D West side of SR 63 in Johnson Cemetery, 1 mile north of Graysville

Grave of Jane Todd Crawford, Johnson Cemetery, Graysville, Sullivan County.

Pioneer Heroine of Abdominal Surgery
Jane Todd was born in Virginia in 1763. In 1805 she and her husband, Thomas Crawford, moved to Green County, Ky. Suffering from a huge abdominal tumor, she rode 60 miles to Danville, Ky., to submit to an operation never before performed. On December 25, 1809, Dr. Ephraim McDowell performed this, the first ovariotomy, in his home. The ordeal lasted 25 minutes. There was no anesthesia. Mrs. Crawford recovered completely. Years later she came to Graysville to live with her son, Thomas, a Presbyterian minister. She died in 1842 at age 78. She is buried here. The restored McDowell home in Danville is a surgical shrine.

Westernmost Naval Battle of the Revolution

On 25 February 1779 Col. George Rogers Clark captured Ft. Sackville at Vincennes from the British. About 6 miles west at Pointe Coupee on the Wabash River on 2 March 1779 Capt. Leonard Helm commanding 3 boats and 50 volunteers from Vincennes captured a reinforcement fleet of 7 boats carrying 40 soldiers and valuable supplies and Indian trade goods. This small naval battle completed destruction of British military strength in the Wabash Valley.

ID 77.1985.1

CL Erected by the Sullivan County Historical Society 1985

D 0.7 mile south of junction of SR 58 & US 41, between Old US 41/Earl J. Abe Rogers Road & new US 41, Carlisle

Merom Conference Center

Merom Conference Center, Sullivan County.

Dedicated in 1862, Union Christian College served as a preparatory school and college until 1924. In 1936 it became Merom Institute - a rural enrichment center. Now owned by the United Church of Christ it serves as a camp, conference, and retreat center.

ID 77.1989.1

CL Erected by the Merom Improvement Association 1989

D Merom Conference Center, Phillip & 5th Streets at Edward Ovellette Drive, Merom

Merom Bluff Chautauqua, 1905-1936

ID 77.1989.2

CL Erected by the Merom Improvement Association 1989

D Merom Bluff Park overlooking Wabash River near pavilion, Merom

Organized nationally to bring culture to rural communities, Merom's 10 day religious and educational event featured concerts, debates, plays, and lectures. Carrie Nation, William Jennings Bryan, William H. Taft, Warren Harding, and Billy Sunday were among the speakers here.

Merom Founded, 1817

ID 77.1989.3

CL Erected by the Merom Improvement Association 1989

D 1997 Third Street/SR63 north of Market Street intersection, Merom

A log courthouse here served as Sullivan's first county seat from 1819-1842. Merom was an important river port and a stop on the stage route --The Old Harrison Trail. Harrison's troops camped near here on their 1811 march to Tippecanoe.

Fairbanks' Massacre

ID 77.1989.4

CL Erected by Indiana Michigan Power and Sullivan County Historical Society, 1989

D NW corner SR 63/Main Street & CR 925 N/ Market Street, near post office, Fairbanks

A War of 1812 military action occurred in September 1812 three miles west/southwest of here. While escorting supplies from Fort Knox near Vincennes to Fort Harrison at Terre Haute, Sergeant Nathan Fairbanks and approximately a dozen soldiers were ambushed–and most killed---by Indians.

A Civil War Murder

Sullivan

Numerous violent conficts erupted in Sullivan County during the Civil War over differing war sentiments. On July 14, 1864, anti-war Democrat John Drake was fatally shot at a community picnic near here. The Union soldier who shot Drake was apparently never prosecuted.

ID 77.1992.1

CL Erected 1992 Indiana Historical Bureau and Sullivan County Historical Society

D Main Street/SR 63 & North Street, east side of highway, north edge of Fairbanks

Birthplace John Shaw Billings, M.D. April 12, 1838-March 11, 1913

Switzerland

His was *"The most important contribution yet made to American medicine."* Civil War surgeon, pioneer planner of modern hospitals, early advocate of preventive medicine. Billings published the Surgeon-General's first medical Index Catalogue in 1880.

ID 78.1966.1

CL Erected by Indiana Sesquicentennial Commission, 1966

D SR 250 & Lake Geneva Road, SW corner at Allendale Village, west of East Enterprise & south of Allensville

Dr. Elwood Mead (1858-1936)

ID 78.1980.1

CL Switzerland County Historical Society, 1980

D SR 250 & SR156, NE corner, one block west of Ohio River, Patriot

Portrait of Dr. Elwood Mead, Patriot, Switzerland County, Indiana Picture Collection, MS. Section, Indiana State Library.

"Engineer Who Made the Desert Bloom" Patriot, Ind., native; supervised Hoover Dam construction in Colorado R.; Lake Mead named for him; appointed Director, U.S. Bureau of Reclamation, President Coolidge; served under Presidents Hoover and Roosevelt, top authority on irrigation, reclamation.

Tippecanoe Battleground 2.1 Miles East

ID 79.19??.1

CL Indiana Historical Bureau

D West side of SR 43 at Prophet's Rock Road & Burnetts Road, 0.2 mile south of I-65 exit 178, Battle Ground. Missing

Tippecanoe Battlefield, map, Battle Ground, Tippecanoe County, from J. P. Dunn's, Indiana & Indianans, Vol. I, paage 265, 1919.

Urged by the Prophet, Tecumseh's brother, Indians attacked army of Gen. W. H. Harrison Nov. 7, 1811. The victory by Harrison broke Indian power.

Tecumseh Trail

Portrait of Tecumseh, from J. P. Dunn's, Indiana & Indianans, Vol. I, page 272, 1919.

ID 79.1953.1

CL Women's Civic Council of Tippecanoe County

D SR 43, 3.8 miles north of SR 43 & State Street at roadside park adjacent to Wabash River, West Lafayette

Used by Indian tribes and often traveled by Chief Tecumseh prior to defeat of his warriors by Gen. William Henry Harrison at the Battle of Tippecanoe on November 7, 1811.

Major General Joseph J. Reynolds 1822-1899

Living in Lafayette at the outbreak of the Civil War he recruited and trained Indiana soldiers, served as Colonel of the 10th Regiment, helped secure West Virginia for the Union and was breveted for his action at Chickamauga and Missionary Ridge.

Portrait of Major General Joseph J. Reynolds, Lafayette, Tippecanoe County, Indiana Picture Collection, MS. Section, Indiana State Library.

ID 79.1963.2

CL Indiana Civil War Centennial Commission 1963

D In storage.

The Wabash River

79.1973.1

Erected by the Indiana Historical Society 1973

SR 43, Mascouten Park & boat ramp adjacent to Wabash River, 1.1 miles north of intersection of SR 43 & State Street, West Lafayette

The Wabash River, Tippecanoe County.

Side one:
was called "Wah-bah-shik-ki" by the Miami. The French called it the "Oua-ba-che." It was the principal route connecting Quebec and New Orleans. The Miami, Potawatomi, Mascouten, Wea, Kickapoo, and Piankashaw Indians lived in the Wabash Valley. Along the river the French established Fort Ouiatanon (1717) and Post Vincennes (1732). The French lost their empire to the British in 1763. The Ottawa chief, Pontiac, who led a revolt against the British, made peace (1765) with the British at Ouiatanon.

Side two:
During the American Revolution George Rogers Clark seized Vincennes and Ouiatanon from the British. In 1778, Lt. Governor Henry Hamilton moved a force of 350 soldiers and Indians to Vincennes by the Wabash route. Clark captured his command in February of 1779. In the 19th century both flatboats and steamboats used the Wabash. By 1852 the Wabash and Erie Canal linked the Great Lakes with the Ohio. The Wabash has been a major highway for travel, trade, and settlement for two centuries. In song and in story it symbolizes Indiana.

Tippecanoe

Perrin Historic District

Perrin Historic District, Lafayette, Tippecanoe County.

ID 79.1992.1

CL Erected 1992 Indiana Historical Bureau and Perrin Neighborhood

D 205 Perrin & Main Streets, east of downtown Lafayette

Platted in 1873, this district was Lafayette's first planned residential area which conformed to geographic contours. It was developed by James J. Perrin, Margaret Cason Perrin, Edward Asher, and Consider Tinkler. Listed in National Register of Historic Places, 1979.

Cairo Skywatch Tower

Operation Skywatch Statue, Tippecanoe County.

ID 79.1995.1

CL Erected 1995 Indiana Historical Bureau.

D CRs 850 N & 100 W, Memorial Park, Cairo

U.S. Air Force commissioned observation tower August 16, 1952 for Operation Skywatch, part of Civilian Ground Observation Corps during Korean War. Constructed by community volunteers. Approximately ninety people alternated shifts to maintain twenty-four-hour watch for enemy planes because there was no national radar system.

Highland Park

ID 79.1997.1

CL Erected 1997 Indiana Historical Bureau and Highland Park Neighborhood Association.

D Between Highland & Pontiac Avenues along Miami Street in the triangle park, south of downtown Lafayette

Neighborhood in late-Victorian "landscape garden suburb" style, designed by Cincinnati firm, Earnshaw and Punshon. Platted 1891, 1893. Houses are of a wide variety of architectural styles. Important for this suburban development was 1892 spur on existing 1888 electric streetcar system. Listed in National Register of Historic Places, 1996.

Highland Park

ID 79.1997.2

CL Erected 1997 Indiana Historical Bureau and Highland Park Neighborhood Association.

D Intersection of Wea & Cherokee Avenues, Lafayette.

Neighborhood in late-Victorian "landscape garden suburb" style, designed by Cincinnati firm, Earnshaw and Punshon. Platted 1891, 1893. Houses are of a wide variety of architectural styles. Important for this suburban development was 1892 spur on existing 1888 electric streetcar system. Listed in National Register of Historic Places, 1996.

Centennial Historic District

Centennial Historic District, Lafayette, Tippecanoe County.

ID 79.1998.1

CL Erected 1998 Indiana Historical Bureau and Centennial Neighborhood Association.

D 6th & Brown Streets at entrance to Centennial Park, Lafayette

Area platted as Bartholomew and Davis Addition, 1829. Neighborhood grew rapidly during citywide expansion after canal (1843) and railroad (1853) arrived. Most structures, of many architectural styles, built 1870-1910. Named after Centennial School, at this site, 1876-1971. Listed in National Register of Historic Places, 1983.

Fort Ouiatenon

Fort Ouiatenon, (reconstruction) West Lafayette, Tippecanoe County.

ID 79.1998.2

CL Erected 1998 Indiana Historical Bureau and The Society of Colonial Wars in the State of Indiana.

D Fort Ouiatenon Historic Park adjacent to blockhouse, S. River Road, 4 miles SW of West Lafayette. Replaces 79.1947.1

First post in Indiana area built nearby in 1717 by French Canada to counter British expansion in valleys of Wabash and Ohio rivers. Served as trade and communication post. French surrendered fort to British in 1761 during the French and Indian War. Fort was occupied by Native Americans after 1763 and destroyed by American soldiers 1791.

Tippecanoe

Ninth Street Hill Neighborhood Historic District

ID 79.2001.1

CL Installed 2001 Indiana Historical Bureau and Historic Ninth Street Hill Neighborhood Association

D 904 State Street at 9th, NE corner, Lafayette

Ninth Street Hill Neighborhood Historic District, Lafayette, Tippecanoe County.

Side one:
Lafayette platted 1825. This area was first known as Prospect Hill. Wealthy families built country estates here 1850s-1860s. Streetcar lines of 1880s transformed Hill into popular suburb. Area declined after World War II.
Side two:
This neighborhood district showcases many American domestic architectural styles from 1850s through 1950s. Revitalization began in 1970s. Neighborhood association founded 1986. Listed in National Register of Historic Places 1997.

Tipton

New Purchase Boundary (Treaty of St. Mary's)

ID 80.1966.1

CL Erected by Indiana Sesquicentennial Commission, 1966

D 2 blocks north of Jefferson Street/SR 28 & SR 19 intersection, Tipton

In October 1818, Purchasing Commissioners Lewis Cass, Benjamin Parke and Governor Jonathan Jennings acquired Indian claims on the land shown on this marker. About one-third of modern Indiana was involved in this transaction. [map]

Tipton

Tipton County Courthouse

Tipton County Courthouse, Tipton.

Romanesque Classical Revival Style building designed by Adolph Scherrer, architect of the 1888 Indiana State Capitol. It is Tipton County's third courthouse and was completed, 1894; placed in National Register of Historic Places, 1984; restored, 1988-1991.

ID 80.1994.1

CL Erected 1994 Indiana Historical Bureau and Tipton County Historical Society

D North entrance of courthouse, Tipton

Union

Maj. Gen. Ambrose E. Burnside 1824-1881

Portrait of Major General Ambrose E. Burnside, Liberty, Union County, Indiana Picture Collection, MS. Section, Indiana State Library.

Born in Liberty, Indiana, Ambrose E. Burnside invented the breech-loading rifle in 1856. Commanded a brigade at First Bull Run and the Army of the Potomac at Fredericksburg. He was commander of the Army of Ohio when Morgan's Raiders were captured.

ID 81.1963.1

CL Erected by the Indiana Civil War Centennial Commission, 1963

D Main & Union Streets, NW lawn, Courthouse Square, Liberty.

Wabash and Erie Canal

ID 82.1947.1

CL Indiana Historical Bureau

D SE corner of Vanderburgh Courthouse lawn, 5th & Vine Streets, Evansville

Completed from Lake Erie to Evansville, 1853. Used till 1865. Passing from 5th St. to 1st Ave., canal widened into basin for docks covering part of this square.

First SWCD In Indiana

ID 82.1976.1

CL none

D Booneville-New Harmony Road, Vanderburgh County 4-H Center, Darmstadt

The first Soil and Water Conservation District in Indiana was organized here in 1940 -- the last in Tipton County in 1974. The contribution of these districts to the conservation and wise use of soil and water resources has been of great social, economic, and environmental benefit to Indiana. The citizens of Vanderburgh County are recognized for their pioneering leadership.

P-47 Thunderbolt Factory

Republic Aviation Corporation, located on this site, was an essential part of Evansville's World War II defense industry. Over 5,000 men and women manufactured 6,242 P-47 Thunderbolts, 1942-1945. P-47 was principal WW II fighter plane, known for its speed, durability, and reliability.

ID 82.1995.1

CL Erected 1995 Indiana Historical Bureau, Vanderburgh County Historical Society, and Whirlpool Corporation

D 5401 US 41 N, east side of highway at Whirlpool Factory (as of 12/2003) visitors entrance, Evansville

Evansville Cotton Mill

Several buildings (1874) remain of Evansville Cotton Manufacturing Co., 1867-circa 1900. It was a major employer on lower Ohio River. Most workers were women. Accessibility of raw cotton via river, coal from local mines, and railroad transportation attracted mill. Infant food products manufactured here since 1916.

ID 82.1996.1

CL Erected 1996 Indiana Historical Bureau

D Bristol Myers Squibb facility, St. Joseph Avenue/SR 62, south of Ohio Street, Evansville

McCurdy-Sears Building

ID 82.1999.1

CL Erected 1999 Indiana Historical Bureau, Vanderburgh County Historical Society, and Old National Bancorp

D McCurdy-Sears Building is located at 101 NW 4th Street. The marker is situated at 5th & Sycamore Streets at a parking lot entrance behind the building, Evansville

McCurdy-Sears Building, Evansville, Vanderburgh County.

Side one:
Built in 1920 for financier and philanthropist William H. McCurdy (1853-1930), president of Old National Bank. Constructed of reinforced concrete with poured concrete floors, employing architectural developments newly pioneered for industrial buildings. Building leased by Sears, Roebuck and Company in 1925 for retail use.
Side two:
This very successful store was Sears' first retail outlet located outside a mail order city. Sears' expansion to department stores was prompted by population shifts from rural to urban areas. Building was remodeled and enlarged 1937, 1943, 1946. Store closed 1975. Renovated and restored 1991. Building listed in National Register of Historic Places 1979.

Ohio River Levee

Ohio River Levee, Dress Plaza, Evansville, Vanderburgh County.

ID 82.2003.1

CL Installed 2003 Indiana Historical Bureau, Vanderburgh County Historical Society, and Evansville-Vanderburgh Levee Authority District

D Eastern portion of Dress Plaza along the Ohio River in downtown Evansville, near the intersection of Walnut Street & Riverside Drive

Side one:
U.S. Congress passed flood control acts 1936-1938 after disastrous floods, including one on Ohio River when water crested at 53.7 feet in Evansville January 31, 1937. This project authorized August 1937; U.S. Army Corps of Engineers began construction 1939. Levee protects residents of city and county from flood water level up to 57 feet.
Side two:
Project, maintained and operated by Evansville-Vanderburgh Levee Authority District, consists of 17 miles of earth levees and concrete floodwalls to prevent flooding from the Ohio River, 19 pumping stations to remove rainwater from the city into the river, and gated structures to prevent flooding through pipes and roadways. Work completed 1994.

Vanderburgh

Sheriff's Residence and Jail

ID 82.2007.1

CL Installed 2007 Indiana Historical Bureau, Woods & woods, LLP, and Vanderburgh County Historical Society

D 208 NW 4th St., Evansville.

Side one: Vanderburgh County formed, Evansville named county seat 1818. This castle-like structure was completed 1890 for county's fourth jail and second sheriff's residence. Stone exterior has step-gables, projecting turrets, crenellated roof lines, simulated portcullis, and central, rounded tower. Tunnel connects the jail to the 1890 courthouse.
Side two: Jail and residence were the focal point of a race riot July 1903, which lasted several days; twelve people were killed and many more injured. County functions moved out 1969. Listed in National Register of Historic Places 1970. County jails were first established 1792 under territorial laws and were included in state constitutions of 1816 and 1851.

Vermillion

Harrison's Crossing - November 3, 1811

ID 83.1960.1

CL Erected by the Indiana Society of Pioneers in cooperation with the Vermillion County Histori-cal Society and the Harrison Trail Commis-sion 1960

D North bound lane of SR 63, 100 yards north of Vermilliion River bridge across from the North Vermillion High School, Cayuga

100 yards south, Harrison's Army crossed the Big Vermillion at sunrise, having just built Boyd's Blockhouse, enroute to the Prophet's Town at the mouth of the Tippecanoe to disperse the Indians there assembled.

Newport Covered Bridge

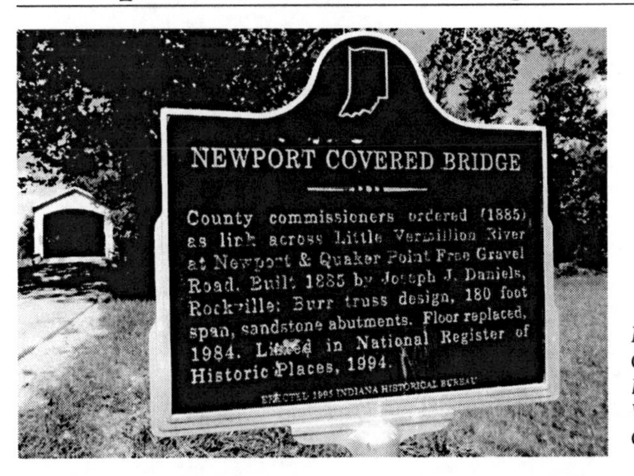

Newport Covered Bridge, marker, Vermillion County.

County commissioners ordered (1885) as link across Little Vermillion River at Newport & Quaker Point Free Gravel Road. Built 1885 by Joseph J. Daniels, Rockville: Burr Truss design, 180 foot span, sandstone abutments. Floor replaced, 1984. Listed in National Register of Historic Places, 1994.

ID 83.1995.1

CL Erected 1995 Indiana Historical Bureau

D CR 50 S, south end of Newport Covered Bridge over Little Vermillion River, Newport.

Eugene Covered Bridge

Eugene Covered Bridge, Vermillion County.

County commissioners ordered (1873) to replace unsafe bridge over Big Vermillion River at Eugene. Built 1873 by Joseph J. Daniels, Rockville: Burr truss design, 180 foot span, using existing abutments. Closed to vehicle traffic, 1974. Listed in National Register of Historic Places, 1994.

ID 83.1995.2

CL Erected 1995 Indiana Historical Bureau

D N. Main/CR 00 & CR 100 W over Big Vermillion River, south end of bridge, Eugene

The Hillsdale Steps

ID 83.1997.1

CL Erected 1997 Indiana Historical Bureau & Friends and Residents of Hillsdale

D Lincoln & Second Streets, Hillsdale

The Hillsdale Steps, Vermillion County.

Hillsdale platted 1872. Railroads were instrumental in town's development. Businesses located near depot at base of hill; residential areas were built on side and top of hill. Concrete steps were constructed 1903 by John H. Self to facilitate access to town areas. These "stone" steps provide a scenic connection with the community's past.

Vermillion County Jail

ID 83.2001.1

CL Installed 2001 Indiana Historical Bureau and Vermillion County Indiana Historical Society, Inc.

D 220 E. Market Street, Vermillion County Historical Society, Newport

Side one:
First county jail built 1828 of logs at southwest corner of courthouse lawn. Second jail built 1836 of brick. Third jail and sheriff's residence built 1868 of brick in Italianate Style. This 1868 structure became sheriff's residence only, when jail addition built 1896 of rusticated stone in Romanesque Revival Style.
Side two:
Facility ceased operation 1992. Structure owned by Vermillion County Historical Society since 1992. Listed in National Register of Historic Places 1999. County jails were first established in 1792 under laws of the Northwest Territory; they continued under laws of the Indiana Territory and state constitutions of 1816 and 1851.

Terre Haute

The home of Paul Dresser, author of the state song, "On the Banks of the Wabash." Located close to national center of population, city noted for industry, mining, transportation, education.

ID 84.1947.2

CL Terre Haute Chamber of Commerce

D Dresser Drive and 1st Street, Fairbanks Park, Terre Haute. Missing

Vigo

Birthplace of Paul Dresser (1859-1906)

Birthplace of Paul Dresser (1859-1906), Terre Haute, Vigo County.

ID 84.1966.1

CL Erected by the Indiana Historical Bureau, 1966

D Dresser Drive & 1st Streets, Fairbanks Park, Terre Haute.

Composer of Indiana State Song, "On the Banks of the Wabash," and other songs popular in the Gay Nineties. His famous brother, Theodore Dreiser, wrote *An American Tragedy* and other novels.

Chauncey Rose 1794-1877

ID 84.1966.2

CL Erected by Indiana Historical Bureau. 1966

D NE corner Chestnut & Seventh Streets, Terre Haute

Portrait of Chauncey Rose (1794-1877), Terre Haute, Vigo County, Indiana Picture Collection, MS. Section, Indiana State Library.

Home of early business and civic leader who built his fortune on honesty, frugality and hard work. He used his wealth generously for the care of orphans, medicine for the sick and the education of youth.

Birthplace of Paul Dresser (1859)-(one block west)

ID 84.1966.3

CL Erected by Indiana Sesquicentennial Commission, 1966

D In the median at Third and Farrington Streets, Terre Haute

Composer of Indiana's State Song, "On the Banks of the Wabash", "My Gal Sal", and many more, popular in the gay 90's era. His famous brother, author Theodore Dreiser, wrote *An American Tragedy* and other novels.

Eugene Victor Debs 1855-1926

ID 84.1976.1

CL Erected by Eugene V. Debs Foundation 1976

D SW corner of Marks Field, Indiana State University, Terre Haute. Missing

Portrait of Eugene V. Debs, Terre Haute, Vigo County, Indiana Picture Collecton, MS. Section, Indiana State Library.

Father of industrial unionism, five time Socialist candidate for President of the United States, pacifist, humanitarian. Birthplace marker, one block east on North Fourth Street; home, 451 North Eighth Street.

[Charles Gene Abrell]

This bridge commemorates the memory of CHARLES GENE ABRELL, Corporal, First Marines of the United States First Marine Division, posthumous holder of the Congressional Medal of Honor. Born August 12, 1931. Died June 10, 1951.

ID 84.1982.1

CL Erected by Indiana War Memorials Commission and United War Veterans Council of Vigo County, 1982

D SR 63 at Wabash River, north side of city, Terre Haute

Home of Eugene V. Debs

Debs (1855-1926) was leading pioneer in industrial unionism, social reformer, and peace advocate. Founded American Railway Union, 1893; cofounded American Socialist Party, 1900; and ran five times for United States presidency. Home built in 1890; declared National Historic Landmark, 1966.

ID 84.1992.1

CL Erected 1992 Indiana Historical Bureau and Eugene V. Debs Foundation

D 451 N. Eighth Street, Terre Haute

Union Hospital

Union Hospital, Terre Haute, Vigo County.

In 1892, near this site, Union Hospital was founded by Leo J. Weinstein, M.D., and Benjamin F. Swafford, M.D., with the support of local citizens. This hospital established Terre Haute's first School of Nursing in 1900.

ID 84.1992.2

CL Erected 1992 Indiana Historical Bureau and Union Hospital, Inc.

D NW corner, 1606 N. Seventh Street & 8th Avenue, Terre Haute

Birthplace of the Coca-Cola Bottle

ID 84.1994.1

CL Erected 1994 Indiana Historical Bureau, Vigo County Historical Society, the Coca-Cola Company

D NE corner, Third & Voorhees Streets, Terre Haute

World-famous trademark created in 1915 on this site at Root Glass Company, by Chapman J. Root, T. Clyde Edwards, Earl R. Dean, and Alexander Samuelson. Bottle design selected in national competition. [illustration]

Crossroads of America

ID 84.1998.1

CL Erected 1998 Indiana Historical Bureau and Vigo County Historical Society, replacing 1988 marker.

D NW corner of Seventh Street & Wabash Avenue, Terre Haute

Crossroads of America, marker, Terre Haute, Vigo County.

U.S. Highway 40, the old National Road which opened the west for settlement, and U.S. Highway 41, a major north-south route, were designated part of the original federal highway system in 1926. Their intersection in Terre Haute at Wabash Avenue and Seventh Street became the "Crossroads of America."

Markle Mill Site

ID 84.2001.1

CL Installed 2001 Indiana Historical Bureau and Leadership Terre Haute

D 4900 Mill Dam Road, Terre Haute. Missing

Abraham Markle (1770-1826) had gristmill and dam built here 1817. Mill had an early horizontal water wheel in a splatter box located within the stone foundation of the structure. Wooden part of mill destroyed by fire 1938. Markle was one of founders of Terre Haute Land Company. Also ran nearby general store, sawmill, and distillery.

Wea Tribe at Terre Haute

Vigo

Side One:
This bountiful area on the Wabash River was occupied early by American Indians. French and later Americans recognized this strategic area called terre haute (high land). At least one Wea village was present in area by late 1700s. Wea Chief Jacco Godfroy and others ceded these lands to U.S. in 1809. Town of Terre Haute platted by Americans 1816.
Side two:
Before leaving for 1824 meeting with U.S. agents, Chief Jacco and others ran a notice in the Terre Haute newspaper, which said they were leaving their "wives and children in the white settlement and . . . solicit the white people not to mal-treat them." Most Wea were forced to move from Indiana. Descendants of Chief Jacco still live in Indiana.

ID 84.2004.1

CL Installed 2004 Indiana Historical Bureau and Native American Foundation of Western Indiana

D Fairbanks Park, First & Oak Streets, Terre Haute

Camp Wabash 1862-65

Wabash

Site of 11th Congressional District military camp used to rendezvous, recruit and organize the 75th, 89th, 101st, 118th and 153rd Indiana Regiments during the Civil War.

ID 85.1962.1

CL Erected by Indiana Civil War Centennial Commission 1962

D NW corner Chestnut & Columbus Streets along Wabash River, Wabash

First Electrically Lighted City

ID 85.1966.1

CL Erected by Indiana Sesquicentennial Commission, 1966

D Wabash County Courthouse, SE lawn, Wabash Street, Wabash

On March 31, 1880, officials of Wabash began experimenting with Charles F. Brush's carbon-arc lights. Four 3,000 candlepower lamps were placed atop the courthouse and used to illuminate the town until September, 1888.

Frances Slocum

ID 85.1967.1

CL Society of Indiana Pioneers, 1967

D Frances Slocum Cemetery entrance, CRs 650 W & 900 S, Mississinewa Lake, Somerset

Frances Slocum Grave, Somerset, Wabash County.

Captured as a child by the Delaware Indians in 1778 from her Pennsylvania home, she grew up with the Indians, married a Miami chief, and lived in Indiana till her death, 1847.

Paradise Spring Treaty Ground

Paradise Spring Treaty Ground, Kin-com-a-ong Spring, Wabash, Wabash County.

ID 85.1992.1

CL Erected 1992 Indiana Historical Bureau and Wabash County Tourism

D Allen & Market Streets, Paradise Spring Historical Park, Wabash

At treaty ground (two blocks east) in October, 1826, Potawatomi and Miami tribes signed treaties with the United States ceding lands north of the Wabash River. The treaties included provisions for land for a canal and the Michigan Road.

Miami Indian Mills

Miami Indian Mills, Mill Stone, Richvalley, Wabash County.

ID 85.1995.1

CL Erected 1995 Indiana Historical Bureau and Richvalley Lions Club.

D Mill & Jefferson Streets, Community Center and Lions Club, Richvalley

This millstone is a remnant of the grist and saw mills built near here for Miami Indians by United States government as part of 1818 Treaty of St. Mary's. Treaty also established several Miami reservations in area. Possibly first industrial site in what became Wabash County.

St. Patrick's Roman Catholic Church

ID 85.2000.1

CL Installed 2000 Indiana Historical Bureau and Eugene and Anne Driscoll Family

D Main & Harrison Streets, Lagro

St. Patrick's Roman Catholic Church, Front Entrance, Lagro, Wabash County.

Side one:
Congregation founded 1836, serving Irish who immigrated to area to work on construction of Wabash and Erie Canal, 1834-1837. Many Irish bought land and stayed as permanent residents using their religious and cultural interests to build Lagro, originally platted 1834, into a thriving trade center.
Side two:
Church dedicated first building 1838; used for activities until razed in 1960s. This brick structure, built 1870-1873, designed in Victorian Gothic Style; original bell still in use. Brick made in Huntington and Lagro. Features include hand-carved altars and statues, stained glass windows, and oak and walnut curved stairway. Listed in National Register of Historic Places 1999.

Brethren Annual Meetings

Side one: Church of the Brethren founded 1708 in Europe. By 1778, Brethren met annually to determine church policy. First annual meeting in Indiana was in Elkhart County 1852. North Manchester Church of the Brethren hosted annual meetings 1878, 1888, 1900; last two meetings held here in Harter's Grove. Had enormous social and economic impact on area.
Side two: Business meetings and preaching by prominent Brethren leaders drew thousands from U.S. In a fair-like atmosphere, visitors had access to modern conveniences of the time, including in 1888, electric lamps. Area residents cooperated in providing visitors with housing, transportation, vast quantities of food, goods, and clean, running water.

ID 85.2006.1

CL Installed 2006 Indiana Historical Bureau and North Manchester Historical Society

D Harter's Grove, Warvel Park, west of Market Street, between 7th and 9th Streets, North Manchester

Thomas Riley Marshall

Side one: Born 1854 in North Manchester in this house on Main Street. Was Governor of Indiana 1909–1913. Under his leadership, Indiana General Assembly enacted legislation, called the "Marshall Constitution," to improve government efficiency by amending the Constitution. Indiana Supreme Court declared the legislation unconstitutional July 5, 1912.
Side two: He was elected vice president under Woodrow Wilson. Marshall generally supported Wilson's proposals. He refused to assume powers of presidency after Wilson's stroke in 1919, believing it would be unconstitutional. Marshall was only the third vice president to serve two full terms. He died 1925 and is buried in Crown Hill Cemetery, Indianapolis.

ID 85.2007.1

CL Installed 2007 Indiana Historical Bureau and North Manchester Historical Society

D 405 North Market Street, North Manchester.

Williamsport, Warren County

ID 86.1992.1

CL Erected 1992 Indiana Historical Bureau.

D Warren County Courthouse lawn, Williamsport

Williamsport, Warren County Seat, was home, 1879-1896, of James Frank Hanly, Governor of Indiana, 1905-1909. The courthouse, built 1907, was designed by J.W. Royer, Urbana, Illinois. Warren County was established 1827.

Pine Village Football

ID 86.2002.1

CL Installed 2002 Indiana Historical Bureau, Pine Village Town Board, Businessmen, and Lions Club

D SR 55 at Pine Village Fire Station, Pine Village.

Side one: Local team was important Indiana precursor to modern professional football organizations. Clinton Beckett introduced football to Pine Village High School 1898. Town and high school teams played on bottomland, northwest of here, starting local football tradition. Town team, the Villagers, managed by C. J. Shackleton and later by Claire Rhode.

Side two: Team became "professional" 1915, claiming state and regional championships. Jim Thorpe, All-American, played for Villagers in 1915 Thanksgiving Day game against Purdue All-Stars; Villagers won 29 to 0. Team was a founder of Indiana Football League 1917. Following World War I, the Villagers played intermittently until 1927.

Angel Mounds

Angel Mounds, Mound B, Evansville, Vanderburgh County.

ID 87.1966.1

CL Erected by Indiana Sesquicentennial Commission, 1966

D Angel Mounds State Historic Site, 8215 Pollack Avenue, Evansville

Site of a palisaded Middle Mississippi Indian village occupied circa 1500 A.D. This 450 acre site includes eleven man-made mounds, town plaza and village area for a population of about 1,000. Excavated by the Indiana Historical Society, 1939-1965.

Morgan's Raid July 8-13, 1863

Morgan's Raid, Salem, Washington County, Indiana Picture Collection, MS. Section, Indiana State Library.

ID 88.1963.1

CL Erected by the Indiana Civil War Centennial Commission, 1963

D South side of Washington County Courthouse, Salem

At this point Gen. John Hunt Morgan routed poorly armed militia and occupied Salem - July 10, 1863. The town was looted and $1,000 ransom exacted from each mill owner.

Brock Cemetery

ID 88.1981.1

CL Erected with donations by the Washington County Cemetery Commission, 1982

D SR 135 at Brock Creek bridge, SW corner, 0.5 mile north of Salem

Located 40 rods west of this spot. Est. before 1812. Salem's early settlers are buried here including Brocks, Kemps, Hendersons; also John Zink, a ranger with Col. Dawalt, fatally wounded by Indians after the Pigeon Roost Massacre.

Illinoian Glacier Boundary

ID 88.1995.1

CL Erected 1995 Indiana Historical Bureau.

D NE corner of SR 135 & Lick Skillet Road, 8 miles north of Salem

Nearby is the boundary of the Illinoian Glacier, which covered all but approximately 6,250 square miles in south, central area of Indiana. Most of Indiana's topography was affected by four separate glacial advancements during Pleistocene epoch, circa one million years ago.

Washington County Courthouse/ Salem Downtown Historic District

Washington County Courthouse, Salem.

ID 88.1998.1

CL Erected 1998 Indiana Historical Bureau and Washington County Community Foundation.

D North side of Washington County Courthouse, Salem

Side one:
County formed 1814 by General Assembly of Indiana Territory. Commissioners selected county seat and named it Salem. This third courthouse completed 1888 using locally quarried limestone. Designed in Richardsonian Romanesque Style by Harry P. McDonald, Louisville. Listed in National Register of Historic Places, 1980.
Side two:
Town platted 1814; historic district area includes original plat. Continues as geographical, governmental, business, and social center of county. Nineteenth and early twentieth century commercial buildings-in Italianate, Gothic, and Classical styles-surround public square. Listed in National Register of Historic Places 1997.

Washington

Skirmish Near Pekin

ID 88.2005.1

CL Installed 2005 Indiana Historical Bureau and East Washington Lions Club

D Near 5751 East Greenbriar Road West, Pekin

Side one:
On July 8, 1863, Confederate General John Hunt Morgan and his men crossed the Ohio River at Brandenburg, Kentucky and entered Indiana. As a diversion on July 11, Confederate Captain William J. Davis and his troops crossed the Ohio River at Twelve Mile Island, Kentucky and were attacked. Davis and part of his force escaped into Indiana.
Side two:
Heading to Salem on July 11, Davis and some of his men were captured near Pekin by 73rd Indiana Volunteers and a detachment of the 5th U.S. Regulars. Davis and several other soldiers were taken to New Albany and secured in the county jail. On July 13, Morgan's Indiana raid ended as he rode east out of Harrison on the Indiana-Ohio state border.

Wayne

Oliver P. Morton Home

ID 89.1962.1

CL Erected by the Indiana Civil War Centennial Commission 1962.

D US 40/W. Main Street & Willow Grove Road, Centerville

Oliver P. Morton, Civil War Governor (1861-1867), Centerville, Wayne County, Indiana Governors' Portraits Collection, Indiana Historical Bureau.

Residence of Oliver P. Morton, Governor of Indiana during the crucial years of the American Civil War, 1861-65. U.S. Senator, 1867-77. Morton was the first native-born governor of Indiana.

Iron Brigade Commander

One-quarter mile south of this marker is the home of General Solomon A. Meredith, Iron Brigade Commander at Gettysburg. Born in North Carolina, Meredith was an Indiana political leader and post-war Surveyor-General of Montana Territory.

ID 89.1963.1

CL Erected by Indianapolis Civil War Roundtable and Indiana Historical Society 1963

D US 40/W. Main Street & South Gay Street, Cambridge City

East Germantown Civil War Band

Band organized in East Germantown; members enlisted in 1862. Assigned to the Twelfth Regiment of Indiana Volunteers. Fought with General Ulysses S. Grant. Marched with General William T. Sherman from Atlanta to sea.

ID 89.1978.1

CL Erected in Memory of D. W. Kocher

D US 40 & Milton Street/ Germantown Road, East Germantown/ Pershing

Overbeck House and Studio

Overbeck Home & Studio, Cambridge City, Wayne County.

Indiana's first art pottery, a nationally-recognized product of the American Arts and Crafts Movement, was produced 1911-1955 by the Overbeck sisters. Their 1830s Federal Style house, one block south, was listed in National Register of Historic Places, 1976.

ID 89.1992.1

CL Erected 1992 Indiana Historical Bureau and Jerry and Phyllis Mattheis

D US 40/E. Main and S. Pearl Streets, Cambridge City

Cambridge City

ID 89.1992.2

CL Erected 1992 By Indiana Historical Bureau

D US 40/E. Main & Foote Streets, Cambridge City

Cambridge City, Historic District, Wayne County.

A transportation center, platted 1836 along the Whitewater River, the Cumberland/National Road, and the Whitewater Canal route. Four steam railroads served the town; interurban electric railroad opened 1903. Cambridge City Historic District listed in National Register, 1991.

Levi Coffin

Levi Coffin Home, State Historic Site, Fountain City, Wayne County.

ID 89.2002.1

CL Installed 2002 Indiana Historical Bureau and Levi Coffin House Association, Inc.

D 113 US 27 North, Fountain City

Side one:
Levi Coffin (1798-1877), a Quaker abolitionist, lived in Newport (now Fountain City) with his family 1826-1847. Moved from North Carolina because he and his wife, Catharine, opposed slavery. Advocated, and sold in his store, free-labor products not produced by slaves. House built circa 1839; designated a National Historic Landmark 1966.
Side two:
Coffin's *Reminiscences* (1876) documented work in Underground Railroad and antislavery movement. The Underground Railroad refers to a widespread network of diverse people in the nineteenth century who aided slaves escaping to freedom from the southern U.S.

Indiana's First Woman's Rights Convention

ID 89.2003.1

CL Installed 2003 Indiana Historical Bureau, Indiana Women's History Association, Indiana Commission for Women, and Town of Dublin

D 2224 Cumberland Road/US 40 & Davis Street, Dublin

Side one:
A convention was called for by reform-minded Congregational Friends meeting at Greensboro, Henry County, January 1851. Convention held October 14-15, 1851 at Dublin adopted resolutions for political, social, and financial rights for women. Women and men who favored abolition, temperance, and suffrage attended.
Side two:
The 1852 convention formed Indiana Woman's Rights Association to promote united action for woman's rights. Association's 1853 convention demanded equality in all political rights and functions. It voted to be auxiliary to American Woman Suffrage Association 1870. It became Indiana Woman's Suffrage Association.

Charles C. Deam

Portrait of Charles C. Deam, Bluffton, Wells County, Indiana Picture Collection, MS. Section, Indiana State Library.

Side one:
Born 1865 near Bluffton; died 1953. Resided most of his life on land south of here where house, study, and arboretum located. A Bluffton druggist, he was avid collector of botanical specimens throughout state 1890s-1920s. Documented important biological transition taking place between eras of virgin forests and intensive agricultural cultivation.
Side two:
Appointed Indiana's first State Forester (1909-1913, 1917-1928); Research Forester 1928-1940. Author of books on trees, shrubs, grasses, and flora of Indiana. Collections in Deam Herbarium, Indiana University and Deam Arboretum, Bluffton. Charles C. Deam National Wilderness Area, 12,953-acre preserve, established in southern Indiana 1982.

ID 90.2001.1

CL Installed 2001 Indiana Historical Bureau and Wells County Historical Society

D Triangle Park, intersection of Wayne & Market near Wabash River, River Road & Washington, Bluffton

The Wolcott House

ID 91.1961.1

CL Erected by Gamma Upsilon Chapter Psi Iota Xi

D 500 N. Range Street/US 24/US 231, north edge of Wolcott

The Wolcott House, White County.

The Wolcott House, marker, White County.

This gracious Italianate home was built c. 1859 by Anson Wolcott, land baron, businessman, attorney, and founder of the town of Wolcott. The plans were drawn by Architect T. Tilly of Chicago. Three generations of the Wolcott family were culturally and politically influential in Indiana and have contributed much to this state.

Indiana Normal [School], 1852-1886

Founded originally as Farmington Academy in the southwest part of town, in 1858 Joseph Baldwin opened the Indiana Normal. This was Indiana's first Normal school and the fifth in the United States.

ID 91.1976.1

CL None

D S. Main & Pearl Streets in front of community center, Burnettsville

Monon, Indiana

Monon, Indiana, Train Caboose, White County.

ID 91.1982.1

CL Presented by the Monon Historical Society, 1982

D US 421/Market Street & E. Third Street, Monon

Monon-Intersection of the New Albany and Salem (org. 1847) and the Indianapolis, Delphi and Chicago (1878) railroads. These roads later merged to become "The Monon Route," Indiana's beloved "Hoosier Line," and provided over a century of passenger service to the state. The "Monon" was known nationwide for fine passenger and dining service until 1967. One of the first 1st class railroads to completely dieselize (1947), it merged with the Louisville & Nashville (L&N) July 30, 1971.

White

Trooper Paul Vincent Minneman

ID 91.1992.1

CL Erected 1992 Indiana Historical Bureau, State Police Alliance, and David Morrison

D NW corner of SR 16 & CR 1450 E adjacent to the United Methodist Church, 0.5 mile west of the Cass-White county line

Site of gun battle May 25, 1937, with infamous Brady Gang after bank robbery in Goodland. Minneman (1904-1937) died from his wounds, the first trooper to be killed by criminals' bullets since formation of Indiana State Police in 1933.

Whitley

Wm. Wells 1770-1812

ID 92.1959.1

CL Erected by the Society of Indiana Pioneers

D Whitley County Museum/Home of Marshall, 108 W. Jefferson Street, Columbia City

Portrait of Wm. Wells (1770-1812), Columbia City, Whitley County, from J. S. Currey's, The Story of Old Ft. Dearborn, page 58, 1912.

Miami captive at 14; adopted by Little Turtle; appointed chief scout by Wayne in 1793; granted farm near Ft. Wayne by Congress for "valiant and conspicuous service." Died in Ft. Dearborn Massacre.

Home of Thomas R. Marshall

Portrait of Thomas R. Marshall (1854-1925), Indiana Governor & U.S. Vice President, Columbia City, Whitley County, Indiana Picture Collection, MS. Section, Indiana State Library.

Born in North Manchester, March 14, 1854, he practiced law in Columbia City until his election as Governor of Indiana (1909-1913). Served two terms as Vice-President (1913-1921). Died June 1, 1925, and was buried in Indianapolis.

ID 92.1966.1

CL Erected by Indiana Sesquicentennial Commission, 1966

D Whitley County Museum/Home of Marshall, 108 W. Jefferson Street, Columbia City

Site of Little Turtle's Miami Village

Portrait of Little Turtle, Columbia City area, Whitley County, from J. P. Dunn's, Indiana & Indianans, Vol. I, page 270, 1919.

Little Turtle (Mishikinoqkwa), c. 1747-1812, was born and raised here on the Eel (Kenapocomoco) River. The Miami village was destroyed by American troops in 1812 and most of the tribe was removed from Indiana by 1843.

ID 92.1966.2

CL Erected by Indiana Sesquicentennial Commission, 1966

D E. Old Trail Road, CR 450 E, 5 miles east of Columbia City

Whitley

Eel River Battlefield - War of 1812

ID 92.2001.1

CL Installed 2001 Indiana Historical Bureau and Youth of First Presbyterian Church

D Junction of S. Raber, E. Mowrey & Paige Roads at the Eel River bridge, NE corner along Paige Road, 2.8 miles SE of Whitley County Courthouse, Columbia City

After General William Henry Harrison relieved Fort Wayne, he ordered Colonel James Simrall in September 1812 to prevent further Miami Indian attacks in the area. The Miamis fled as troops destroyed villages, crops, and supplies along Eel River; Miamis then stood to fight a losing battle on this site.

Kentucky

Battle of Perryville

ID K.Y.1963

CL Erected by the Indiana Civil War Centennial Commission, 1963

D Perryville, Kentucky. Missing.

This marker is dedicated to all the Indiana men who served the Union at the Battle of Perryville. Fourteen regiments of Indiana Volunteers and five batteries of light artillery participated. The dedication and courage of the Hoosier soldiers present were well symbolized by the heroic stand make by Lt. Charles Parsons and his battery at this spot.

Recommended Reading

Allison, Harold. *The Tragic Saga Of The Indiana Indians*. Paducah, Kentucky: Turner Publishing Company, 1986.

Anderson, Harold H. *An Indiana History Of Morgan's Raid*. Wabash, Indiana: self-published by author, 1989.

Baker, Ronald L. *From Needmore To Prosperity: Hoosier Place Names In Folklore And History*. Bloomington: Indiana University Press, 1995.

Baker, Ronald L., and Marvin Carmony. *Indiana Place Names*. Bloomington: Indiana University Press, 1975.

Balesl, Charles John. *The Time Of The French In The Heart Of North America: 1673-1818*. Chicago, Illinois: Alliance Francaise Chicago, 1992.

Barnhart, John D. *The Impact Of The Civil War On Indiana*. Indianapolis, Indiana: Indiana Civil War Centennial Commission, 1962.

Barrows, Robert G., and David J. Bodenhamer, eds. *The Encyclopedia Of Indianapolis*. Bloomington: Indiana University Press, 1994.

Bigham, Darrel E. ed. *Indiana Territory 1800-2000: A Bicentennial Perspective*. Indianapolis: Indiana Historical Society, 2001.

Black, Harry G. *Trails To Hoosier Heritage*. Hammond, Indiana: HMB Publications, 1981.

Black, Harry G. *Highways And Byways Of Indiana*. Hammond, Indiana: HMB Publications, 1988.

Blashfield, Jean F., and Nancy Jacobson. *Awesome Almanac--Indiana*. Fontana, Wisconsin: B & B Publishing, 1993.

Bodnar, John. *Our Towns: Remembering Community In Indiana*. Indianapolis: Indiana Historical Society, 2001.

Boomhower, Ray E. *Destination Indiana: Travels Through Hoosier History*. Indianapolis: Indiana Historical Society, 2000.

Born, Emily. *Power To The People: A History Of Rural Electrification In Indiana*. Indianapolis: Indiana Statewide Associations of Rural Electric Cooperatives, 1985.

Boswell, Jessie P. *Historical Markers And Public Memorials In Indiana, 3rd ed*. Indianapolis: Historical Bureau of the Indiana Library and Historical Department, 1929.

Bowman, Heath. *Hoosier*. Indianapolis, Indiana: Bobbs-Merrill Company, 1941.

Brill, Marlene Targ. *Indiana*. New York:, NY: Benchmark Books, 1977.

Brockman, Paul. *Guide To Ethnic History Collections*. Indianapolis: Indiana Historical Society, 1997.

Buley, R. Carlyle. *The Old Northwest: Pioneer Period 1815-1840, 2 vols*. Bloomington: Indiana University Press, 3rd printing, 1962.

Burgess, Dale W. *Just Us Hoosiers And How We Got That Way*. Indianapolis, Indiana: Unified College Press, 1966.

Carmony, Donald F. *A Brief History Of Indiana*. Indianapolis: Indiana Historical Bureau, 1966.

Carmony, Donald F. *Indiana, 1816-1850: The Pioneer Period*. Indianapolis: Indiana Historical Bureau and Indiana Historical Society, 1998.

Capstone Press Geography Department. *Indiana*. Mankato, Minnesota: Capstone Press, 1997.

Cavinder, Fred D. *More Amazing Tales From Indiana*. Bloomington: Indiana University Press, 2003.

Cavinder, Fred D. *The Indiana Book Of Records, Firsts And Fascinating Facts*. Bloomington: Indiana University Press, 1985.

Cayton, Andrew R. L. *Frontier Indiana*. Bloomington: Indiana University Press, 1996.

Clark, Andrew L. *The Wabash And Erie Canal: The Lower Division*. Mt. Vernon, Indiana: Windmill Publications, 1999.

Clifford, Eth. *Freedom's Road: A History Of The Black People In Indiana*. Indianapolis, Indiana: David-Stewart, 1970.

Cockrum, William Monroe. *Pioneer History Of Indiana*. Oakland City, Indiana: Press of Oakland City Journal, 1907.

County Histories. Too numerous to list all books. Rich sources of local history information.
Counts, Willmer, and John Dilts. *The Magnificent 92: Indiana Courthouses*. Bloomington: Indiana University Press, 1999.
Crenshaw, Gwendolyn J. *Bury Me In A Free Land: The Abolitionist Movement In Indiana 1816-1865*. Indianapolis: Indiana Historical Bureau, 1986.

Deam, Charles C. *Flora Of Indiana*. Indianapolis: Wm. B. Burford Printing for the State of Indiana, 1940.
Delorme. *Indiana Atlas And Gazetteer, 2nd ed.* Yarmouth, Maine: Delorme, 2000.
Dillon, John Brown. *A History Of Indiana From Its Earliest Exploration By Europeans To The Close Of Territorial Government In 1816.* New York, NY: Arco Press, 1971.
Dunn, Craig L. *Iron Men, Iron Will: The 19th Indiana Regiment Of The Iron Brigade.* Indianapolis: Guild Press of Indiana, 1998.

Edmunds, David R. *The Potawatomi: Keepers Of The Fire*. Norman: University of Oklahoma Press, 1978.
Eggleston, Goerge Cary. *Life In Early Indiana.* Fort Wayne, Indiana: Public Library of Fort Wayne and Allen County, 1953.
Esarey, Logan. *The Indiana Home*. Bloomington: Indiana University Press, 4th reprint, 1976.
Fatout, Paul. *Indiana Canals*. West Lafayette, Indiana: Purdue University Studies, 1993.
Funk, Arville L. *Hoosiers In The Civil War*. Chicago, Illinois: Adams Press, 1967.
Funk, Arville L. *Revolutionary War Era In Indiana.* Corydon, Indiana: Alfco Publication, 1975.
Funk, Arville L. *Tales Of Our Hoosier Heritage*. Chicago, Illinois: Adams Press, 1965.
Funk, Arville L. *The Hoosier Scrapbook*. Corydon, Indiana: Alfco Publication, 1981.
Furlong, Patrick J. *Indiana: An Illustrated History.* Northridge, California: Windsor Publication, 1985.

Gibbs, Wilma L., ed. *Indiana's African American Heritage: Essays From Black History News And Notes.* Indianapolis: Indiana Historical Society, 1993.
Gillis, Ruth J. *Indiana Books By Indiana Authors: A Guide To Children's Literature.* Bloomington: Indiana University Press, 1990.
Goodall, Hurley C. *Voices From The Past: A Collection Of References To The African American Community In The State Of Indiana, 2 vols.* Muncie, Indiana: self-published by author, 2000.
Goodall, Hurley C., compiler. *Underground Railroad: The Invisible Road To Freedom Through Indiana.* Muncie, Indiana, self-published by author, 2000.
Gray, Ralph D., compiler and editor. *Indiana History: A Book Of Readings.* Bloomington: Indiana University Press, 1994.
Gray, Ralph D., ed. *The Hoosier State: Readings In Indiana History*. Grand Rapids, Michigan: W. B. Eerdmans Publishing Company, 1980.
Griner, Ned H. *Gas Boom Society.* Muncie, Indiana: Minnetrista Cultural Foundation, 1991.
Gross, Anthony. *The Wit And Wisdom Of Abraham Lincoln*. New York, NY: Barnes and Noble, 1994.

Hamlin-Wilson, Gail, Donald B. Ricky, and Nancy K. Capace. *Encyclopedia Of Indiana Indians: Tribes, Nations And People Of The Woodland Area, 2 vols.* St. Clair Shores, Michigan: Somerset, 1998.
Havighurst, Walter. *The Heartland: Ohio, Indiana, And Illinois*. New York, NY: Harper & Row, 1974.
Hawkins, Hubert H., ed. *Living Indiana History/Heartland Of America.* Indianapolis, Indiana: David-Stewart Publishing, 1967.
Hawkins, Hubert H. *Indiana's Road To Statehood.* Indianapolis: Indiana Sesquicentennial Commission, 1964.
Heiss, Willard, ed. *Indiana Source Book*. Indianapolis: Indiana Historical Society, 1992.
Henry, Joanne Landeers. *A Clearing In The Forest: A Story About A Real Settler Boy*. New York, NY: Four Winds Press, 1992.
Hesser, Leon F. *The Taming Of Our Wilderness: Indiana's Transition From Indian Hunting Grounds To Hoosier Farmland 1800-1875.* Bloomington, Indiana: First Books, 2002.

Hoover, Dwight W., and Jane Rodman. *Pictorial History Of Indiana.* Bloomington: Indiana University Press, 1996 reprint.

Hoppe, David, ed. *Where We Live: Essays About Indiana.* Bloomington: Indiana University Press, 1989.

Horvath, Dennis E., and Terri Horvath. *Indiana Cars: A History Of The Automobile In Indiana.* Indianapolis: Hoosier Auto Share & Swap Meet, Inc., 2002.

Horvath, Dennis and Terri Horvath. *Cruise IN: A Guide To Indiana's Automotive Past And Present:* Indianapolis: Publishing Resources, 1977.

Hunter, Curtis W. *It Happened In Indiana.* Indianapolis: self-published by author, 2001.

Indiana Civil War Centennial Commission. *A Chronology Of Indiana In The Civil War 1861-1865.* Indianapolis: 1965.

Indiana Jewish Historical Society. *Indiana Jewish History.* Fort Wayne, Indiana: Indiana Jewish Historical Society, 1990.

Indiana University, Department Of History. *Indiana Magazine Of History.* Quarterly. Bloomington: Indiana University, Department Of History, 1913-present.

Indiana Women, 150 Years Of Raised Voices: Sesquicentennial Of Indiana's First Woman's Rights Convention, Dublin, Indiana October 14-15, 1851. Indianapolis: Indiana Women's History Association, 2001.

Jackson, Marion T., ed. *The Natural Heritage Of Indiana.* Bloomington: Indiana University Press, 1997.

Jarboe, Betty, and Kathryn Rumsey. *Studies On Indiana: A Bibliography Of Theses And Dissertations Submitted To Indiana Institutions Of Higher Education For Advance Degrees 1902-1977.* Indianapolis: Indiana Historical Bureau, 1980.

Kaelble, Steve. *Indiana: Crossroads Of Industry And Innovation.* Encino, California: Cherbo Publishing Group, 2000.

Knollenberry, Bernhard. *Pioneer Sketches Of The Upper Whitewater Valley, Quaker Stronghold Of The West.* Indianapolis: Indiana Historical Society, 1945.

Leary, Edward A. *The Nineteenth State: Indiana.* Indianapolis: E. Leary & Associates, 1966.

Leffers, Mary Jeanne. *Indiana Invaded: Morgan's Raiders In Indiana.* Bloomington: Guardian Publishing Company, 1994.

Lindsey, Alton A. *Natural Features Of Indiana.* Indianapolis: Indiana Academy of Science, 1966.

Lindley, Harlow. *Indiana As Seen By Early Travelers.* Indianapolis: Indiana Historical Commission, 1916.

Ling, Bettina. *Indiana.* New York, NY: Children's Press, 2003.

Lockridge, Ross F. *The Story Of Indiana.* Oklahoma City, OK: Harlow, Publishing Corporation, 1951.

Long, John Hamilton, ed., and Peggy Tuck Sinko, compiler. *Indiana Atlas Of Historical County Boundaries.* New York, NY: Simon & Schuster, 1996.

Madison, James H. *Indiana Through Tradition And Change: A History Of The Hoosier State And Its People 1920-1945.* Indianapolis: Indiana Historical Society, 1982.

Madison, James H. *The Indiana Way: A State History.* Bloomington & Indianapolis: Indiana University Press and Indiana Historical Society, 1986.

Martin, John B. *Indiana: An Interpretation.* Bloomington: Indiana University Press, 1992.

Marsh, Carole. *Indiana: Most Devastating Disasters & Most Calamitous Catastrophes.* Decatur, Georgia: Gallopade Publishing, 1998.

Marsh, Carole. *Indiana History: Surprising Secrets About Our State's Founding Mothers, Fathers And Kids.* Atlanta, Georgia: Gallopade Publishing, 1997.

Marsh, Carole. *The Hard-To-Believe-But-True Book Of Indiana History, Trivia, Mystery, Legend, Lore And More.* Decatur, Georgia: Gallopade Publishing, 1998.

Miller, John W. *Indiana Newspaper Bibliography 1804-1980.* Indianapolis: Indiana Historical Society, 1982.

McPherson, Alan. *Temples Of Knowledge: Andrew Carnegie's Gift To Indiana.* Kewanna, Indiana: Hoosier's Nest Press, 2003.
McPherson, Alan. *Indian Names In Indiana.* Monticello, Indiana: The Blasted Works Printer, self-published by author, 1993.
McPherson, Alan. *Hoosier: Illustrated Origins Of Indiana's Sobriquet.* Monticello, Indiana: The Blasted Works Printer, self-published by author, 1996.
Moore, Leonard J. *Citizen Klansman: The Ku Klux Klan In Indiana 1921-1928.* Chapel Hill University Of North Carolina Press, 1991.
Moore, Powell, A. *The Calumet Region: Indiana's Last Frontier.* Indianapolis: Indiana Historical Bureau, 1977.
Morris, Harvey. *The Underground Railroad.* Salem, Indiana: Washington County Historical Society, 1993.

Newman, Ralph G. *Preserving Lincoln For The Ages: Collectors, Collections And Our 16th President.* Fort Wayne: Louis A. Warren Lincoln Library And Museum, 1989.
Norberg, John. *Wings Of Their Dreams: Purdue In Flight.* West Lafayette, Indiana: Purdue University Press, 2004.

Peckham, Howard H. *Indiana: A History.* Urbana: University of Illinois Press, 2003.
Phillips, Clifton J. *Indiana In Transition: The Emergence Of An Industrial Commonwealth 1880-1920.* Indianapolis: Indiana Historical Bureau, 1968.
Pohlen, Jerome. *Oddball Indiana: A Guide To Some Really Strange Places.* Chicago, Illinois: Chicago Review Press, 2002.
Price, Nelson. *Indiana Legends: Famous Hoosiers From Johnny Appleseed To David Letterman.* Carmel, Indiana: Guild Press Of Indiana, 1997.

Rafert, Stewart. *The Miami Indians Of Indiana: A Persistent People 1654-1994.* Indianapolis: Indiana Historical Society, 1996.
Ramage, James A. *Rebel Raider: The Life Of General John H. Morgan.* Lexington: University Press of Kentucky, 1986.
Ratts, Stacey, Hayly Lewis, and Lawrie Ragle. *Crossroads Of America: A Portrait Of Historic South Central Indiana.* Marcelene, Missouri: D-Books Publishing, Inc., 2000.
Riley, Martha Chrisman. *Singing Indiana History.* Delphi, Indiana: Riverside Productions, 1992.
Rudolph, L. C., and Judith E. Endelman. *Religion In Indiana: A Guide To Historical Resources.* Bloomington: Indiana University Press, 1986.

Sanders, Craig. *Limited, Locals And Expresses In Indiana 1838-1971.* Bloomington: Indiana University Press, 2003.
Sayers, Evelyn M., ed. *Handbook On Indiana History.* Indianapolis: Indiana Department Of Education, 1987.
Shangle, Barbara. *Discovery Indiana.* Beaverton, Oregon: America Products Publishing, 2000.
Shedd, Randall R. *Indiana Landscapes.* Bloomington: Indiana University Press, 1992.
Shumaker, Arthur W. *History Of Indiana Literature, Prior To World War II.* Indianapolis: Indiana Historical Bureau, 1962.
Sieber, Ellen, and Cheryl A. Munson. *Looking At History: Indiana's Hoosier National Forest Region 1600-1950.* Washington, D. C.: USDA, National Forest Service, 1992.
Simons, Richard S. *Rivers Of Indiana.* Bloomington: Indiana University Press, 1985.
Simons, Richard S., and Francis H. Parker. *Railroads Of Indiana.* Bloomington: Indiana University Press, 1997.
Somerset Publishers. *Indiana Biographical Dictionary.* St. Clair Shores, Michigan: Someset Publishers, 2nd ed., 1999.
Swain, Gwenyth. *Indiana.* Minneapolis, Minnesota: Lerner Publication Corporation, 1992.
Sweeney, Margaret. *Fact, Fiction And Folklore Of Southern Indiana.* New York, NY: Vantage Press, 1967.

Taylor, Robert M., and Connie A. McBirney. *Peopling Indiana: The Ethnic Experience.* Indianapolis: Indiana Historical Society, 1996.

Taylor, Robert M., and Robert G. Burrows. *Indiana Professionals In History: A Directory.* Indianapolis: Indiana Association of Historians and the Indiana Historical Bureau, 1987.

Taylor, Robert M., et al. *Indiana: A New Historical Guide.* Indianapolis: Indiana Historical Society, 1989.

Thompson, Kathleen. *Indiana.* Austin, Texas: Raintree Steck-Vaughn, 1996.

Thompson, Dave O., and William L. Madigan. *150 Years Of Indiana Agriculture.* Indianapolis: Indiana Sesquicentennial Commission, 1966.

Thornbrough, Emma Lou. *Indiana Blacks In The 20th Century.* Bloomington: Indiana University Press, 2000.

Thornbrough, Emma Lou. *This Far By Faith: Black Hoosier Heritage.* Indianapolis: Indiana Committee for the Humanities, 1982.

Thornbrough, Emma Lou. *Indiana In The Civil War Era 1850-1880.* Indianapolis: Indiana Historical Bureau and Indiana Historical Society, 1965.

Trogdon, Wendell. *Winding Are The Roads: Slow Lanes, Scenic Routes.* Mooresville, Indiana: Backroads Press, 2002.

Trogdon, Wendall. *Backroads Indiana.* Evanston, Illinois: Highlander Press, 1994.

Troyer, Byron L. *Yesterday's Indiana.* Miami, Florida: E. A. Seemann Publishing Company, 1975.

Van Allen, Elizabeth J. *James Whitcomb Riley: A Life.* Bloomington: Indiana University Press, 1999.

Vander Meer, Phillip. *The Hoosier Politician: Office Holding & Political Culture In Indiana 1896-1920.* Urbana: University of Illinois Press, 1985.

Warren, Louis A. *Lincoln's Youth: Indiana Years 1816-1830, 2nd ed.* Indianapolis: Indiana Historical Society, 2002.

Weinzaptel, Connie A., Darrel E. Bigham, and Susan Branigin. *New Harmony, Indiana.* Charleston, South Carolina: Arcadia Publishing, 2000.

Welsbacher, Anne. *Indiana.* Edina, Minnesota: Abdo & Daughters, 1998.

Willkie, Wendell L. *One World.* New York, NY: Pocket Book Inc., 1943.

Wilson, D. Ray. *Indiana Historical Tour Guide.* Carpentersville, Illinois: Crossroads Communications, 1994.

Wilson, George R. *Early Indiana Trails And Surveys.* Indianapolis: Indiana Historical Society, 1991 reprint.

Wilson, George R., and Gayle Thornbrough. *The Buffalo Trace.* Indianapolis: Indiana Historical Society, 1946.

Wilson, Jefferey, compiler. *Indiana In Maps: Geographic Perspectives Of The Hoosier State.* Bloomington: Indiana University Geography Department, 2000.

Wilson, William E. *The Angel And The Serpent.* Bloomington: Indiana University Press, 1984.

Wilson, William E. *The Wabash.* New York, NY: Rinehart, 1940.

Winslow, Hattie Lou. *Camp Morton.* Indianapolis, Indiana: Butler University, 1935.

Wood, Mary Elizabeth. *French Imprint On The Heart Of America: Historical Vignettes Of 110 French Related Localities In Indiana And The Ohio Valley.* Evansville, Indiana: Unigraphics, 1976.

Zavatsky, George and Michelle Zavatsky. *Kids Love Indiana: A Parent's Guide To Exploring Fun Places In Indiana With Children Year Round!* Columbus, Ohio: Kids Love Publications, 1999.

Index by County

Index by Marker Name

Printed in the United States
114599LV00001B/131-238/P

9 781434 316448